STEAMBOATS ON
NORTHWEST RIVERS

STEAMBOATS ON
NORTHWEST RIVERS
BEFORE THE DAMS

Bill Gulick

CAXTON PRESS
Caldwell, Idaho
2004

Library of Congress Cataloging-in-Publication Data

Gulick, Bill, 1916-
Steamboats on Northwest rivers / Bill Gulick.— 1st ed.
    p. cm.
ISBN 0-87004-438-9
1. Inland water transportation—Northwest, Pacific—History. 2. River steamers—Northwest, Pacific—History. 3. Ship captains—Northwest, Pacific—History. 4. Inland water transportation—Alaska—History. 5. River steamers—Alaska—History. 6. Ship captains—Alaska—History. I. Title.
HE631.N67G85 2004
386'.22436—dc22
                    2003019733

Cover photo

Mitchell Point, Columbia River.
Photo courtesy Mike Mellum.

Lithographed and bound in the United States of America
CAXTON PRESS
Caldwell, Idaho
170054

CONTENTS

x

ILLUSTRATIONS

Map

INTRODUCTION

When a proposal recently was made to breach four dams on the lower Snake to expedite the passage of salmon and steelhead, a great hue and cry went up from tug and barge operators and port districts, who claim this rash act would end river transportation forever and bring economic ruin to the region. Though I doubt such a drastic measure to save the fish will ever be taken, I must speak up to correct the misconception that navigation on the rivers of the Pacific Northwest could not exist if the dams were removed.

Historically, for 100 years before the dams were built on the Columbia-Snake river system, steamboats carried cargo and people to the farthest reaches of the rivers during a lively, colorful era equal to that on Mark Twain's Mississippi. Where water flowed, sturdy steamboats and bold captains went—with no dams, locks, or artificial aids to navigation needed.

The dam-building period began in 1938 with the construction of Bonneville Dam, forty-five miles east of Portland on the Columbia. It ended with the completion of Lower Granite on the Snake River, thirty-eight miles downstream from Lewiston, Idaho, in 1975. By then, the Columbia still ran free for only 145 miles from Bonneville to the sea and in a fifty-one-mile stretch called the "Hanford Reach" upstream from Pasco. On the lower

Columbia River Maritime Museum
Two steamboats, the *Henderson*, left, and the *City of Portland*, race between Portland and Rooster Rock as part of the promotion for the 1952 premiere of the motion picture *Bend of the River. The Henderson* won the race but blew a gasket doing it.

Snake, the four dams, locks, and still pools upriver from its juncture with the Columbia made a seaport of Lewiston, 465 miles inland from the mouth of the Columbia.

Economically, much can be said in praise of the ease and efficiency of transporting cargo by tug and barge. But few passengers are attracted to this mode of travel. On the other hand, traveling by steamboat always has been and still remains a delightful way to see new country, with the cargo being transported a secondary consideration.

The first steamboat to appear on the lower Columbia was the Hudson's Bay Company side-wheeler, *Beaver*, which started operating in 1836. This was the same year the Marcus Whitman party of missionaries came West over what would become the Oregon Trail, setting in motion a series of events that assured the Pacific Northwest's becoming American rather than British property.

Included in the missionary party was a cantankerous, hard-to-get-along-with carpenter-mechanic named William H. Gray, whose name would loom large in the making of history in the new country. He is important to this book because he taught four of his sons the ways of wild Western waters so well that they all became steamboat captains.

The most remarkable of these sons was William Polk Gray, who for sixty years piloted steamboats on wilderness rivers from southwestern Idaho to northern Alaska. Along with fifty or so other captains, who became as famous to their fans as baseball stars today, their names and feats were known to all travelers and river dwellers, just as the distinctive tone of each boat's whistle was recognized by all hero-worshiping boys who dreamed of growing up to be river captains.

It is their story I propose to tell in this journey down the rivers of the past. The details are true—with dialogue created in some instances to make the story more readable. The reader is invited to come along for the ride . . .

* * *

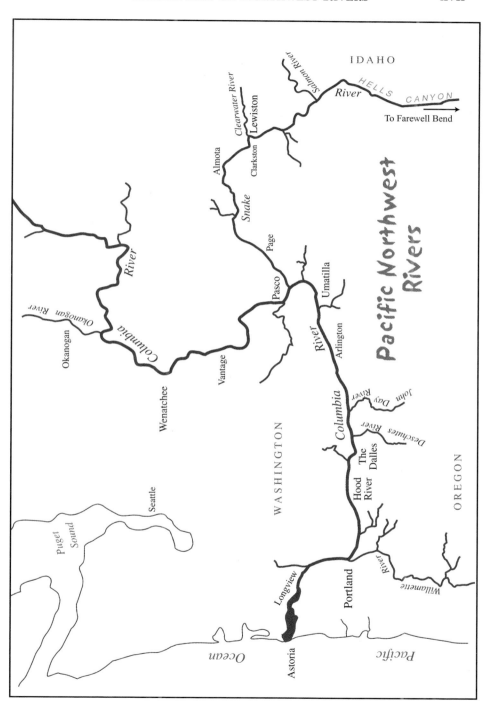

Idaho Historical Society photo
Captain William Polk Gray piloted steamboats in the Pacific Northwest and Alaska for sixty years. Gray's father, William H. Gray, played a key role bringing Oregon under the sphere of influence of the United States.

The most eager Beaver

Even though he was relegated to the role of a carpenter and mechanic in the Oregon-bound missionary party in 1836, William H. Gray thought himself to be as well qualified to be a medical practitioner as Doctor Marcus Whitman or a minister as the Reverend Henry Spalding, even though officially he was neither, for he came from a long line of Scotch doctors and preachers.

Frequently quarrelling with his fellow workers, he was a disagreeable, yet indispensable sort of man. Blunt and tactless, he made few friends among the missionaries, but his skills as a carpenter and a mechanic were always in demand, for in this remote part of the country his was a treasured talent.

"We can't get along with William Gray," members of the missionary party said in exasperation. "But we can't get along without the things he can do for us, either."[1]

Gray was unmarried when he came to Oregon and helped build the Whitman Mission at *Waiilatpu* in the Walla Walla Valley and the Spalding Mission at *Lapwai* in what would become Idaho. He decided he wanted a mission of his own among the Flathead Indians, which would require him to find a wife and obtain some knowledge of medicine. Concocting an ambitious scheme to drive a herd of Indian horses east to the settlements, trade them for cattle to be taken west the following spring, then spend the winter obtaining a wife and some medical skills, he persuaded the Reverend Spalding to give the plan his grudging approval, though getting rid of a man who had been a thorn in his side for a year must have borne some weight in Spalding's decision.

"Gray is an individualist who has plenty of initiative but little of the cooperative spirit," a fellow missionary declared. "He is too often inclined to do good on his own hook. He is uncommonly persevering in whatever he attempts, and I cannot learn that he has ever failed in anything, except in becoming a scholar." [2]

Later, he would succeed in that, too, for his *History of Oregon*, published in 1870, became a classic in its field.[3] Traveling east from the Flathead country in late spring, 1837, Gray's party reached fur rendezvous in the valley of Green River in mid-June. Although he had planned to cross the plains to St. Louis under the protection of the returning fur brigade, when he learned that it would not leave for ten days, he impatiently decided to proceed without it. Jim Bridger advised him against such a rash act, warning that the Sioux would attack his small party, kill the Indians in it, and steal the horses.

William Gray ignored the advice.

Near Ash Hollow, in Sioux country, Bridger's prediction came true. The Indians who were with Gray were killed and the horses stolen, Gray himself barely managing to escape with his life. Despite his later self-justification for his behavior, the verdict among the Flathead Indians and the mountain men was that he had cravenly deserted the Indians in a pinch, trading their horses and lives to the Sioux for his own.[4]

When he reached Boston and told the American Board for Foreign Missions what had happened, they were horrified, refused to give him permission to establish a mission of his own, but did agree to send out reinforcements and aid him in his search for a suitable wife. After being introduced to and courting Mary Dix for only six weeks, they were married and made preparations for their trip to the Oregon country and a life dedicated to missionary work among the Indians. Eventually, she gave birth to nine children, four of whom became river captains, and supported him in everything he undertook to do, even though he soon left the missionary field.

Denied a mission of his own, he moved to Salem, Oregon, in the Willamette Valley in 1842, where he got involved in the real passion of his life—politics. At that time, the residents of the Pacific Northwest were into the third decade of the Joint Occupancy Treaty with Great Britain under whose terms the region was open to settlement by both nations, with its eventual sovereignty to be decided by a majority vote of the people who lived in it. A strong supporter of *Manifest Destiny*, William H. Gray, (whose middle name honored the eloquent Revolutionary War patriot, Patrick Henry) never for a moment doubted that the region should and would become American property.

Although a few land-hungry emigrants were beginning to trickle into the Willamette Valley from the United States, most of its residents were mountain men recently put out of work by the lowly silk worm, whose product was beginning to replace the staple of the fur trade, beaver hats. Whether French-Canadians dependent upon the Hudson's Bay Company or free trappers selling their gather to American traders, a third of these men were loyal to England, another third to the United States, while the remaining third preferred no government at all, for to them a government of any kind meant laws and taxes.

Because of his skills as a carpenter and mechanic, William H. Gray had found employment with the Hudson's Bay Company, one of whose retired trappers, a French-Canadian named Joseph Gervais, had the distinction of being the first permanent white settler in the Oregon country. Coming west with the overland section of the Astor party in 1811, Gervais had stayed on with the North West Company when it took over Fort George, continued with it when it became the Hudson's Bay Company, then decided that he liked the Willamette Valley so well that he wanted to end his days in it.

An American trapper, Ewing Young, who also had settled in the area, did die there in 1841, causing a problem. Though he owned a large herd of cattle and considerable property, he had left neither an heir nor a will. This troubled his American compatriots, for there was no court to settle his estate.

"An executor was appointed," a contemporary historian wrote, "but meanwhile, Young's stock ran wild in the Chehalem Valley and wolves and panthers were soon attracted to the easy prey. The settlers finally had what was called a 'Wolf Meeting' on February 3, 1843. It was agreed that each person present should be assessed $5 to pay a bounty on all wolves, lynxes, bears, and panthers killed."[5]

His father had instigated the meeting, William Polk Gray later claimed, its secret purpose being more political than wolf-eradicating. At the second meeting on March 6, the real intent of the men present—both Americans and French-Canadians—was revealed:

"A resolution was unanimously adopted for the appointment of a committee of twelve to take into consideration the propriety of taking measures for civil and military protection of the colony."

The meeting that would sway the destiny of Oregon was held two months later, May 2, 1843, in a Hudson's Bay Company warehouse at Champoeg. Whether the name of this town derived from the French champ (field) or from the local Indian word champooick is open to question; regardless, local pronunciation then and now is "Sham-POO-egg."

Many of the British subjects thought this was merely another "Wolf Meeting" to further organize protection against predatory animals. As soon as they became aware of its true intent, most of the French-Canadians withdrew, indignant over the use of the warehouse for what they considered "seditious purposes." But the Americans present were determined to continue the meeting, even if it had to be held in a nearby field.

There was much talk of inalienable rights to self-government. Some of the Americans were grateful to Dr. John McLoughlin and the Hudson's Bay Company for all the help they had received. But Joe Meek, an outspoken-by-no-one American ex-trapper, ended the discussion when he demanded: "Who's for a divide? All in favor of the report and an American government follow me!"

Legend relates that a line was drawn on the ground and that when the milling ceased fifty men were on Meek's side of the field, and fifty were on the British side. The two men standing in between were undecided: Etienne Lucier and his friend F.X. Matthieu, both French-Canadians.

"Lucier hesitated because someone had told him that should the United States Government come into control here it would tax the windows of his house. Matthieu, who lived with Lucier, argued convincingly otherwise. In the end the pair took their position with those favoring organization on Joe Meek's terms."[6]

So, by a skinny 52-50 vote, the residents present decided to set up an American-style government. The report of the committee was then disposed of article by article and a number of officers were chosen. A committee of nine Americans was named to draw up a program.

"When the legislative committee made its first report at a mass meeting at Willamette Falls, (Oregon City) on July 5, it created four legislative districts. One of them was called 'Champooick,' and included the settlement of Champoeg and its judicial center."

Joe Meek, who liked to think big, no doubt was in on the district's planning, for its eastern boundary was set at the crest of the Rocky Mountains and took in what later became Idaho and parts of Montana and Wyoming. For a time, the town of Champoeg thrived as a center of both government and commerce. Oregon Territory was organized in 1848. By then, William Polk Gray had arrived on the scene.

"I was born in Oregon City in 1845," he later told historian Fred Lockley. "My father named me William Polk Gray. I remember when I was about four or five years old some one asked my father what my middle initial stood for. Father said, 'I named him after President Polk. When I named him the president had taken a strong stand on 54-40 or fight. Polk reversed his attitude on that question and I have been sorry I called my boy after him ever since. Sometimes I have a notion to wring the youngster's neck, I am so disgusted with President Polk.'"[7]

Knowing his father to be a man who usually did what he said he would do, young Willie Gray for years ran and hid like a rabbit whenever visitors came and his father started arguing politics. As an expansionist, his father greatly favored owning not only Alaska, but all of Canada, too.

"He thought the United States should take in all the continent of North America. When Secretary Seward went up to

Brought over from England by the Hudson's Bay Company in 1836, the *Beaver* was the first steamship at work on the lower Columbia and Northwest coast. Stripped down to a single stack in 1860, when this faded photograph was taken, the *Beaver* wasn't pretty. But she still could do her job.

Alaska, he took my father with him, on account of father's familiarity with the Indian customs and languages.

"Father came back from Alaska greatly impressed with Seward's statesmanship. He said Seward was a high type of American. At that time Thomas Nast and others were cartooning Seward and showing Alaska as an iceberg with a solitary polar bear guarding it. I remember hearing father say when some one sneered at Seward's purchase of Alaska: 'The only criticism I have to make of it is that he didn't also buy British Columbia at the same time.'"[8]

Though William Gray Sr. had been involved in the beginnings of government in the Oregon country, he was too impatient a man to waste his time as an active politician. After taking up a Donations Act claim for a square mile of land in the Salem area, he soon traded it for another on the Clatsop Plains not far from Astoria. It was there that he decided young Willie Gray, now four years old, should start going to school. The fact that the boy had to walk two miles each morning and evening he considered just good exercise. After several years on the

Clatsop Plains, the family moved to Astoria, where eight-year-old Willie Gray went to a school run by a Scotchman named Sutherland.

"The only part of the Bible that he knew well," Gray later said, "was if you spare the rod, you will spoil the child. There was no danger of his students getting spoiled, believe me, for he put in the major part of his time using the rod."

By 1855, when Willie Gray reached the age of ten, many momentous changes had come to the Oregon country. In 1836, the same year his father crossed the American continent with the missionary party, the steam-powered ship *Beaver* made its way across the Atlantic Ocean and ascended the Columbia River 100 miles to Fort Vancouver on the north shore, where Hudson's Bay Company Factor, Doctor John McLoughlin, saluted its arrival with a volley from the post's brass cannon.

Truth was, Doctor McLoughlin hated the stinking little steamer, for it represented a new-fangled invention in a world whose ways were changing too quickly to suit his tastes. Though he knew that both British and American inventors had been playing around with steam engines for years, he felt the confounded things were so heavy, undependable, and dangerous that the very idea of putting one aboard a ship was ridiculous. But in the case of the *Beaver*, the builders had done just that.

According to an article published in the *London Times*, the first-ever steamship built specifically to navigate the waters of the Pacific Northwest had been launched on the Thames in 1835. The article proclaimed:

> *It is safe to say that no vessel has attracted anywhere near as much attention as this pioneer of the Pacific Ocean. Over 150,000 people, including King William and a large number of the nobility of England, witnessed the launching, and cheers from thousands of throats answered the farewell salute of her guns as she sailed away for a new world.*
>
> *Much speculation is indulged in as to the success of her cruise. The machinery was placed in position, but the side-wheels were not attached, so she was rigged and started for*

her destination under canvas, with Captain Home in command. The bark Columbia *sailed with her as a consort.*[10]

Designed to burn soft coal—the stinky, smelly, smoky stuff that was making all the big cities of England such hellholes to live in—the *Beaver's* bunkers could hold only enough coal to fire her boilers for two days. How far could she sail in that time? Doctor McLoughlin wondered. She could burn wood, too. But how many forests grew on the high seas?

To McLoughlin, it would have been no great loss if the *Beaver* had capsized under the weight of her useless machinery. But from the day the two ships cleared Land's End and moved out into the open sea, the *Beaver* proved to be so much better a sailer that time and again she had to reef or lower her sails and wait for the *Columbia* to catch up. A hundred feet long, with a twenty-two foot beam, an eleven-foot depth, and drawing eight feet of water, she was double-planked out of solid English and African oak, had a copper-sheathed bottom, and displaced 187 tons. Her side-wheels, were set well forward.

Understandably proud of her, Captain Home told anybody willing to listen that he did not know whether the superior craftsmanship of her designers, the quality of the materials put into her, or sheer luck made her sail so well, but he was sure that the 163-day passage of the *Beaver* to the mouth of the Columbia was a record that would stand for a long time. Despite Doctor McLoughlin's old fashioned misgivings, Captain Home felt that the career of the *Beaver* in northwest waters was going to be a long and happy one. The fact that his brigantine-rigged little ship arrived at the mouth of the Columbia on March 21, a week ahead of its much larger escort, was an omen of things to come.

Because of the early spring runoff, high tides, contrary winds, and constantly shifting sandbars in the lower river, it took both ships two weeks to work their way up to Fort Vancouver, with the bigger ship, the *Columbia*, continuing to have problems—going aground, having to be kedged out of the mud by the ship's boat, or towed off sandy shoals by the *Beaver* until at last reaching anchorage just off Fort Vancouver. There, the post's blacksmiths' and craftsmens' skills were used to bring

Penrose Library, Whitman College
Wandering artist John Mix Stanley did this painting of The Dalles, with Mt. St. Helens in the background, about 1848. Mt. St. Helens blew its top on May 18, 1980, losing its symmetry and 1,200 feet off its crest.

the paddle wheels, guards and connecting engine machinery above decks and install them.

Her log records the first trip made under steam as: "Monday, May 16 (1836)—Variable winds and fine weather. Carpenters shipping the paddle wheels. At 4 P.M. the engineers got steam up and tried the engines and found (them) to answer very well. . .

"May 31—At 9:30 a party of ladies and gentlemen from the fort came on board. At 9:45 weighed anchor and ran down the river under steam and entered the upper branch of the Wilhammet (sic); ran under half power until we cleared the lower branch at 3:30, and ran up towards Vancouver."

Visiting the fort at that time, the Reverend Samuel Parker, who had come out from Boston to select a site for a mission to the Indians and was about to return home by sea, took a ride on the boat:

On the 14th (June, 1836) we took a water excursion in the steamboat, Beaver. The novelty of a steamboat on the Columbia, awakened a train of prospective reflections upon the probable changes which would take place in these

John Mix Stanley did this painting of Fort Walla Walla in 1847, looking down the Columbia River past towering bluffs known as Wallula Gap. Two vertical basaltic rocks known as the "Two Sisters," are still visible today.

remote regions, in a few years. It was wholly an unthought of thing when I first contemplated this enterprise, that I should find here this forerunner of commerce and business. On the 18th of June, I took passage on the steamboat, Beaver, *for Fort George to join the barque,* Columbia, *for the Sandwich Islands.. As the* Beaver *was commencing her first voyage on the Pacific under steam the people of the fort, and those residing around, assembled upon the shore of the Columbia, and as she moved majestically from her anchorage, they saluted us with cheers.*"[11]

The *Beaver* had two Bolton and Watt engines, designed by the man who invented the steam engine, James Watt, propelling with a side-lever action. Her thirteen-foot paddle wheels supported buckets six-and-a-half feet long. Her boilers used low-pressure steam, which turned the paddle wheels thirty times a minute, driving her along at nine miles an hour in the river or eight knots at sea.

Although Doctor McLoughlin doubted that the steamer could operate profitably and hated its stink and noise, he admitted that it had made a tremendous impression on the Indians of the lower Columbia. No doubt it would have a similar effect on the natives of Puget Sound, British Columbia, and Russian Alaska.

Yakima Nation Collection
Indians fish for Salmon at Celilo Falls in the 1950s before the cataract was covered by the backwaters of a dam. Celelo Falls was know as "The Chutes" by early trappers. Goods and passengers were unloaded from steamboats below the falls and then reloaded on other vessels above it.

By equipping it with anti-boarding nets, a couple of six-pounders, rifles and pistols with which the crew could defend itself, the Beaver would avoid the kind of disaster that had over-whelmed the *Tonquin*[12]. At the same time, its trading missions to the north would get it out of the Factor's sight and smell, as well as impressing the Indians with the might of the Hudson's Bay Company.

With only twenty tons of coal in her bunkers and no more of the "black stones that burn"—as the Indians called it—available in this part of the world, two weeks of off-and-on cruising between Fort Vancouver and the mouth of the Columbia exhausted that source of fuel. Because the brigantine rigging was not compatible with steam sailing, the masts, spars, and yards were removed at Fort Vancouver before the paddle wheels were installed. From that time forward, the *Beaver* would move

Columbia River Maritime Museum
End of the *Beaver*. Working as a tug in British Columbia in 1888, the *Beaver* struck a rock near the Vancouver Harbor entrance. Before she could be dislodged, the wake of a larger passing boat rolled her over and broke her back.

only on steam power. If her experiences on the lower river were any criterion, she would consume twenty cords of wood a day when steaming under full power, which meant she would steam one day, then lay by two while the necessary quantity of wood to keep her going was brought aboard.

Even so, she earned her keep. She first proved her worth when the *Columbia*, anchored off Fort George (formerly Astoria), and about to sail for England, was ordered by McLoughlin to come upriver to Fort Vancouver and add some furs to her cargo. With the wind and current against her, she could make no progress, so the *Beaver* chugged downriver, put a line on her, and gave her a tow.

Whether Doctor McLoughlin liked it or not, it had just been demonstrated that steam power would be the future of traffic on the rivers of the Pacific Northwest.

Chapter 1 footnotes

1. Clifford M. Drury, *Henry Harmon Spalding*, Caxton Printers, Caldwell, Idaho, 1939, pgs. 128-129.
2. Ibid, p. 130.
3. William H. Gray, *History of Oregon, 1792-1849*, Portland, Ore., Harris & Holman; New York American News Company, San Francisco; H.H. Bancroft Co., 1870.
4. Ex-mountain man William Craig, who married a Nez Perce woman and became Spalding's neighbor at Lapwai, was particularly critical of Gray and Spalding and resented them for years, though he eventually did make peace with Spalding.
5. J..A.Hussey, *Champoeg: Place of Transition,* Portland; Oregon Historical Society Press, 1967.
6. Ibid..
7. Fred Lockley, "Reminiscences of Captain William Polk Gray," *Oregon Historical Quarterly,* December, 1913, V. XIV, N. 4, p. 321.
8. Ibid, p. 322.
9. Ibid, p. 323.
10. Lewis & Dryden, *Marine History of the Pacific Northwest*, pp. 15-17, 1895; reprint Antiquarian Press, 1962, New York, Edit ed by E.D. Wright. London Times, 1835.
11. Washington Irving, *Astoria*, 1837; reprint Lippincott, 1961. After the Astor ship Tonquin deposited men and goods to establish Fort Astoria near the mouth of the Columbia in late May, 1811 the ship sailed north to engage in trade with the Nootka Indians on the coast of British Columbia. Due to the stupidity of Captain Jonathan Thorn, the Indians became enraged and attacked, with the ship's gunner exploding its six-ton store of powder, killing all the whites and a hundred or so Indians, the tale eventually related by a native named Lamansee, then retold by Washington Irving in his book Astoria.
12. E..D. Wright, *Marine History of the Pacific Northwest*, 1925, pp. 20-23.

CHAPTER TWO
Home-made steamboats

S team power came to the Columbia River when the paddle
wheels were installed on the *Beaver* in 1836. But this did
not mean the end of the age of sail, for, as Doctor
McLoughlin caustically observed, neither coal mines nor forests
existed on the high seas. Steamboats on the rivers of the heavily forested Northwest proved their worth, for a sharp axe and
a strong back were all the equipment needed to keep the boats
running. But ocean-going ships for many years were a mixture
of steam and sail.

The first of these to come to the Pacific Northwest, the Army
transport *Massachusetts* was built in Boston in 1845, the year
William Polk Gray was born.[1] Meant to carry troops where they
were needed, her first mission came in the spring of 1848 when
she was loaded with soldiers, guns, and supplies, and dispatched with all possible speed around the Horn and up the
West Coast to the mouth of the Columbia, where she arrived in
May 1849.

Four years old and living in Astoria at that time, young
Willie Gray must have seen her after she crossed the bar under
steam power. Though he might not have wondered how the
ship's cannons and troops could be used against a hostile Indian
tribe (what was called the "Cayuse War" was raging at the time)
living 350 miles inland, he surely would have been puzzled by
her appearance. Like other curious boys, he would have asked,

"She's a steamer, you say?"

"Aye, that she is."

"Where are her paddle-wheels?"

"She doesn't have any, Willie. She's screw-propelled."

In maritime-wise Astoria at that time a number of people had heard of such ships, though they weren't too sure how they worked. Experts knew that at sea screw propellers performed as well or better than paddle-wheels, for when in stormy seas a paddle-wheel could be tilted and lose its purchase on the water, while a submerged screw propeller would not. But how well a screw propeller would serve in the river, where there was more silt and sediment to be stirred up, was open to question.

During the day-long trip up the Columbia to the anchorage off Fort Vancouver, which was made under reduced speed, the screw-propelled ship behaved well enough. After greeting the ship's arrival with a salute from the brass cannon of the fort, which now was under American management, the staff stationed there entertained Captain Bertrand and the ship's officers with a dinner. Next day, the troops disembarked and began forming an encampment that would transform the former Hudson's Bay Company trading post into an American military base which would retain the Fort Vancouver name.

Although the Cayuse War was over by now and there was no need to impress the Indians with the naval might of the United States, Captain Bertrand did carry a deck load of visitors as far upriver as Rooster Rock, just downstream from where a six-mile series of rapids called the Lower, Middle, and Upper Cascades began.

Dropping back downriver, the transport anchored near Portland for ten days, loading a deck cargo of newly milled lumber which Captain Bertrand planned to carry to the new Army base being built near San Francisco. Because of the vast number of prospectors pouring into the Sacramento area since the discovery of gold at Sutter's Mill in January 1848, most of the traffic these days was headed for California rather than Oregon.

"Frankly, I'm worried about losing a lot of my crew to the gold fields," Captain Bertrand told the commandant at Fort Vancouver. "On our way out from New York, we called at Hawaii

Bill Gulick photo
Rowena Crest, about nine miles east of The Dalles, Oregon, looking upriver.

rather than San Francisco, so we had no problem with desertion. Now, I'm afraid we will."

Before the discovery of gold in California, plans had been made by the Pacific Mail Steamship Company to establish fast steamer mail service between New York and Portland. But the gold rush soon changed that. When the first Pacific Mail steamer, the *California*, sailed from New York in late spring, 1848, she was scheduled to stop at Monterey, then come north to Portland. But when she touched at Buenos Aires on the way south, fifty South Americans who had heard of the strike swarmed aboard as paying passengers. At Panama on the west coast, 700 frantic men with money in their hands screamed to be taken aboard.

Knowing that his ship could legally carry only 250 passengers, the captain decided that since these were not American waters, American law did not apply. In view of the fact that the fifty people who had come aboard at Buenos Aires were South Americans, who probably were used to being crowded anyway, they were shoved below decks into steerage, while 350 of the waiting Americans who were waving money at him were taken aboard as passengers.

Reaching Monterey safely despite her overload, the *California* discharged the steerage and deck passengers there, then, forgetting that her destination was supposed to be Portland, returned to Panama and picked up the 350 cash customers left stranded there. Notwithstanding its agreement to serve Portland, the ship continued to make the highly profitable Monterey-Panama run for the next two years.[2]

In May, 1850, a new Pacific Mail steamer, the *Carolina*, did manage to sail west from New York and then up the Pacific Coast to the Columbia and Portland. Only half the size of the California, she was a wooden twin-screw vessel, which also carried a rack of sail. Establishing what was advertised to be a monthly service between San Francisco, Astoria, and Portland, she maintained that schedule until the weather turned bad and the seas grew stormy, under which conditions the month often turned out to have six or seven weeks in it.

Having learned by now that the prospectors in California were willing to exchange their gold dust for lumber, beef, potatoes, salmon, and butter, Willamette Valley farmers and Portland businessmen decided that it would be to their advantage to acquire a steamship of their own. When a majority interest in the side-wheeler *Gold Hunter*, which had been built by an independent company for the Sacramento River trade, came on the market, a hastily thrown-together combine of Portland businessmen raised enough money to buy a controlling interest in the ship. Proud of the fact that they now owned what was bound to be a highly profitable steamship, the Portland merchants filled her hold with cargo and sent her on her way south rejoicing.

Unfortunately, when the *Gold Hunter* reached San Francisco, the minority shareholders residing there bought back enough shares from the ship's officers to give them a controlling interest, then put her into service between San Francisco and Panama. Quite literally, the Oregon owners had been "sold south."[3] In response to this treachery, a group of enterprising residents of Astoria said,

"Serves you Portlanders right for trusting Californians who are all born scoundrels and thieves. We intend to keep our money at home by building our own steamboat."

Which they proceeded to do . . .

Because William H. Gray lived in the Astoria area and was a skilled carpenter and mechanic, it is highly likely that he took part in building the homemade boat. Called the *Columbia*, it was framed on the bank just below the dock. Planned strictly for river use and powered by steam generated in a wood-fired boiler, its captain was an experienced riverman named Jim Frost, who had piloted steamboats on the Mississippi for many years.[4]

"He helped us design it," the investors said. "We've got the parts for the engine ordered from San Francisco and are going to put it all together when they arrive. It'll be the best darned steamboat on the river."

Since her only competitor was the *Beaver*, soon to be taken north into Canadian waters by the Hudson's Bay Company, the *Columbia* did have the field all to itself for the time being. But times were changing as the country developed. Under a new law passed by the Oregon Territorial Legislature, George Flavel, a recent arrival from San Francisco, was going into the bar-piloting business. Said to be well qualified in the trade, he was in the process of forming a Bar Pilots Association which would set standards and fees for men guiding ships over the bar.

The builders of the home-designed-and-owned steamboat slid the nearly completed craft into deep water in early June 1850. Even the most loyal stockholders admitted that the boat was not much for looks.

"She's an ugly-duckling cross between a ferry boat and a scow," they said. "But she floats. Now if her engine will run and turn the paddle-wheels, we'll call her a success."

Double-ended with a blunt stem and stern, the boat was a side-wheeler, ninety feet long, with a sixteen-foot beam and a hold depth of four feet. Unlike her distant relatives on the Mississippi, she was without an ornament of any kind, having not a single piece of gingerbread scrollwork on her. As boats went, she looked boxlike and clumsy. But when her wood-fired boiler was heated up and steam was fed into her cylinders, her paddle-wheels turned and she moved through the water at a slow but steady rate.

Which was all that counted.

Lacking sleeping accommodations and a galley, she was not much for comfort, her passengers having to pack their own food and blankets aboard and sleep unsheltered under the open sky. Even so, the day of her maiden voyage from Astoria to Portland, July 3, 1850, was a memorable one in the annals of American steam-boating in the Pacific Northwest. Every Astorian who could find an excuse to make the trip was aboard as the *Columbia* left the dock, except George Flavel, who was awaiting an incoming ship to pilot across the bar. When the *Columbia* returned triumphantly a week later, the passengers who had made the trip gave the stay-at-homes an enthusiastic report on the trials and triumphs of the voyage.

Captain Frost was a mighty cautious man, they said. Like most of the people aboard, he'd never gone any farther upriver than Tongue Point, so once he passed it he had no idea where the main channel ran. Feeling that anybody who had navigated the Mississippi as long as he had ought to be able to find his way up the Columbia, Captain Frost wasted no money hiring a pilot with local knowledge. Hailing a pair of Indian youngsters he saw fishing from a small boat a couple of miles above the Point, he asked them if they knew the channel. They said they did, so he paid them a dollar to come aboard as guides.

At first there was a communications gap, with the two Indian boys talking Jargon and him with a Deep South drawl, but by using a lot of sign language, they finally managed to understand one another. Taking it slow and making only fifty miles the first day and not wanting to risk steaming in the dark, Captain Frost pulled in to the bank and tied the bow of the boat to a tree for the night.

Tieing up for the night proved to be a mistake, for when the captain snubbed the boat off, the tide was out. Around midnight, it came back in, lifting the bow of the boat six feet and nearly pulling it under. Although everybody aboard was asleep at the time, a deckhand fortunately woke up, told Captain Frost what was happening, and he had the line slacked off before the boat was pulled under.

Somewhat embarrassed, he said he'd never seen a tide like that on the Mississippi. On the Columbia as far upriver as Portland, he was told, it happened twice a day. Every day.

Other than that near-disaster, the trip to Portland went smoothly. By the middle of the afternoon the *Columbia* was steaming along so well that Captain Frost took her into the Willamette River and chugged on up to the falls below Oregon City, her whistle tooting all the way. Along both banks, people cheered until they were hoarse, shooting off Fourth of July fireworks in celebration.[5]

Following the success of her initial trip, the home-designed-and-built steamboat established regular service between Astoria and Oregon City on a twice-monthly basis, charging twenty-five dollars per passenger each way and the same amount for a ton of freight. Connecting with the Pacific Mail Steamship Company vessels to and from California, as well as towing sailing ships, barges, and keelboats at a brisk four miles an hour, the *Columbia* had a monopoly on the lower river trade for six months.

But even as she and the investors who had built her enjoyed the revenue from their enterprise, a professional shipbuilder was going to work at Milwaukie, Oregon, just downriver from Oregon City, with plans to build a steamboat the likes of which had never been seen in the Pacific Northwest.

His name was Lot Whitcomb . . .

Emigrating from Wisconsin to Oregon in 1848, Lot Whitcomb named the town he platted on the banks of the Willamette River seven miles upstream from Portland "Milwaukie." Since he had become its postmaster, as well as the owner and publisher of the local newspaper, his somewhat lame explanation—that the town's name had been derived from three Clackamas Indian words whose meaning never had been explained to him, rather than from his own misspelling of the Wisconsin city's name, Milwaukee—had to be accepted at face value.[6]

After all, if the postmaster and newspaper publisher of a town didn't know how to spell its name, who did? So Milwaukie it remained.

Most newcomers to Oregon shared the misconception that Portland was on the Columbia River. It was not. What initially was called "Stumptown" had been staked out on the west bank of the Willamette River twelve miles upstream from its juncture with the Columbia. Because there was deep water from its mouth twelve miles to Portland, upstream to Milwaukie at River Mile 19, then on to Oregon City at River Mile 27, steamboats could navigate the Willamette all the way up from Astoria without difficulty most of the year. The lone hazard was just below the mouth of the Clackamas River, two miles downstream from Oregon City, where the rapids were shallow at periods of low water.

In this land of a nine-month-long rainy season, bottomless mud-holes, and poor roads, navigable rivers were by far the best way to travel. So Lot Whitcomb, who owned everything in sight, had good reason to believe that the town he had platted was going to be the most important port on the Willamette River. By building and launching the biggest and best steamboat ever to ply the inland waters of the Pacific Northwest, he was well on his way toward becoming a very important and wealthy man.

Not surprisingly, he decided to call the new steamboat the *Lot Whitcomb*.

"From her keel to her pilot house, she's going to be a first-class steamboat," the brash, handsome, black-mustached, energetic young entrepreneur proclaimed to anyone who would listen. "Her keel is a stick of prime Oregon fir without a knot in it. She'll measure 160 feet in length, have a 24-foot beam, be five feet eight inches deep in the hold, and will displace 600 tons."

"She'll be a side-wheeler, like the *Beaver*?"

"Right. Only much bigger, of course. Her side-wheels will be eighteen feet in diameter, set in housings well back from center. Fully loaded, we estimate she'll draw about three feet of water."

Designed by Jacob Kamm,[7] a qualified marine engineer with a degree from the best school in Missouri, and built to his exact specifications in New York and New Orleans, the engine had been shipped by way of San Francisco.

Born in Switzerland in 1823, Jacob Kamm had been eight years old when his father resigned his commission in the French Army and took his family to America in search of a better life. In New Orleans four years later, Jacob became an orphan at the age of twelve when his father, mother, and all the other children in the family died during an epidemic of yellow fever. Left to fend for himself, he worked as a copy boy for a daily newspaper for a couple of years, then, seeing no future in that, took passage up the Mississippi on a riverboat headed for St. Louis.

En route, a slick-talking stranger robbed him of all his money except ten cents, so he was forced to take employment as a cabin boy aboard the small steamer *Ark*. It was there that his interest in marine engineering began. Working first as a fireman, then as a mechanic aboard several river packets, he found that both jobs affected his chronic asthmatic condition adversely, making breathing difficult, so he studied textbooks, attended classes, and saved all the money he could in order to get a diploma from the Engineers Association of Missouri, following which he became part owner of the steamer *Belle of Hatchie*.

Increasingly frequent asthmatic attacks forced him to sell out and seek a change in climate. Leaving the miasmatic lowlands of the Mississippi and emigrating to California in 1849, Kamm's health did improve. While working as an engineer on a steamboat running on the Sacramento River, he met Lot Whitcomb, who told him of his plans to develop navigation in Oregon, persuading him to come to Milwaukie as a partner in the company and to design and install the engine for the boat Whitcomb planned to build there.

Blueprinted in twenty-two sections, then manufactured and shipped to the West Coast by way of New Orleans and Panama, the boilers pipes, valves, and fittings went together exactly as Jacob Kamm intended them to. When fired up, the engine performed as flawlessly as a Swiss watch. In fact, when Captain J. C. Ainsworth arrived, he proclaimed the boat to be as good as any craft he had ever skippered on the Mississippi.[8]

Big, bluff, and hearty, Captain Ainsworth was a man people liked on sight, for there was no pretense to him. With a top speed of twelve miles an hour, the *Lot Whitcomb* promised to be the fastest boat on the river, a handsome craft, combining the traditions of Hudson River steamers with a few touches of Mississippi River boats. Twin smokestacks set well forward rose above a pair of boilers whose steam pressure turned the enclosed side-wheels with a great deal of power. She had a long cabin deck, a small Texas, and a modest-sized pilot house placed just behind the chimneys. All her upper works were painted white and were without an ornament, though each wheelhouse did bear her name in big black letters.

Designed with what her owners called "simple elegance," she had ample mixed-passenger cabin space, a dining hall, and a small sheltered ladies' cabin where the fair sex would not have to endure such male crudities as tobacco chewing, spitting, cigar smoking, drinking, and strong language. On the lower or freight deck, a substantial amount of cargo could be carried.

Following flowery speeches by Mayor Kilborn, Governor Gaines, and a stirring serenade by the Fort Vancouver brass band—all of which were duly noted by the local newspaper, *Western Star*, which Lot Whitcomb owned—the boat *Lot Whitcomb*—with Lot Whitcomb himself on board—got under way. Her first order of business was to compete with the clumsy, lumbering, slow, Astoria-built *Columbia*, which now had a monopoly on the traffic of the lower river.

Charging twenty-five dollars for the trip between Milwaukie and Astoria, just as the *Columbia* did, the *Lot Whitcomb* took most of the trade away from the older boat on her first round-trip. In retaliation, the *Columbia* reduced its fare from Astoria to Oregon City to fifteen dollars. Relying on the elegance, speed, and comfort of their new boat to beat the competition in all ways but price, the *Lot Whitcomb* cut its fare to twenty dollars, announcing in January 1851 that it would leave Milwaukie on Mondays and Thursdays at noon, touching at Portland, Fort Vancouver, Milton, St. Helens, Cowlitz, and Cathlamet on the way to Astoria, with the return trip subject to favorable tides, scheduled for a more-or-less noon departure from Astoria on Wednesdays and Sundays, "Board not included in the above rates."

Though the *Lot Whitcomb* got the larger share of the traffic for a couple of months, she did suffer the embarrassment of getting hung up on a reef at the mouth of the Clackamas River when the water across a riffle there proved to be too shallow for the boat's keel to clear. This misadventure happened as the steamboat was heading toward the rapid against a blinding, low-angle mid-afternoon sun, and Captain Ainsworth, who had

Click Relander Collection, Yakima Valley Regional Library
Beacon Rock, on the Columbia River, near Vancouver, Washington. A Lewis and Clark landmark.

never been this far upriver before, misjudged the depth of the water.

Because the boat grounded while moving under full power, no amount of jockeying with first one wheel and then another turning first in one direction and then in the other would work her clear. But Captain Ainsworth was too old a hand at running aground on bars and snags to be concerned with that.

"If we can't lower the sandbar, we'll just have to raise the river," he grunted. "First thing tomorrow, we'll get a crew of workmen to bring up some timbers from Lot's mill and build some cofferdams and weirs to raise the water level enough to float us off. The channel over that reef has to be deepened any-way, else all the river boats will have to stop two miles down-stream from Oregon City."

Since a sawmill was among the many other enterprises Lot Whitcomb owned and operated in Milwaukie, getting enough timbers and skilled workmen to build the cofferdams and weirs was no problem. But damming the Clackamas and Willamette

Rivers enough to raise their levels so that the grounded boat could be floated off turned out to be much more of a project than anticipated, requiring two weeks to complete.

After bringing the boat back to Milwaukie, where she was docked and careened to make sure no serious damage had been done to her keelson, the *Lot Whitcomb* went back into service on the Oregon City-Astoria run.

With plenty of water in the rivers during late spring and early summer and the engine performing perfectly under Jacob Kamm's precise control, the steamboat set new speed records, making the 120-mile run from Astoria to Oregon City in just ten hours against the current, with the final eight-mile stretch from Milwaukie to Oregon City done in only fifty minutes. Using a trick learned on the Mississippi, Captain Ainsworth told Jacob Kamm to have the stoker toss half a dozen pitch-filled pine knots into the furnace just before the boat pulled into the landing, making billows of thick black smoke roll out of the chimneys and putting on a show for potential passengers.

Just as the *Beaver* had done back in 1836, the *Lot Whitcomb* undertook a towing job in March 1851. Owned by the Pacific Mail Steamship Company, the iron-hulled propeller ship, *Willamette*[9] had been built on the East Coast, rigged as a schooner, and then brought around the Horn to Astoria under sail. Putting a hawser on the vessel, the *Lot Whitcomb* towed the *Willamette* upriver to Portland, where, during the next few months, her engines were installed, her propeller connected, and she was put into service on the lower river run. Scheduled to meet the bi-monthly Pacific Mail ship plying between San Francisco and Astoria, she was in direct competition with the *Lot Whitcomb*, of course, which did not seem to bother Captain Ainsworth a bit. In fact, it inspired him to challenge the rival boat to the first-ever steamer race on the Columbia River.

On a warm summer day in early July the *Willamette* cast loose her lines from the Portland dock just a few minutes after 1 p.m., heading downriver for Astoria just as the *Lot Whitcomb* tied up and put out her landing stage to discharge Portland ticketed passengers from Oregon City and Milwaukie. Seeing the other boat pull away, Captain Ainsworth stuck his head out of the pilot house and shouted down at the First Mate,

"It's a great day for a race, wouldn't you agree?"

"I certainly would, sir!"

"Then pull back your landing stage and cast off your lines! We'll take on the *Willamette* in spite of her head start. I mean to pass her before she clears Sauvie Island Slough!"[10]

Scrambling aboard with or without downriver tickets as the landing stage was swung in, a dozen or so startled passengers managed to find footing on the deck as the lines were cast off. While they cheered lustily, the big side-wheels, which had barely stopped turning, came to life again, pulling the boat out into the river in a long arc, then pointing her bow downstream in the direction the screw-propelled *Willamette* had taken.

Unaware that she was being challenged to race, the *Willamette* was moving down the river, which here was constrained between ranges of steep hills, at three-quarter speed, so the *Lot Whitcomb* soon began to close the quarter-mile gap between the two boats. Seeing the *Whitcomb* gaining on her and hearing a pair of whistle-toots as Captain Ainsworth gave fair warning he was coming after her, the master of the *Willamette* accepted the challenge, gave two whistle blasts of his own, then poured on full power.

Because her screw was under water and did not disturb its surface, the propeller boat ran quietly, while the buckets of the side-wheeler made a thunderous noise as they churned the water.

With the two boats running neck and neck abreast of each other as they raced the length of Sauvie Island Slough, passengers lined the rails of both steamers, cheering and shouting at the top of their lungs. At the lower end of the nine-mile-long island, the channel narrowed until it was barely wide enough for two boats abreast, with the shallower water restricted by an invisible mud bank under the surface to port. Since both captains were familiar with the hazards here, neither had an advantage, so far as local knowledge was concerned.

But as the captain of the *Willamette* knew very well, if a blade of his screw-propelled boat dug into the bottom and got twisted or bent, repairing it would be a major problem. On the other hand, a damaged bucket on a side-wheeler could be fixed with a lot less effort and expense. So as the two racing boats

Bill Gulick photo
The Two Sisters are a landmark on the Columbia River..

moved into the narrowing neck of the slough, Captain Ainsworth was not surprised to see the *Willamette* move to starboard, seeking the deeper water of the right-hand channel, while the *Lot Whitcomb* stayed to port. Risking grounding on the mud bank to cut across the short side of the arc, the *Lot Whitcomb* forged into the lead by two boat lengths as the vessels cleared the lower end of Sauvie Island and moved into the deeper waters of the Columbia itself.[11]

Acknowledging the cheers of the crowd by leaning out of the pilot house and lifting his cap, Captain Ainsworth shook a jubilant fist at the passengers, then bent down to the engine room's speaking tube and grunted, "Good work, Jacob! You can release your tie-down on the safety valve now."

In the years that followed, a number of steam-powered boats with engines designed and manufactured by Jacob Kamm were built in Milwaukie and Oregon City, operating as passenger and freight carriers on the Columbia and Willamette Rivers below and above the falls. The tiny, iron-hulled propellers, *Eagle* and *Black Hawk*, were only forty feet long, carrying no more than a dozen passengers and a ton of freight, plying the Willamette between Portland and Oregon City.

An even smaller craft, the *Hoosier*, was built out of a ship's longboat, which had been slightly altered to accommodate an engine originally designed to be a pile-driver. When the engineer-captain-owner found business slack on the lower Willamette run, he put the vessel on rollers, portaged it around the falls, and put it into service to Dayton on the Yamhill and Salem on the Willamette.

He made history of a sort one day when he snapped the shaft of the *Hoosier* while trying to scramble over a rapid four miles downstream from Salem. Not at all concerned, he unshipped the shaft—which had broken into two pieces—shouldered one piece himself, gave the other to a deckhand, then walked into Salem and found a blacksmith shop. There, he had the two pieces welded back together, then he and the deckhand carried the shaft back to the vessel and put it in place, following which the boat resumed its trip.[12]

Chapter 2. footnotes

1. James A. Gibbs, *Pacific Graveyard*, Binfords & Mort, Portland, Oregon, 1950, p. 259. Marine historian Gibbs writes: "When the Massachusetts entered the Columbia, she claimed to be the largest vessel that had yet crossed the bar (700 tons). She carried both a full suit of sail and the Ericsson propeller, along with her steam plant, making her one of the more modern government vessels of her time."
2. Eliot Grinnel Mears, *Maritime Trade of the Western United States*, Stanford University Press. 1920, p. 110.
3. Randall V. Mills, *Sternwheelers Up Columbia*, Pacific Books, Palo Alto, California, 1947, p. 15.
4. Ibid, pp. 16, 17.
5. R. C. Clark, *History of the Willamette Valley Oregon*, Chicago, The S.J. Clarke Publishing Company, 1927, p. 463.
6. *Sternwheelers Up Columbia*, op. cit., pp. 16-18.
7. Ibid.
8. Ibid, pp. 19, 20.
9. Ibid.
10. Ibid.
11. Ibid.
12. Ibid.

Columbia River Gorge

A lthough the Columbia River was navigable to steamboats for most of its 1,250-mile length, two sets of rapids
in the lower river presented major obstacles to continu-
ous passage. The first was the Cascades, where a six-mile
stretch of white water 145 miles inland from the sea turned the
narrow, rock-strewn channel into a raging torrent. Upstream, a
fifty-mile section of quiet water, in which the great river cut its
way through the heart of a 10,000-foot-high mountain range,
extended to The Dalles, where the Columbia's flow was again
impeded by a fourteen-mile stretch called the "Long Narrows."
Pinched into a channel only 160 feet wide, the river literally
turned on edge here, racing along at a speed recorded by Lewis
and Clark at thirty miles an hour.[1] At Celilo Falls, the river
dropped twenty vertical feet during periods of low water in late
summer, while the volume became so great during spring flood
that the river's surface leveled out into a roaring pour of white
foam.

Because the Columbia was broken into three sectors, com-
monly called the lower, middle, and upper river, a steamboat
operating on it was confined to the stretch of river upon which
it was launched. In early days between 1836 and 1850, traffic
existed only on the lower river from its mouth to the Cascades.
Most of the boats were side-wheelers, like the first one, the
Beaver.

With the Cayuse Indian war over and the gold rush to

California tapering off, emigration to Oregon increased substantially in 1851. As promised, the Army built posts at intervals all along the Oregon Trail, including a fort at The Dalles which was manned by a small detachment of troops. Despite the good climate, abundant sunshine, and proven fertility of the interior country east of the Cascade Mountains, most of the emigrants still regarded the Willamette Valley as the promised land, heading there either over the Barlow Road[2] in the high Cascades or along the water-level route through the Columbia River Gorge.

As business began to develop above the Cascades, a merchant, D. F. Bradford, and a boat-builder, Van Bergen, put together a hull and an engine for a small side-wheeler, the *James P. Flint*. Compared to the *Lot Whitcomb*, it was a modest-sized steamboat, measuring only sixty feet in length with a beam of twelve feet. But to the emigrants who put their wagons and cattle aboard for the fifty-mile downriver trip from The Dalles to the Upper Cascades, as well as the soldiers whose horses and supplies were carried upriver to the newly established fort, she was a welcome change from walking and a sign that civilization at last was reaching this remote corner of the Pacific Northwest.

Unfortunately, with the coming of autumn and the chill rains, traffic on the middle river dwindled to the point of nonexistence, so Bradford and Bergen decided if business would not come to their boat, they must take their boat to the business. Winched up onto the low north bank of the river, skids were placed under the boat and she was dragged by the brute force of half a dozen yoke of oxen six miles downriver, then returned to the water below the Lower Cascades.[3]

For the next year, the *James P. Flint* did a fair business transporting emigrants down and soldiers up the lower river. It became evident from the way her valves wheezed and her bearings pounded that unless her engine was given an extensive overhaul, it was not going to last much longer. But her owners said no money was available for an expensive overhaul at the moment, so her wheezing and pounding got progressively worse. On September 15, 1852, the inevitable happened. Blowing a valve just upstream from a spire of jagged rock on the

Penrose Library, Whitman College
Portage railway around the Cascades about 1865. Earlier tracks were wood topped with metal strapping.

north bank—appropriately named Cape Horn by Lewis and Clark—she lost power, drifted helplessly with the current, bashed a gaping hole in her bottom on a sharp lava reef, then sank where she struck, leaving only her upper works visible above water.

Though her hull was a total loss and gradually rotted away, her engine was recovered, repaired so that it functioned after a fashion, then was reincarnated for a couple more lifetimes, first to power a sawmill on the lower river for a few years, then as a clanking steam engine on a homemade boat on the Yangtze River in China, where it operated for the rest of its days . . .

With the coming of spring 1853, several events of importance to the Pacific Northwest occurred. In March, Congress passed legislation establishing Washington Territory, breaking what formerly was known as the Oregon Country into roughly equal portions, with the Columbia River as the dividing line.[4]

Because of the lack of business on the lower Columbia, the *Lot Whitcomb* had been "sold south" to California and now was operating on the Sacramento River. Unable to compete with the newer boats, the *Columbia* had given up the struggle, her hull being tied at a dock in Astoria while her engines were removed and placed in a smaller boat, the *Fashion*, which started running from Portland to the Lower Cascades. When a spring freshet tore the hull loose from the dock, sweeping it over the bar and out to sea, the boat that had once been the pride of Astoria "went south," too, in a sense, for when last seen her storm-scattered timbers were floating in the direction of California.[5]

In Oregon City that summer, the first-ever iron-hulled boat was built by a foundryman named Thomas V. Smith, who had recently come out from Baltimore. First called the *Belle of Oregon City*, then simply the *Belle*, the boat was ninety-six feet long and twenty-six feet wide. When finished, she was put into service on the lower Willamette run, where she established a standard for speed and dependability never before seen in this part of the country.[6]

Leaving the warehouse at the base of the falls at 7:30 each morning, the *Belle* stopped at Oregon City at 8:00 A.M., Milwaukie at 8:30, and arrived at Portland at 9:30. After giving businessmen travelers time for a full morning's work and a leisurely noon meal, the boat started back at 2:00 P.M., reaching home at 4:00 P.M. in plenty of time for the storekeeper to close up shop and get home for supper. Fare between the two terminals was two dollars. Compared to the time and effort required to travel the muddy or dusty roads of the area, this was the easy way to go.

As time passed, the *Belle* proved to be not only a dependable boat but also a durable one. Expanding her service to Fort Vancouver, the Cowlitz River, and the Columbia to the Lower Cascades, she proved her worth during the Indian wars of 1856-58, transported prospectors and settlers upriver as the interior developed in the 1860s, and continued to operate until 1869, when she finally went to the scrapper.

Even then, *Belle* lived on, as other boats did before and after her, when the dismantled sheet iron of her hull was shipped to China and her engines, still faithfully turning over, were used to power a sawmill.

Meanwhile, the master builder, Jacob Kamm, was hard at work designing and ordering parts for his latest concept in steamboats—a stern-wheeler. Financed by the Abernethy and Clark Company, in which Kamm and J. C. Ainsworth also had an interest, parts for the engines were manufactured in accordance with Jacob Kamm's detailed specifications in Baltimore, while the hull took shape in Milwaukie. To be called the *Jennie Clark* after the lovely wife of the

Penrose Library, Whitman College
The Oregon Pony was a primitive steam engine that pulled portage cars at the Cascades, 1862.

principal stockholder, the craft would be the finest, most expensive, most efficient boat ever to ply the Columbia River.[7]

The cost of the engines, according to Jacob Kamm, who kept meticulous track of every penny, was $1,663.16. Brought around the Horn on the clipper ship *Golden Racer*, the freight charges were $1,030.02. In an attempt to economize, Jacob Kamm had specified that the wheel by which the ship was steered be "neat and plain finish and not costly." Contrary to his instructions, it turned out to be of the most expensive mahogany the builders could find, inlaid with solid silver and polished until it gleamed. If Jacob Kamm complained, his remarks were never published.

Ainsworth and Kamm agreed that a stern-wheeler was the best type of boat for the inland waters of the Pacific Northwest. Until now, all the others had been side-wheelers or propellers, but experience had shown them to have serious disadvantages. Propellers fouled in shallow water, blades bent, and shafts snapped. Side-wheelers required docks with deep water on both sides and were hard to manage in swift currents and winding channels.

A stern-wheeler was able to nose into or alongside a sandy beach, depending in its slow-turning wheel and twin rudders to keep it in place. With her two engines connected so that one man could handle them both, the *Jennie Clark* maneuvered easily. Each cylinder had a four-foot stroke, their sixteen-foot connecting rod turning a stern-wheel that was fifteen feet in diameter. Because the slats of the wheel were simply lengths of one-by-four inch wood, they could easily be replaced by even a poor carpenter, while repairing a damaged metal bucket on a side-wheeler was a major problem, requiring a mechanic's skill.

With a stern-wheeler, Jacob Kamm said, it would be possible to split the wheel into two sections set side by side. By using three rudders—one on each end and one in the middle—and the engines turning in opposite directions, such a boat could spin on a dime, like a puppy chasing its tail. Operated as a tug in tight quarters, this sort of boat would be extremely useful.

The length of the *Jennie Clark* was 115 feet, her beam 18 1/2 feet, and she was four feet deep in the hold. She had a single cabin, over which the boilers were centered; the two engines were set well aft, close to the stern-wheel, so there was little lost motion. A single black smokestack rose from the boiler, with the pilot house set well forward and as high as possible for good vision lines. In uncharted waters, it was most important that a boat's captain be up where he could "read the river" in all kinds of weather.

From the day she was launched in February 1855, it was clear to Captain Ainsworth and the crew of the *Jennie Clark* that she was going to be Queen of the River for years to come. She responded to her helm at the slightest touch, her stern-wheel bit into the water with powerful authority, and she handled the most delicate landings with ease. Although there was little doubt she could show her heels to anything else on the Portland-Astoria run, the only boat that might have challenged her to a race, the *Lot Whitcomb*, was now in California . . .

The creation of Washington Territory in 1853 and subsequent treaties made with the Indians in 1855 caused unrest east of the Cascades. Until then, there was neither reason nor need for river transport to that side of the mountains. But as travel though the Columbia River Gorge increased, the Indians became resentful and restless, so the U.S. Army established posts at The Dalles and the Cascades. To supply them, the small side-wheeler *Belle* ran on the section of river between the Lower

Cascades and Fort Vancouver, while two more side-wheelers, the *Mary* and the *Wasco*, ran the fifty-mile stretch between the two posts.[8]

At first, portages on both sides of the river went along narrow trails cut into the rocky banks of the Gorge, over which goods and people moved via pack or saddle trains. Then two enterprising brothers, Daniel and Putnam Bradford, built a six-mile-long rail line of wooden stringers topped by strap iron on which flatcars pulled by mules carried freight. On the Washington side of the river at the Upper Cascades, a small settlement called Bradford's Store was built. Usually, the steamboat *Mary* docked there, while its counterpart, the *Wasco*, tied up to the landing on the Oregon shore.

On Tuesday, March 25, 1856, the *Mary* and the *Wasco* came downriver from The Dalles, running light, to pick up loads. For some months, rumors had circulated that the Yakimas, a loose affiliation of fourteen related bands living north of the Columbia, were so unhappy with the terms of the treaty they had been forced to sign the previous summer that they were going to start a war against the whites. But few settlers took the threat seriously.[9]

The *Mary* tied up by Bradford's Store and put ashore her downriver cargo, while the *Wasco* did likewise on the south shore. During the night, both boats lay at their docks, waiting for dawn when they would take on wood and freight, fire up, and head back upriver. Early the next morning, Captain Baughman and the Mate of the *Mary* went ashore to supervise the loading of fuel and cargo. The cook, Dick Turpin, and his young helper, John Chance, who had just finished serving breakfast to the crew, were clearing away the dishes.

Suddenly, a volley of bullets raked the landing. Caught in their cabin, an entire family of settlers was shot, scalped, dragged to the river, and dumped in. Men at the sawmill ran for the store. All but one made it. He was shot dead. Captain Baughman and the Mate sprinted for the woods. Three members of the crew, running through crossfire, got to the boat and scrambled aboard.[10]

Aboard the boat, the crew members grabbed what few arms

they had and returned fire. Buckminister, the engineer, had a revolver; John Chance, the helper, an old Dragoon pistol. Dick Turpin, the cook, seized the only really useful weapon aboard, a rifle. After firing it a couple of times, he jumped into a flatboat tied alongside, was wounded, then, crazed with fear, fell overboard and drowned, taking the rifle with him.

With the crew putting up a stiff defense on the boat, the Indians turned their attention to attacking the whites holed up in Bradford's Store, which gave the crew a chance to get a fire going beneath the boilers with the scant fuel on hand. As soon as steam pressure began to mount, Chenoweth, the pilot, ran across the hurricane deck and into the pilot house. From ashore, the attacking Indians raked the deck with a withering fire.

Exposing himself as he chopped the lines securing the boat to the dock, young John Chance was wounded in the upper left arm, but managed to scramble back and lie flat in the flimsy shelter of the cabin. Lying prone, Chenoweth worked the wheel with his feet as the boat floated clear of the dock, taking steering directions from John Chance as the boat drifted downstream toward the tumult of the rapids, into which it would be sucked unless the paddle-wheels started turning.

Sluggishly, the wheels began to move, taking the boat away from the north shore and out of firing range of the Indians, who could be heard shouting their frustration. Watching from shore, the besieged people in Bradford's Store saw black smoke rising beyond the trees and feared that the Indians had set the steamboat afire. But as the *Mary* moved out and became visible in the river, with its boiler pressure rising and the paddle-wheels taking hold, Chenoweth stood up and pulled the whistle cord defiantly. The sound of his mechanical jeering at the Indians told the settlers that he was going for help. The besieged whites cheered lustily. But the odds were still against the *Mary*, for she did not have enough fuel aboard to move her very far.

Guiding the boat in a wide arc back toward the north shore a quarter mile upriver, Chenoweth nosed in to a landing below a settler's cabin, hoping the raiding Indians were not in the vicinity. At the moment, they were not, nor was the white settler. Dashing ashore, crew members grabbed wood from the pile outside the cabin, rails from fences, unchopped logs, and whatever fuel they could find, then dragged it aboard. Pulling out into the river again, the *Mary* headed toward The Dalles and help, fifty miles away.

On the Oregon shore, the *Wasco*, also caught with cold boilers, worked frantically to build up a head of steam. When she did, she pulled out into the river and followed the *Mary*.

Meanwhile, the blockhouse at the Middle Cascades and the landing at the Lower Cascades also had been attacked by the Indians. Both were poorly defended, the arsenal at the blockhouse consisting solely of a small cannon, while the settlers at the lower landing had no guns at all. But the cannon, booming away at random, kept the hostiles at bay near the blockhouse, while the settlers piled up bales of goods to shield themselves against the bullets. After darkness fell, the whites scrambled into small keelboats and catboats at the landing, cut loose, and began drifting downriver toward Fort Vancouver.

When they and a friendly Indian runner who had raced ahead to carry news of the attack to the military post reached the fort, a young Army lieutenant named Phil Sheridan (the same one destined for national renown later during the Civil War) assembled a company of dragoons and twenty Portland volunteers, commandeered a pair of steamboats, the *Fashion* and the *Belle*, and headed upriver to the rescue.

At The Dalles, the *Mary* and the *Wasco* took on federal troops. The eager but underpowered *Mary* tied a line to a flatboat loaded with horses and men as a tow, only to find that the river's current often pushed the flatboat ahead of the steamer. Although Colonel George Wright,[11] leader of the troops from The Dalles, had hoped to trap the Indians between his force landing above them and another led by Lieutenant Sheridan[12] below, his second in command, Lieutenant Colonel Edward Steptoe,[13] spoiled the surprise by following the book of regulations too closely.

Suddenly, from his command, into the clear morning air rose the brassy blare of a bugle blowing "Charge!" The troops heard it and obeyed. But so did the Indians. When the trap closed, not a hostile was in sight.

Although the attackers had failed to overwhelm the defenders at the Cascades, casualties among the whites had been heavy. Eleven civilians and three soldiers were dead, with three more mortally wounded. Twelve others had wounds and a number of cabins, warehouses, and bales of freight awaiting shipment had been burned.

But the value of having steam-powered boats on the middle river had been proved beyond doubt. During the next two years of conflict with scattered bands of recalcitrant Indians living in eastern Oregon and Washington Territory, boat-building above The Dalles and Celilo Falls developed, assuring transportation up the Columbia as far as Canada and up the Snake into northern Idaho.

When the Indian wars finally ended and peace came to the interior country in 1858,[14] settlers were drawn to the fertile land by its abundant sunshine and rich soil. At first, they came in trickles. But when gold was discovered in the Idaho mountains in 1860, the trickles became a flood. The quickest, easiest way to get to the diggings from western Oregon was by steamboat. Despite the formidable obstacles of portages, rapids, and navigational hazards, a colorful era of steamboat traffic began, with a number of venturesome individuals about to win or lose fortunes.

The most colorful of them was William Polk Gray, who would pilot steamboats on the rivers of the Northwest for the next sixty years . . .[15]

Chapter 3 footnotes.

1. Bernard DeVoto, Editor, *The Journals of Lewis and Clark*, Houghton Mifflin, 1953, p. 266.

2. Robert Ormond Case, *Last Mountains*, Doubleday, 1946. Forced to choose between taking the wheels off their wagons and rafting them through the dangerous rapids of the Gorge or crossing the mountains on the terrible Barlow Road, the emigrants invariably wished they had gone the other way, no matter which route they took.

3. Randall V. Mills, *Stemwheelers Up Columbia*, Pacific Books, Palo Alto, Calif., 1947.

4. As its first Governor, former Army officer Isaac Ingalls Stevens promised to find a northern route for a trans-continental railroad on his way west from Saint Paul, then to "extinguish title to their lands" by making treaties with the Indians of the regions. Within two years time, he kept his promise—with dire results, as we shall see.

5. Randall Mills, op. cit., p. 24.

6. Ibid, p. 25.

7. Ibid, pp. 25, 26.

8. Ibid, p. 32.

9. In the Treaty of 1855 negotiated my Governor Stevens, the Yakimas were promised that no whites would trespass on Indian lands without their permission. When that promise was violated, they went to war.

10. Randall V. Mills, *Stemwheelers Up Columbia*, op. cit., pp. 33-35. In his *History of the Columbia River Valley*, V. 1, S.J. Clarke Co., Chicago, 1928, pp. 890-905, Fred Lockely gives a detailed account of the attack as related by the survivors, upon which all later stories are based.

11. Carl P. Schlicke, *General George Wright, Guardian of the Pacific Coast*, University of Oklahoma Press, 1988, pp. 122, 123.

12. Ibid.

13. Ibid.

14. After an Indian-white war that lasted two years and cost the United States Government $6 million, the Treaty negotiated in 1855 was finally ratified by the Senate and signed by the President in 1858, thus becoming the law of the land, establishing Indian land, water, fishing, and sovereignty rights. It is still valid today, as a number of cases carried up to and confirmed by the Supreme Court have verified. Copies of the Treaty, (which I have examined) are available at the National Archives and in federal repositories such as the Whitman College Library in Walla Walla.

15. Quoted in the Preface of *Stemwheelers Up Columbia*, by Randall V. Mills, 1947, Captain Gray said: "Every change in the stage of water makes a change in the currents and around boulders, bars, and reefs, and when the rapid comes in sight every attribute of sight and brain is concentrated on the surface of the currents. The banks and cliffs are not noticed. The shimmer of the water on the bars, the exhaust of the engines of the boats, and the pressure of the water on the rudders were my guide."

Gold rush to British Columbia

Just as Willie Gray's father believed that a four-year-old child should be able to walk two miles a day to attend school, so did he feel that a ten-year-old boy was mature enough to go into business for himself.

"Father had a theory that it was a pretty good scheme for his boys to get to work early as possible," Gray later wrote. "As a matter of fact, we never had much time to get into mischief."[1]

In 1855, the custom house and the post office were located in what was called Upper Astoria, while Lower Astoria claimed the sawmill, the stores, and most of the population.

"Doctor C. J. Trenchard started a subscription paper," Willie Gray said, "and I went around to all of the stores and residences of Lower Astoria and got the people to agree to pay me to deliver their mail before I said anything to my father about it. I was to go twice a week for the river mail and make two extra trips a month for the steamer mail that came from California and from the East. The stores paid from 75 cents to $1.50 a month, while the private individuals paid 25 to 50 cents a month.

"I guess that was about the first city mail delivery in Oregon, as that was back in 1855. I started for the mail in the morning, summer and winter, at 5:30 o'clock. It kept me busy until school time distributing it. I often had from twenty-five to forty pounds of mail, and for a ten-year-old boy, climbing around the cliffs, that was a pretty good load."

Willie Gray hated the subscribers, he said, who made him

bring four or five bulky papers to one address and paid him only 25 cents a month. Tough as it was, he did it, earning from $30 to $35 a month. His mother wanted him to save the money. But his father said,

"It's Willie's money. Let him spend it as he pleases."

Having recently discovered girls, what pleased Willie most was to curry their favor by buying them ten cent peaches and 25 cent oranges imported from California, which made him the most popular boy in school among the older girls.

"I never was much of a hand at saving," he admitted. "When a pretty girl or two wanted oranges and I had the money, they generally got the oranges."

Following the gold rush to California in 1849, news of a strike anywhere in the West drew an influx of prospectors eager to make their fortune. In 1858, word that gold had been found in British Columbia on the Fraser River and its tributaries attracted a horde of Americans north to the new bonanza. Among them was the William H. Gray family.

"When I was 13 years old, we moved to British Columbia and I began working with canoes and bateaux on the Fraser River," Willie Gray later wrote. "A good many people got drowned on the Fraser, as it is a dangerous river, but father used to say that danger was all in a day's work, and one must take what comes. We ran from Fort Hope to Yale. Father was an expert wood-worker, having learned the cabinet maker's trade, and I worked with him in the building of sloops and river boats."

After living with his family for a little over a year in the lower Fraser River town of Fort Hope, William H. Gray heard of a new strike on the Similkameen River 140 miles to the east across the mountains, so decided to go there with his two older sons, leaving his wife, three daughters, and two younger sons in Fort Hope.

"We found gold on the south fork," Willie wrote. "Father built two rockers, and for the next few months we kept busy. At the end of that time our supplies were running very short. I was 13 years old, and father decided I was old enough to assume responsibility, so he sent me to Fort Hope to secure supplies. There was only an Indian trail, but I knew the general direc-tion. I had to ford streams and cross rivers, but I had learned to swim when I was eight years old so that didn't bother me."[2]

Because they were short of provisions, Willie took along only two sandwiches, thinking he could make the trip in two days by riding from dawn till dark and that his provisions would be sufficient. But he had ridden only twenty miles when he overtook a big, burly, "hard character" known to the prospectors in that country as "Big Jim." Blocking Willie's way, the man demanded,

"Hey, kid, have you got anything to eat?"

"Only a couple of sandwiches," Willie said.

"I haven't had anything to eat for two days. Give 'em to me."

Because the man was much bigger than he was, Willie decided he had better hand over the sandwiches. Bolting them down, Big Jim complained because there were no more. Noting that the man's horse was worn out, Willie tried to move past him, but Big Jim said,

"Where you headed, kid?"

"Fort Hope."

"So am I. We'll stay together for company. Your horse is a good deal fresher than mine. I may need him."

A short while later as they were making their way across a narrow cliffside trail 200 feet above a gorge, Big Jim's exhausted horse stumbled and gave out, its rider managing to kick free of the stirrups and slide out of the saddle before it fell to its death on the rocks below.

Down to one horse between them now, the boy and man "rode and tied" for the four and a half days it took them to reach Fort Hope—that is, one of them rode for a mile while the other walked, then the rider tied the horse and walked, letting the horse rest until the walking man behind caught up, who then would ride and pass the other man to a spot a mile beyond, where he would dismount, tie, and repeat the process. Hard character though Big Jim may have been, he at least did not ride off and leave Willie afoot in the wilderness, as he could have done.[3]

"All we had to eat during that time was a fool hen that he knocked down," Willie said. "When I got home, I went in the back door. My mother saw me and said, 'Oh, Willie, what has happened to your father?'"

"He's all right. But I'm nearly starved. Can I have something to eat?"

Loading a pair of packhorses with bacon, beans, rice, and other supplies, Willie headed back across the mountains to their camp. When some prospectors he met along the way learned that diggers in the Similkameen country were making ten dollars a day on the average, they followed him, hoping to stake claims on undeveloped ground. But his father was not content.

"When I returned, father thought he could strike richer diggings, so he left a man and myself to work with the rockers while he went down to what is now the site of Roslyn, B.C. I averaged eight dollars a day while father was gone. The bedrock was white clay, which we threw out with the tailings."

A few years later, Willie said, he learned they had made a mistake, for some Chinese miners took over the abandoned diggings and made fifteen to twenty dollars a day apiece from working their old clay tailings.

"The clay had rolled back and forth in our rockers and the gold had stuck to it. When it had weathered and disintegrated, the gold was released and the clay washed away in the Chinamen's sluice boxes."

On his trip, William Gray Sr. looked over the country and decided to locate near Osoyoos Lake, on the headwaters of the Okanagon in the Columbia River watershed, just south of the border in American territory. Going back to Fort Hope, he secured riding and packhorses, then, with his wife, daughters, and sons, started for what was to be their new home.

"This was in October, and winter had begun," Willie said. "We traveled day after day through the rain and snow, camping at night, usually in the snow. Timber was scarce where father had selected his ranch, so we hauled logs down the mountains, split them and built our cabin by standing the split logs on end. We chinked the cracks with moss and mud."

After living in the area a short while, Willie's father found that its prospects were not as good as he thought they were, so decided to undertake a new, ambitious project. He would build a boat, he told his family, launch it in the Okanagon River, then take it down through 300 miles of unchartered Columbia River rapids to just above Celilo Falls, where he would load a cargo of supplies and transport them back up the Columbia and Snake to the Idaho mines, where a gold rush had just begun, and sell them for a substantial profit.

Never mind that such a thing had never been done before. To William H. Gray, doing the difficult was ordinary.

"We had no tools, and of course no nails," Willie Gray said. "We went into the mountains, whipsawed out the lumber, hauled it down to the water, and father, with the help of us boys, built a boat, fastening it together with trunnels or wooden pegs."

Nails could have been purchased from a store in Fort Hope 200 miles away, his father knew, but freight would have added a dollar a pound to their cost, so he decided that wooden pegs would do equally well.

"We built a boat 91 feet long with a 12-foot beam, drawing empty twelve inches of water. The next thing was caulking her, but I never saw my father stumped yet. He hunted around and found a big patch of wild flax. He had the children pick this and break it to use as oakum to caulk the cracks in the boat. We also hunted all through the timber and found gum in the trees, which we melted for pitch to be used in the caulking.

"He had no canvas for sails, so he made some large sweeps. Father christened her the *Sarah F. Gray*, for my youngest sister. He launched her on May 2, 1861, and started on his trip down the river on May 10."

Accompanying William Gray on the trip was his oldest son, twenty-two-year-old John Henry Gray, who would man one of the sweeps.

"To give you an idea of the determination of my father," Willie said later, "he took that boat, without machinery, sails or other equipment except the sweeps, through Rock Island Rapids and through Priest Rapids, both of which he negotiated successfully. He arrived on the Deschutes (just upriver from Celilo Falls) on May 23. He left me to bring the family down, and I certainly had a very exciting time of it."

At that time, the Gray family consisted of his mother, three older sisters, Caroline, 20, Mary Sophia, 19, Sarah F., 17, younger brother, Albert William, 11, James T., 8, and Willie himself, 16. As the oldest male member of the family, young William Polk Gray would be in charge of taking the party overland through the same three hundred miles of unsettled wilderness his father and older brother were traversing in their homemade boat.

"A. J. Kane[4] had joined our family to go with us from our ranch to The Dalles," Willie wrote later, failing to mention that Andrew J. Kane was a big man, weighing three hundred pounds. As Agent on the Nez Perce Reservation a year earlier, he had tried to stem the tide of illegal white trespassers on the Reservation by arresting and ejecting members of the Elia Davidson Pierce party in the Clearwater country, only to have his honorable efforts negated when the white men bribed a young Indian woman, Jane Silcott[4], to show them a back way into the gold-bearing region. Making a big strike, they publicized it, bringing thousands of men stampeding into the area.

"My mother, sisters, and brothers, with Mr. Kane and myself, started July 4, 1861. The first day out, Mr. Kane's horse became restive and threw him against the saddle horn, rupturing him badly. We bound him up, but for the rest of the trip he could barely ride and was practically helpless. This threw the responsibility of bringing the family through safely on me, but I was sixteen years old and felt quite equal to it."

At that place and time, the Indian wars of the 1856-58 period had recently been brought to an end by the brutal acts of Colonel George Wright, a Regular Army officer who had taught the Indians east of the Cascades how horrible war could be when waged by white men with superior weapons. After defeating the hostiles in two one-sided battles and capturing 875 Indian horses, Colonel Wright set the warriors afoot permanently by letting his officers select seventy-five of the best horses for their own use, then gave orders that the remaining 800 be shot and killed.

The slaughter required two days, sickening many of the soldiers forced to do it, but it taught the Indians a lesson they would never forget. In this open country of vast distances, a man set afoot was no man at all. He became what the Spanish conquistadors in the Southwest a hundred years earlier called a *reducido*, a "reduced one," a man emasculated by being set afoot.[5]

This was a piece of knowledge that young Willie Gray soon would find very useful.

Below the mouth of the Okanagon River, the party swam the Columbia, passed through the Grand Coulee country and arrived at what would become known as the White Bluffs region.

"We planned to go to The Dalles by way of the Yakima and Simcoe valleys," Willie said. "But while we were still on the Yakima side of the Columbia, a cattleman came to our camp. He said that a man and his wife had just been killed at Moxee Springs the night before and that it would be almost certain death for us to go by way of the Yakima and Simcoe valleys. We at once recrossed the Columbia and started down the east bank. We camped opposite the mouth of the Yakima."

During the next day's travel, they met a couple of prospectors who warned them to look out for the Indians at the mouth of the Snake River a few miles to the south, where an unfriendly band had charged the two white men twenty dollars to take them across the river in a canoe, while their three horses swam beside it. Because the Gray party contained several women and children, an almost helpless older man, and was being led by a sixteen-year-old boy who no doubt could be easily intimidated, it was highly likely that the Indians would extort as much money from them as they could.

"That night, I staked my riding horse near camp, as usual, and turned the other horses loose to graze," Willie said, "knowing that they would not wander away. During the night, the Indians drove off all our loose horses. We were stranded with my one saddle horse and no way of continuing our journey unless I could recover the horses."

When Willie declared that he intended to follow the trail of the stolen horses and get them back, his mother was greatly alarmed, though she realized that it was the only thing to do.

"I followed the trail for twelve miles to just beyond the juncture of the Yakima and Columbia Rivers (near present-day Pasco)," Willie wrote. "There was a big Indian camp with many tepees near the river. I rode up to the biggest tepee, where I heard the tom-toms and the sound of Indians dancing."

Deciding to put on a bold front, Willie dismounted, threw

back the tepee flap, and stepped inside. Like most young white men raised in the Pacific Northwest, he spoke Chinook Jargon, which all the Indians understood, as well as he did English. In Jargon, he declared,

"Some of you Indians stole my horses last night. If they are not back in my camp an hour after I get there, I'll give the order that every horse you own be shot."

Utter silence was his only response.

Leaving the tepee, he mounted his horse and rode back toward camp. Before he had gone very far, he heard the thud of running horses.

"Four Indians were plying their quirts, riding after me. They were whooping and howling. Just before they got to me, they divided, two going on each side. I never looked around. One of the Indians rode his horse square across the trail in front of me. I spurred my horse and raised my quirt. I knew the Indian character well enough to realize that the only way I could carry out my bluff was by appearing perfectly fearless."

When he got back to their camp, Willie found his mother crying, saying she had prayed for him all the time he was gone. Having started before breakfast and ridden thirty miles, he was very hungry, he said, so sat down to eat the big meal his mother prepared for him.

"As I sat down to my delayed breakfast, we heard the thud of running hoofbeats. Our horses charged into camp, covered with lather. I hurried out, caught and staked them, then came back and finished my meal."

After the party had moved on to the juncture of the Snake with the Columbia, on whose shore there was another large camp of Indians, Willie Gray sought their help in crossing the Snake, which here was a sizeable river. Again, he entered the biggest tepee and put on a bold front, saying in Chinook Jargon to the Indians seated within:

"I want one canoe for my women and children and three canoes to help swim my horses across. You have delayed us by driving our horses off, so I want you to hurry."

For a few moments, the Indians sat impassive as statues. Then one of the chiefs grunted an order, several of the younger men got up, went down to the water's edge and got canoes.

His mother and the children got into one with their packs and were ferried across the Snake to its south shore, where they took the trail to Wallula, eleven miles distant. Willie and his brother Albert got into the second canoe, while one of the Indians guiding the swimming horses manned the third vessel. When they reached the other side, Willie asked the Indian in charge,

"How much?"

"What you think?" the Indian grunted deferentially.

Willie handed him five dollars, which the Indian took without a word of complaint, apparently glad to be rid of a person who claimed to have the power to kill all his people's horses.[6]

Reaching Wallula and rejoining his family that evening, Willie found that the former Hudson's Bay Company post, Fort Walla Walla, now had become a river port, with the stern-wheeler, *Tenino*, under the command of Captain Leonard White, now making regular scheduled runs up the Columbia and Snake between Celilo Landing and Lewiston.

"Having brought my mother and the children to Wallula on horseback from Osooyos Lake," Willie wrote, "I put them aboard the steamer *Tenino*, and they proceeded to Portland."

Living in the ruins of the old adobe fort abandoned by the Hudson's Bay Company when the Americans took over the region, Willie herded stock for a local rancher, J. M. Vansycle, while his father tried to secure machinery for the boat he had built and brought downriver.

"He found, however, that he was unable to raise the money to purchase the machinery, so he rigged her with a mast and sail and secured a load for the nearest landing to the newly discovered mines at Oro Fino."

Joining his father at Deschutes Landing, Willie took charge of the *Sarah F. Gray* while Gray, Sr., went to Portland and tried to obtain a cargo to be taken to Lewiston. By then, it was late summer, and the rumor had circulated among the merchants that it was impossible to navigate the Snake River with an unpowered boat.

"Father was unable to secure a cargo. But he was a very determined man. If he once set out to do a thing, he would not stop short of its accomplishment."

Deciding to buy a cargo on his own, he mortgaged his horses, his property in Astoria, and his boat, then, with the assistance of a few personal friends who advanced him money, he bought a large stock of goods for the mines, had them shipped upriver, then hauled around the falls and rapids to Deschutes Landing.

"We were loaded and ready to leave in the latter part of August," Willie said. "We arrived at Wallula on September 15. When we got there, our entire crew deserted, declaring it was too dangerous to attempt to navigate the Snake River."

Managing to hire a new crew of seven men, plus his son Willie and a younger friend of his named Jim Baker, Gray, Sr., and the clumsy, unpowered craft left Wallula on September 20, 1861. It took them three days to reach the mouth of the Snake, a distance of only eleven miles, for the prevailing winds were directly against the boat, making it necessary to cordell and pole most of the way. Once into the Snake, where the current against them was even stronger, the real troubles began.

"Jim and I would take ropes upstream until we found a place where a rope could be made fast. Then we would come down-stream in the skiff, bringing the lower end of the rope to a cap-stan on the boat, were it could be made fast. Then the capstan would be turned and the boat slowly wound up against the cur-rent."

The 140-mile trip to Lewiston was "difficult," Gray later wrote in a masterpiece of understatement. By the end of the forty days it required, he and his young friend Jim Baker had demonstrated "that there was not a single rapid in the Snake River that could not be swum."

"We were both strong swimmers and perfectly at home in the water," he said. "Our skiff was overturned in the rapids scores of times in cordelling up to Lewiston. The skiff was small and we had to carry a full coil of inch-and-a-half rope, as well as a coil of smaller rope, and oftentimes, when the line was wet, we had a bare two inches of free board going through the rapids.

"Not content with being wet all day long and being tipped out of our skiff, Jim and I would dare each other to swim dangerous places in the river."

Bold and fearless though Willie and his young friend were, they found the challenge of Five-Mile Rapid in the lower Snake almost too much for them, for there were no rocks or tree trunks on either shore to which a line could be secured. Willie's father thought they could find a rock in mid-stream to which they could attach a rope, but Willie disagreed, saying, "It can't be done, Pa. It's impossible"

"My son," his father replied, "'can't' isn't in my dictionary. Anything can be done if you want to do it badly enough."

"But the rapids are full of whirlpools and the skiff is bound to be overturned when we try to fasten a line to the rock."

"If you are overturned, you and the skiff both will come downstream, Willie. You may not come down together, but you will both come down. You will then go back and make another attempt—and continue to do so until you have succeeded."

Getting into the skiff, Willie and Jim went back upriver and managed to get a loop over a rock above Five Mile Rapid. No sooner had they done so than the skiff was caught in the raging current, overturned, and the two boys were spilled into the water.

"We went through the rapid at a terrific rate, sometimes under water, sometimes on top. We finally got through, swam to the overturned skiff and succeeded in getting back to the boat."

They had fastened a piece of wood to the end of the line, which floated free in the river. Chilled through and through and badly scared, they clambered aboard the *Sarah F. Gray* and were moving toward one of the lockers when Willie's father demanded, "Where are you going?"

"To get some dry clothes."

"There will be time enough for that when you have secured the end of the line. Go do it."

Which they did.

"After that experience," Captain William Polk Gray wrote many years later, "there has never been any combination of wood, iron, or water that has ever scared me."[7]

It was October 30 when they finally arrived in Lewiston. Many times during the trip, Willie said, he had been worried that they would wreck the *Sarah F. Gray*, lose the boat and its contents, and bring financial ruin to the family. But the hazardous venture turned out to be highly successful.

"Provisions were getting short in the mines. Father sold his flour for $25 a sack, or fifty cents a pound. Beans also brought fifty cents. Blankets were eagerly bought at $25 a pair. We sold all our bacon at 60 cents a pound. Father had made a very profitable voyage, had not only carried out his plan but came out with a handsome profit."

Chapter 4 footnotes

1. Fred Lockley, "Reminiscences of Captain William P. Gray," Oregon Historical Quarterly, V. XIV, Number 4, December, 1913, p. 323.
2. Ibid, p. 324.
3. Ibid, p. 325.
4. Ibid, p. 327. Andrew J. Kane had a reputation for being as honest as he was big, a rare virtue among Indian agents at that time. But his best efforts could not prevent the newly established Nez Perce Reservation from being overrun with white prospectors.
5. J. Frank Dobie, who wrote *Coronado's Children*, *The Longhorns*, and many other books about the Southwest, used the term to aptly describe the plight of a man set afoot in horse country. Men used to riding were poor walkers.
6. "Reminiscences," Gray, op. cut., p. 329.
8. Ibid, 331.

Colonel Wright—explorer steamboat

With the Indian treaties ratified and the interior country opened to settlement, the directors of the Oregon Steam Navigation Company felt that a steamboat launched above Celilo Falls would be a money-maker. Even as William H. Gray began hauling supplies to the new military post of Fort Walla Walla, the timbers, ironwork, engine parts, and boiler sections for a stern-wheeler designed to operate on the upriver sector of the Columbia were being shipped to the launching ways just below the mouth of the Deschutes River. In honor of the military leader whose firm actions had recently opened up the interior country, the boat would be called the *Colonel Wright*.[1]

Selected as captain of the boat for her maiden voyage was a veteran Willamette River pilot named Leonard White, a man capable of taking a steamboat anywhere water slightly denser than a light dew flowed. One of his many eccentricities was his firm belief that the King's English would be greatly simplified if words were spelled the way they were pronounced. In the frequent letters he wrote to editors of local newspapers, he put this theory into practice. For instance, he wrote the editor of the Eugene, Oregon, paper:

> *I anticipat that navigashun wil be opened as far as Ugen Siti the kuming winter, if the good inhabitants wil alou us to Bush-hwak above Korvalis (Corvalis). . .the*

Bill Gulick photo
Palouse Falls, 198 feet high.

smal timber that gros along the eg wil be ov yus for Bush-hwaking.[2]

Most readers of that day knew that "Bushwhacking" was a Missouri hill country term for shooting somebody in the back from ambush. What they probably did not know was that it had other meanings, too. Pulling a boat against the current by grasping bushes along the bank, was one. In the early 1800s the speaking style of a politician who sawed the air with his hands as he spoke, was another.[3] Being a literate man, Captain Leonard White no doubt knew them all.

Launched at the mouth of the Deschutes River in late summer, 1859, the *Colonel Wright* made regular runs as far upriver as Wallula Landing for the rest of the year. Equipped with a mast carrying a huge square sail, which was used when the wind was favorable, the boat was a wood-burner, which caused problems, for no trees grew along that stretch of river, so cordwood cut in the mountains and floated downstream made fuel expensive.

In the spring of 1860, an army quartermaster engaged the *Colonel Wright* to carry supplies to the mouth of the Palouse River, sixty miles up the Snake. The next summer, June 1861, Seth Slater, a Portland merchant, offered a full cargo of supplies to be taken upriver to the closest landing point feasible near the Idaho mines.

The first trip of the *Colonel Wright* turned out to be an exciting one. An *Oregonian* reporter going along for the ride wrote:

After entering the Snake River the captain touched at

an island where an enormous tree had lodged from a former high water, and the crew and volunteer passengers were landed with axes to add to the supply of fuel. Upon disturbing the trunk of the tree, a nest of rattlesnakes was also disturbed and a vicious war ensued in which a dozen snakes were killed, two of tremendous size.[4]

Below the mouth of the Palouse, a water-powered ferry had recently been installed, with cables stretched between two tall wooden towers carrying pulleys attached to a big wooden wheel on the flat-bottomed ferryboat by which it was angled into the current and propelled across the river. Sagging low over the water, the heavy rope cable was

Penrose Library, Whitman College
Palouse Falls. From a painting by John Mix Stanley.

beneath the level of the boat's pilot house, mast, and stack, so Captain White reduced power and brought his boat to a halt a few yards downstream.

"Ahoy the ferry!" he shouted into a megaphone after coming out on deck. "You're impeding navigation on my river. Will you be so kind as to lower your goddam cable?"

"Beggin' your pardon, Cap'n, but you're wrong on several counts," the ferryboat operator shouted back. "First place, this ain't your river. Second place, it ain't navigable. Third place, I got a franchise from the Territorial Legislature to operate this ferry. Have you got a license to operate your boat?"

"The Snake is a federal river, you damn fool, and I've got a right to run my boat wherever it flows. If you'll lower your blasted cable, I'll show you how navigable the river is."

After several minutes of heated argument, the owner of the ferry grudgingly slacked off the cable so that it sagged a few feet under the surface of the water in the center of the channel up which the *Colonel Wright* would pass. Unfortunately, the threshing stern-wheel picked up the slacked-off cable as the boat crossed over it, snapping it in two. Left behind and temporarily out of business, the angry, disgusted ferryman could only watch, curse, and hope for the worst as the boat churned on upstream into the white-water rapid just below the mouth of the Palouse.[5]

And the worst nearly happened. Running in full early summer flood, Palouse Rapid was the strongest the boat had encountered during its maiden voyage up the Snake. For two hours the stern-wheel threshed and the engine labored under a full head of steam, while Captain White used his considerable skills, trying first one channel, then another, until he finally managed to coax the boat through the rapid.

After a few miles of relatively quiet water, the boat found itself battling yet another rapid, this one so bad that the square sail was raised to utilize a favoring wind, and a line was put out and carried ahead. With the threshing stern-wheel pushing, the power capstan pulling, and the wind aiding both, the boat climbed foot by foot through the thundering, pounding, tossing current. Just as it appeared that the *Colonel Wright* would be successful in its attempt to ascend the rapid, a sudden gust of wind from astern filled the big square sail, driving the boat ahead with such a surge that it overtook the cable before its slack could be reeled in, causing the heavy wet rope to wrap itself around the paddle-wheel in a hopeless snarl. Cutting off the power, Captain White nosed the boat into the bank, where its crew spent an hour cutting the line free. The *Oregonian* reporter wrote:

> *A little further up the river, the boat overtook a party of mounted Indians who were engaged in trying to ascertain its speed by first walking their horses, then trotting, then*

galloping them. Their experiments amused the passengers
for some miles until a rocky bluff shut them off from view.[6]

After tying up for the night, which was made much shorter
by music, song, and improvised entertainment by the passengers and crew, the steamer proceeded on upriver at dawn the
next day, reaching the mouth of the Clearwater in the middle of
the afternoon. Despite the difficulties encountered in ascending
a dozen rapids, the *Colonel Wright* had needed only two days to
cover the same distance that William H. Gray and his clumsy
barge had required forty to traverse.

Just as the Snake carried one-third the volume of water that
the Columbia did, the Clearwater, in whose watershed the gold
fields lay, was less than half the size of the Snake. Even though
his new boat required only twenty-eight inches of water under
her keel, Captain White doubted that it could go very far up the
Clearwater. Still, he decided to keep going until he ran out of
water.

Reaching Indian agency headquarters at Lapwai, Captain
White stopped to pick up Chief Lawyer[7] of the Nez Perces, who
cried when he saw the boat: "Look! Here comes a water wagon!"
Taken aboard with the head chief was Agent Cain, which added
considerable weight to the boat, for, as noted earlier, he weighed
more than 300 pounds.

As the boat chugged on up the narrowing, increasingly shallow river, whose white granite reefs and gravel bottom could be
clearly seen beneath the translucent waters, the reason for its
Indian name, *Kooskooskee*, which translated into "Clearwater,"
became evident.

Twenty-five miles upstream from Lapwai at the mouth of the
North Fork of the Clearwater, Captain White decided he could
safely go no farther. Pulling in to the bank there, he unloaded
Seth Slater's merchandise, then declared this spot, 507 miles
inland from the mouth of the Columbia, to be the head of navigation for this branch of the great river.

During the next three weeks, the *Colonel Wright* and another steamer recently built and launched above Celilo Falls, the
Okanogan, made two trips to what was first called Slaterville,
then renamed Orofino, Spanish for "fine gold." As the water

level fell in mid-summer, it became evident that the practical head of year-round navigation must be the tongue of land where the Clearwater joined the Snake, thirty-seven miles downriver. Adjacent to this spot, which still legally lay within the boundaries of the Nez Perce Reservation—upon which no white man could trespass without permission—a boom town named Lewiston came into being.

Though the first trip of the *Colonel Wright* had required three and a half days from Celilo Landing to Slaterville, the return trip riding the crest of the early summer flood took only eighteen hours. Beyond all doubt, Captain Leonard White had proved the Snake to be a navigable river.

Even so, it turned out to be a cantankerous, treacherous river during much of the year, mute testimony to which were the names exasperated steamboat captains gave its many rapids: Perrin's Defeat, Three Island, Copeley's Cutoff, Haunted House, Gore's Dread, Almota Dead March, Steptoe Canyon, and Texas—the last being a euphemism for what one angry captain had called the bare rear end of the proprietor of a much hotter place.

In the newly born town of Lewiston during the summer of 1862, the spirit of expansionism advocated by Alonzo Leland,[8] editor of the local newspaper, the *Radiator*, was running amok with unprecedented speed and vigor. As the northern Idaho mines boomed and stern-wheeler traffic increased on the Snake and Columbia, the merchants began to dream of commercial grandeur. Discounting all previous reports of rapids, whirlpools, and other obstacles to navigation in the Big Canyon upriver, the town promoters dispatched a scouting expedition in early autumn "to determine the possibility of navigating Snake River with light draught steamers to Fort Boise."

The report turned in by the "three reliable men" was highly favorable. The *Radiator* editor declared jubialantly:

> *The entire distance from Lewiston to Fort Boise is only one hundred and thirty-five miles. They found nothing in the river to impede navigation whatever, and pronounced it feasible at any season of the year unless it be by ice. . .*

A new route will now be opened for steam, the results of which cannot now be foretold. We shall penetrate Nevada and Utah Territories by steam, as it is well known that it is only ninety miles from Fort Boise to Salmon Falls on Snake River. Salmon Falls is within 250 miles of Salt Lake. . .

But a few more suns will rise and set before the shrill whistle of the steamer will reverberate along the banks of this noble river, and its echo will be heard for ages yet to come through the ravines, gorges, and canyons, and on the mountaintops of our golden land, as a symbol of ambition, perseverance, and goaheadativeness. . .[8]

Unfortunately for the goaheadativeness of the Lewiston promoters, a couple of serious misstatements had been made. For one thing, the scouts had underestimated the distance by at least 100 miles. For another, their description of the country they were supposed to have scouted bore little resemblance to reality.

In 1819, the red-haired giant, Donald MacKenzie, who weighed 320 pounds, bossed a crew of six French-Canadian *voyageurs* as they paddled, poled, pushed, and pulled a barge from the mouth of the Clearwater to Farewell Bend while he was working for the North West Company. After he had accomplished the feat, he wrote with qualified elation:

Point Successful, Head of the Narrows, April 15, 1819. The passage by water is now proved to be safe and practicable for loaded boats, without one single carrying place or portage; therefore, the doubtful question is set to rest forever. Yet from the force of the current and the frequency of the rapids it may still be advisable, and perhaps preferable, to continue the land transport. . . We had often recourse to the line. There are two places with bold cut rocks on either side of the river, where the great body of water is compressed within a narrow compass, which may render those parts doubtful during the floods, owing to rocks and whirlpools, but there are only two and neither of them are long.[9]

Requiring two months of strenuous effort, the trip was not

repeated. In fact, forty-five years would pass before a boat of any size ventured into the wild rapids of Hell's Canyon again.

By now, Captain Leonard White had quit the Oregon Steam Navigation Company and gone into business for himself. Despite the fact that its boats were earning tremendous revenues by carrying as much as half a million dollars in Idaho gold downriver to Portland on a single trip, the company felt Captain White's $500 a month salary was too high. When they tried to reduce it, he quit in disgust and moved on to another field—building and operating a boat on the upper Columbia River into Canada.

Captain Thomas Stump[11] accepted the lower $350 a month salary, then brought seventeen-year-old Willie Gray aboard as second mate at $100 a month. With passenger and freight traffic between Lewiston and Celilo remaining heavy and profitable, it was not until late spring of 1864 that the Oregon Steam Navigation Company decided that the navigability of the Snake above Lewiston should be tested. By then, gold and silver mines in the Boise area of what had become Idaho Territory had developed to such a degree that prospectors, businessmen, and politicians were pouring into the region, creating a demand for cheap, reliable transportation. There was even talk of moving the capital of the newly-created Territory from Lewiston south to Boise City.

While taking no sides in the controversy, the O.S.N. Company was determined to get its share of the business in southwestern Idaho—either by steaming its boats through the rapids of the big canyon or by transporting the pieces of a boat to be built across the Blue Mountains, putting them together on the river near Farewell Bend, and starting steamboat service on the upper river from there.

Because Captain Stump wanted all the water he could get under his boat's keel so that the rapids would be flattened out, the time chosen for the attempt was late May, when snowmelt in the mountains upriver would supply a maximum flow through the Big Canyon. Because of the risks involved, only two passengers would be carried aboard the *Colonel Wright*: Alonzo Leland, editor of the *Radiator*, and William H. Gray, Willie's father. Though both men agreed that they would not hold

Captain Stump or the O.S.N. Company responsible for their safety, the captain told Willie he was not worried about them, for, in his opinion, "They're both too ornery to drown."

Indeed, both were outspoken, cantankerous men. Having come to the Pacific Northwest with the Whitman-Spalding party of missionaries in 1836, William H. Gray had been in on almost every historical event that had happened since, thus felt it his right to record regional history as he had lived it. As for Alonzo Leland, the fiery-tempered editor carried on a number of feuds with local people who differed with him.

For instance, he called Superior Court Judge Samuel C. Parks, whom he detested, "judge of a most inferior court."

Carrying on a long-distance feud with James Reynolds, editor of the *Idaho-Statesman* down in Boise City, over the proposed relocation of the Territorial capital from Lewiston to Boise City, Leland claimed Reynolds "was so lazy he never worked but once—and that was when he mistook castor oil for bourbon."

In response, Jim Reynolds refused to capitalize the name of the town or the editor of the *Radiator*, referring to them as the "lewiston lelander."[11]

Personally disagreeable though the two passengers could be, both men knew that on this exploring trip upriver aboard the *Colonel Wright* they must mind their manners or risk being tossed overboard, for Captain Stump was the undisputed master of his boat. Alonzo Leland told the captain that despite his earlier endorsement of the report turned in by the scouting party a year and a half ago, he was beginning to doubt its truth himself, and would certainly say so in print if it proved to be wrong. Admitting that he could not swim a lick, he gladly accepted the offer of a life-saving vest made him by Willie Gray, who now was first mate of the *Colonel Wright* at the age of nineteen, earning the princely wage of $150 per month.

"In fact, if you don't mind, I'll take two lifejackets," he said, casting an apprehensive glance over the side at the brown, surging current. "That water looks awfully cold and rough."

After contemptuously declining a flotation device himself, William H. Gray snorted, "A dozen life jackets won't help you if you go overboard in a rapid like Wild Goose."

"Why not?" Leland asked nervously.

"Because the first thing that will happen, you'll hit your head on a rock and be knocked unconscious. Second, there's more foam than water in that kind of rapid, so the water won't support you. Third, when you gasp for breath you'll take foam rather than air into your lungs, so you'll drown inside before you do outside."

"Well, I do thank you for those reassuring words, Mr. Gray," the editor said sarcastically. "But I'll wear two life jackets all the same."

Called up to the pilot house soon after the boat got under way, Willie Gray listened intently as Captain Stump told him what his duties would be on this exploratory trip upriver.

"I want the river charted mile by mile, just in case the O.S.N. Company decides to make commercial runs through the Big Canyon. Note the landmarks on each side of the river and give each rapid a name. Don't pester me with questions as to why I'm steering a certain course. But if I say anything about my navigation, write it down—leaving out the cuss words. Can you do that, Willie?"

"Yes sir."

"Taking notes is good—so long as you don't let them turn to concrete in your head. Always remember that a rapid changes day by day and is different going downstream from going up. Keep reading the river, as well as your notes, and remember what you learn. In time, you may become as good a riverman as your father."

Both William Gray Sr. and Captain Stump knew from experience how rapidly the hazards of a river's bottom could change. Probably neither of them was aware of the hydraulic fact that when the force of a stream's current doubles its carrying capacity increases sixty-four times. Thus, a ten-ton boulder anchored securely to the bottom one day in low water, could go bouncing like a cork to a new location the next in times of flood. But having seen such things happen many times, they were aware of the hazard.

Some years earlier, William H. Gray had gone forty-five miles up the Snake to the mouth of Salmon River with an Indian guide; so he told his son that he would name the points, landmarks, and rapids as he remembered them that far, so that Willie could record them on his chart.

Though the current was strong and the water a murky brown color due to springtime erosion and placer mining operations upstream, no rapids of any consequence impeded the progress of the *Colonel Wright* for the first two hours of the warm spring day. Goat Island, Swallows Nest, Asotin, and Ten Mile Rapids were traversed and noted on Willie's chart. A quarter-mile wide and contained between low basaltic hills now covered with a lush growth of soft, green bunchgrass—which would turn crisp and brown with the coming of summer—the Snake moved with quiet power through empty, rolling hill country. Except for an occasional white settler's log cabin and a handful of slab-roofed Indian pit-houses and tepees pitched on sandbars, few signs of civilization were visible.

Twenty miles upriver from Lewiston on the Idaho side of the river, several large lava boulders near the water's edge created a swirling pool in which the current turned back on itself, forming what Willie's father told him was called Buffalo Rock Eddy.

"My Indian boatman took me ashore to show me some picture writings on the face of the rocks. Best I could make out, the pictures were supposed to be mountain sheep, bears, horses, or maybe even people. They were so crude and primitive it was hard to tell."

"Who painted them?"

"Nobody could say. All my Indian guides knew was that they were 'old—very old.' They weren't much as paintings. Just stick figures like kids draw in school."

At Mile 24, the *Colonel Wright* ascended a short stretch of white water near the Idaho side of the river called "Captain John" Rapid by his Indian boatmen, Gray said, and at Mile 25, one on the Washington Territory side called "Billy Creek" Rapid."

"The Indians told me Captain John was a Nez Perce brave who scouted for Colonel George Wright back in '58 and was proud of it. Who 'Billy' was, nobody knew."

Coming into the Snake from the Washington side at Mile 29, the Grande Ronde River was swollen with late spring snowmelt from the 10,000-foot-high Wallowa Mountains to the southwest.

Looming above the river a mile upstream was a gray, rocky bluff called Lime Point. Here, foothills on either side of the Snake grew higher and steeper, compressing the river into a narrowing space which Gray Sr. said was the lower end of the big canyon.

"We'll get a sample of what's in store for us when we hit Wild Goose Rapid, a few miles farther on. If Captain Stump can drive his boat up it without using his power capstan, I'll take my hat off to him."

"Is Wild Goose worse than what we've seen so far?"

"Much worse. When the Indians took me upriver, we portaged around it. Coming down, we shot it at full speed, coming over a six-foot ledge of white water like we were falling out of a barn loft. When we hit the pool below, it gave us a jolt that shook our teeth loose."

Reaching the foot of Wild Goose Rapid at Mile 33, Captain Stump rang the engine room to slow the speed of the stern-wheel to the point that the boat merely held its own against the current while he peered intently into the glare of the noontime sunlight ahead, studying the rapid. Standing beside him in the pilot house and listening attentively to what he was saying was First Mate Willie Gray, while the William Gray, Sr., and the nervous newspaper editor, Alonzo Leland, stood on the deck outside and below the pilot house. respectfully keeping silent while Captain Stump planned his attack on the rapid.

"Looks like the best bet would be to stay to the right of that long, narrow island, which splits the river into two channels. Lots of water pouring through it, but it's coming straight and fast down the right-hand channel. We'll hit it with all we've got and see what happens."

"What do you make of the left-hand channel, sir?" Willie asked.

"Looks tricky to me. The current doesn't appear to be as fast as it is in the right-hand channel, but it's pinched into such a narrow chute that it forms a sneaky back eddy. The water in half of the channel is racing downstream, while that in the other half is turning back on itself and going upstream. If we hit that spot wrong, we'll lose steering-way and spin around like a cork."

Bill Gulick photo
White sand beach, Snake River south side above Lower Granite Dam. Many beaches in
the thirty-three-mile stretch of river were flooded by the backwaters of the dam.

"Have you considered winching?"

"May have to, Willie. But we'll try straight power first."

For this maiden trip, the *Colonel Wright* had stocked its
engine room with high-quality fuel—dry, seasoned pine cordwood well laced with pitch—which would provide maximum
steam pressure for the boilers. Designed to operate at 185
pounds per square inch, the boilers could stand 200 or more for
brief periods of time, Chief Engineer Chester O'Malley told the
captain. What did he mean by "brief"? Ten, twelve minutes,
maybe. Beyond that, well, he didn't know.

Dropping back into slack water downriver in order to have
room to build up momentum and hit the rapid at maximium
speed, Captain Stump leaned over toward the engine-room
speaking tube and said, "Give me all you've got, Chet! Tie down
the safety valve and hope she doesn't blow!"

"Aye, sir! Let 'er rip!"

In addition to a pair of deckhands who were doubling as stokers, the boat carried a supply of spare planking, soft-patch materials, a master carpenter, and two helpers so that quick repairs could be made in case the boat hit the rocks and holed her sides or bottom. Feeling the deck under his feet vibrate as the thundering of the engine increased to a sustained roar, Willie gripped the nearby railing until his knuckles turned white, rising on tiptoe as he urged the boat on.

"Go, baby! Go!"

Three hundred yards in length, Wild Goose was slightly wider at its lower end than its upper. With the momentum she had gained by hitting the rapid running, the *Colonel Wright* climbed the first hundred yards of the tumbling white water briskly, the second hundred more slowly, then fell back to the point where she was making no progress at all. For half a minute she hung on balance, motionless in the middle of the constricted channel.

Captain Stump leaned toward the speaking tube.

"Got any more, Chet?"

"Sorry, sir. You've got it all."

"Ease off, then. She's shaking herself to pieces."

As the speed of the threshing stern-wheel slowed, the *Colonel Wright* drifted back into quieter water. Letting her rest there for a few minutes to cool down the engines and give the stokers time to build up a new head of steam, Captain Stump then increased power and tested the left-hand channel. Noting that he kept the boat's stern well to the right of where the back eddy turned the current upstream, Willie was not surprised when the captain shook his head, eased off the power, and let the boat drift back downstream.

"Too goddamn risky!" Willie heard him mutter. "If we lose steering-way here, we'll be on the rocks before we can correct it."

Pulling in to the right hand bank, Captain Stump ordered Willie, two deckhands, and two carpenter's helpers ashore with a two-inch-thick line, which they unreeled from the power capstan in the bow as they carried it upstream to a point above the rapids, where they secured it around the base of an immense black lava rock. Leaning out the window of the pilot house, Captain Stump spoke to the senior William Gray, who was standing on the deck just below.

"Did you teach your son how to secure a line, Mr. Gray?"

"By the time he was ten, Captain Stump," Gray answered testily. "If he hadn't learned it by then, I'd have drowned him."

"All right, Willie," the captain called down. "Signal the engine room to tighten the slack, then tell them to give us full power on the winch. We'll see if we can walk her up the rapid."

With the capstan pulling and the stern-wheel pushing, the *Colonel Wright* moved into the white water of the right hand channel once again. This time, the boat moved through the tumbling torrent without difficulty. After reaching slack water above the rapid, the boat pulled in close to shore, giving the line looped about the big lava rock enough slack that it could be loosened and brought aboard by Willie Gray and his crew.

"Make a note, Willie," Captain Stump called down, "that Wild Goose must be lined. For future traffic, it would simplify matters if the O.S.N. Company engineers would bury a big iron ring in the face of the rock we tied to."

"Yes, sir," Willie said. The puzzled frown on his face as he wrote the notation down on his clipboard made the captain realize Willie was dying to ask for a fuller explanation, so Captain Stump gave it to him. "What the engineers will do, Willie, is cinch one end of a line into the ring, let a quarter mile of it float downstream through the rapid to the quiet water below, with a barrel attached to its lower end. When a boat bound upriver comes along—"

"It'll pick up the barrel with a boat hook," Willie blurted impulsively, "fasten the end of the line to its power capstan, then winch its way up the rapid."

"Exactly!"

"That's real clever, sir! I'll write it all down."[12]

Chapter 5 footnotes.

1. Dan L. Thrapp, *Encyclopedia of Frontier Biography,* The Arthur H. Clark Company, Glendale, California, 1988, p. 1602, states: "Wright's operations had mixed results; they were not as decisive as the army claimed, not as meaningless as opposition voices alleged. . . with the Civil War Wright was promoted to Brigadier General of Volunteers and named in October 1861, to command the Department of the Columbia, but was drowned in the wreck of the *Brother Jonathan*, off the northern California coast.

2. *Oregon City Argus*, May 19, 1855; quoted in "Frontier Humor in Oregon," by Randall V. Mills, OHQ, XLIII, No. 4, December 1942, p. 345.

3. *A Dictionary of Americanisms on Historical Principles*, edited by Mitford M. Matthews, University of Chicago Press, 1951, p. 228.

4. "Up Snake River," by L.W. Coe, *Overland Monthly,* August, 1886, Vol. 8, 2nd series. Coe was one of the owners of the Colonel Wright.

5. Ibid.

6. Ibid.

7. Fluent in English, friendly to the whites, and a persuasive talker, Hol-lol-sote-tote soon acquired the name "Lawyer' because he favored negotiating to get what he wanted for his people instead of going to war. *Henry Harmon Spalding*, by Clifford M. Drury, Caxton, 1936, p. 144.

8. "Steamboat Down the Snake," by Merle Wells, *Idaho Yesterdays*, Vol. 5, No. 4, Winter, 1961-62.

9. *The Fur Hunters of the Far West*, by Alexander Ross, London, Smith, Elder, 1855; reprint edited by Kenneth A. Spaulding, University of Oklahoma Press, 1956, pp. 138, 139.

10. "Reminiscences of Captain William P. Gray," by Fred Lockley, *Oregon Historical Quarterly,* XIV, No. 4, December 1913, pp. 321-41.

11. Ibid.

12. Re-created dialog.

CHAPTER SIX
Willie Gray, rapids swimmer

T hree miles upstream from Wild Goose Rapid, at Mile 36,
a moderate stretch of white water toward the Idaho side
of the river was encountered and passed without difficulty. Because a cluster of Chinese miners had settled along a
gulch running back into the mountains, building crude shelters
of stacked rocks, assembling sluice boxes and rockers, and digging panning pools along the shore, the spot was called China
Gardens, Willie's father told him. Why had the word "Gardens"
been added? Because as they always did where good soil, water,
sunlight, and fertilizer were available, the Chinese had established a flourishing kitchen vegetable garden from which they
fed themselves and usually had extra fresh produce to sell.

With the afternoon almost gone and everyone worn out after
a long, tension-filled day, Captain Stump decided this would be
a good place to tie up for the night. When cook Mose Titus asked
Willie to go ashore with him to bargain with the Chinese for
food, Willie was glad to do so, for he was curious about the alien
race of people which more and more of late had settled in this
part of the country. Willing to do any kind of labor for wages
below what a white man would accept, the Chinese were not
recognized as citizens nor welcomed as prospectors in
California, Oregon, or Idaho gold camps. Where they usually
appeared as miners was in remote places such as this in the
depths of the big canyon of the Snake, taking over diggings
deserted by white men after most of the gold had been removed,

settling on sandbars where their patient, careful panning produced a couple of dollars worth of flour gold for a day's work—
far too little to satisfy a white man but a decent day's wage for
an Oriental.

From the excited manner in which the Chinese were chat-
tering with one another and pointing at the *Colonel Wright*,
Willie gathered that seeing a stern-wheeler come this far up the
Snake was a surprising event to them. Though they appeared to
welcome this opportunity to sell their produce to the boat's crew,
the fact that white civilization had reached this remote canyon
gave them a grim foreboding of bad things to come.

Despite the language barrier of sing-song Cantonese,
Southern Negro drawl, Chinook jargon, and Willie's more pre-
cise English, a basis for trade was soon reached. Just as Mose
Titus knew a firm cabbage when he felt one, so were the
Chinese aware of the value of the gold dust in Willie's buckskin
purse, so an offer was quickly made and readily accepted.[1]

Returning to the boat with a bushel basketful of fresh veg-
etables, Mose Titus bustled down to his galley while Willie
found a deck chair forward in the bow where he could finish
recording his notes for the day. As the late spring sun dropped
below the cliffs to the west and the great river whispered past,
he wrote:

> *At the end of our first day of exploring the Big Canyon
> of the Snake, we tied up on the Idaho side of the river at
> Mile 36 just above a rapid called China Gardens. Bought
> some fresh vegetables raised by some Chinese miners who
> live here. Mose Titus thinks they're a strange sort of peo-
> ple—and so do I. But I suppose they think we're strange,
> too.*

Next morning while the stokers built up the fire under the
boilers, the crew ate breakfast. Two hours after sunrise, the
boat cast off her lines and the *Colonel Wright* resumed its cautious exploration of the big canyon of the Snake. As dark brown
cliffs rose ever more steeply on either side of the river, Willie
noted rapids and landmarks such as Cougar Bar, Cave Gulch,
and Deep Creek at Miles 37, 39, and 44. At Mile 48, the largest,

Mouth of the Palouse River. From a painting by John Mix Stanley.

most turbulent river yet seen—the Salmon—poured its raging waters into the Snake from the southeast, breaking through a high, narrow gorge from the Idaho side of the river.

"This was as far up as I went with my Indian guides," Gray Sr. told his son as he leaned close and shouted to make himself heard over the roar of the rapids and the threshing of the boat's stern-wheel. "They told me the Salmon heads in high mountain country three or four hundred miles to the southeast. It's filled with impassable rapids almost all the way, they said."

That was what the Indians had told Lewis and Clark, Willie knew, when the explorers came west in 1805. Clark named it "Lewis's River" because Meriwether Lewis was the first white man to see it. When Lewis told Clark that the river looked unnavigable, Clark insisted on viewing it himself. A few miles of traveling along its upper reaches convinced him that Lewis was right. He wrote in his journal that he found the steep banks of the river impossible to traverse:

> . . .*without a road, over rocky hillsides where the horses were in perpetual danger of slipping to their certain destruction...with the greatest difficulty and risk made five miles and camped.* . .[2]

After losing three horses to injury or exhaustion, Clark gave up, rejoined Lewis and the main party, and sought an easier way across the mountains farther north.

"Just out of curiosity," Gray told his son, "I got out of the canoe and hiked a mile or so up the canyon of the Salmon. It was rough going, believe me. Where the Salmon bursts through those sheer lava rocks yonder there's a gap so narrow the Indians call it 'Eye of the Needle.' Just above it is a race of white water prospectors named the 'Sluice Box' because when you ride downstream through it in a boat it shakes the gold fillings out of your teeth."

Because there was plenty of water in the Snake below the mouth of the Salmon at this time of year, Captain Stump encountered no trouble in the center of the main river channel. But visualizing future navigational problems, he told Willie, "Make a note that at low stage a boat should stay as close to the rough water on the Idaho side of the river as it can, without actually getting into it."

"Yes, sir."

"What likely will happen at that level of water is that the Salmon will dump whatever gravel it has carried during the spring runoff into the Snake, forming a bar that may cause trouble. But there'll always be a deep channel close to the rough water."

Above the mouth of the Salmon, the Snake entered a canyon so narrow, sheer, and filled with tumbling white water that the *Colonel Wright* moved against the current only by using maximum power. At both High Mountain Sheep, Mile 49, and Imnaha Rapid, Mile 51, the boat was forced to pull in to shore and send a crew ahead with a line so that the *Colonel Wright* could winch its way through the raging white water. Telling Willie to note that at one spot in the middle of the stretch of the big canyon the river was only sixty feet wide, Captain Stump added, "If we turned the boat broadside there, both the bow and stern would be high and dry. Of course, the way the Snake pours through this part of the canyon, it'd be driven under in no time at all."

Having found three rapids that must be winched in the first fifty-one miles upriver from Lewiston, Alonzo Leland, formerly

Corps of Engineers photo
The Snake River in Hells Canyon, a few miles downstream from the Chinese mines.

a strong supporter of the explorers who had declared rapturously that they had "found nothing in the river to impede navigation whatever," had to admit that their report was dead wrong. Anxious to promote commercial travel on the Snake, the editor asked Captain Stump if he thought judicious blasting of a few rocks scattered through the three rapids would make them more easily surmounted.

"Might help," Stump grunted, nodding. "But it would be an awful expensive job. Who'd pay for it?"

"Perhaps the merchants of Lewiston would pick up part of the cost, if the O.S.N. Company would pay the rest. Or maybe our territorial representative could persuade the Corps of Engineers to undertake it as a federal project. After all, the engineers are in charge of making improvements in the nation's rivers."

"In its navigable rivers, Mr. Leland," Captain Stump corrected him. "We've' still got a long way to go before we can say the

Snake above Lewiston is navigable."[3]

At Douglas Bar, Mile 56, the terrain on the Oregon side of the river flattened out for half a mile or so back from the water's edge, then began to rise in a series of steep slopes slashed by winding trails which were scarred by the hoofs of many horses. At this spot, William Gray Sr. told his son, the Wallowa band of Nez Perce Indians often cross the Snake on their way to visit their fellow tribesmen living on the Idaho side of the river.

"You mean they ferry the river here?" Willie asked incredulously.

"Not exactly, boy. What they do is they make bull boats out of buffalo hides and willow frames, pile the women, children, old men, and all their belongings in the boats, then pull them across the river behind young bucks mounted on swimming horses."

"Strong as the current is here, I'd think they'd be swept under and drowned."

"They very seldom get into trouble, I'm told by Indians who have crossed here. Usually, they wait till the river is at a much lower stage than it is now. When it goes down, they say, there's a back eddy half way across that will carry a bull boat or a swimming horse straight to the shallows on the Idaho shore. The Indians call this place 'Nez Perce Crossing.'"

Numbering the spot Mile 57 on his chart, Willie wrote that down. Last year, his father said, more than fifty chiefs of the Nez Perce tribe had met with federal commissioners at Lapwai, headquarters of the Nez Perce Reservation, for a week of talks whose purpose had been to reduce the size of the reservation and bring bands now living in the Wallowa Valley to the Idaho reserve. The chiefs of five dissident bands had refused to sign the new treaty, preferring to dissolve the Nez Perce nation rather than give up their freedom. The leader of the rebellious bands had been a Christianized chief named Old Joseph, who was so incensed by the revised treaty that he tore up his Bible and rejected the white man's religion from that time on.[4]

For three more days, the *Colonel Wright* fought her way up the never-ending rapids of the Snake River, her captain, crew, and passengers hoping that beyond the next bend the white water would grow calmer, the confining bluffs would lower and

Corps of Engineers photo
Deep Creek, China Gulch on the Snake River.

recede, and the way would open for clear, easy steaming on toward Boise City. But it was not to be. Instead, the water grew rougher, the canyon narrower, and the cliff walls on either side turned into towering mountains.

At one spot in the depths of the canyon, Captain Stump took a sighting with an improvised hand level which indicated that from the boat's upper deck to a mountain peak directly above, the vertical distance was at least a mile. Ironically, the place where Captain Stump decided to end the attempt to steam any farther up the river at Mile 73 deserved the name Pleasant Valley on Willie's chart, for above the sandbar at river level an attractive vista of flat, fertile-looking land could be seen, a really lovely spot on which to file a land claim and build a cabin. Certainly neighbors would be no problem, for in the seventy-three mile stretch of river between this point and Lewiston only a handful of Indians, Chinese prospectors, and settlers could be found.

But at water level, the Pleasant Valley Rapid was a bad one; during a reconnaissance for half a dozen miles upriver along the shoreline, those ahead appeared to be even worse.

"By my calculations," Captain Stump said, shaking his head, "there's at least a hundred miles more of canyon, rocks, and white water between here and Farewell Bend, where the Oregon Trail crosses the Snake. No steamboat man in his right mind would even consider starting a commercial operation on this stretch of river."

Turning the bow of the *Colonel Wright* downstream at eleven o'clock in the morning, Captain Stump either got careless or underestimated the power of the current pushing the boat downstream. After barreling into a rapid at a high rate of speed, the boat suddenly was caught in a vicious whirlpool circling toward a sheer lava bluff looming above the Idaho shore, yawed sickeningly to the right, then careened into the jagged, projecting rocks, ripping her starboard side from stem to stern with a crunching sound of tearing timbers.

As the boat spun around in the quieter water downstream from the point where she had struck, Captain Stump, who was fighting the wheel, shouted frantic orders.

"Stop engines, Chet! Full power astern! Willie, get a crew ashore with a line. Try to snub her off when we float free. In case she heels over and starts to sink, we've got to keep her bow above water!"

"Aye, aye, sir! Pa, Mr. Leland, everybody lend a hand! Grab hold of the line and take it ashore!"

Never in all his days aboard the *Colonel Wright,* Captain

Stump said later, had he seen a crew pick up a line and carry it ashore with such speed. First Mate Willie, his father, Editor Alonzo Leland, the master carpenter and his two helpers, and both deckhands all grabbed hold of the heavy two-inch line by its ends, its middle, and wherever else they could seize it, leaped over the side and waded up onto the long stretch of sandy beach below the rapid. Turning to brace themselves as the stricken boat hit the end of the line, Willie Gray at one end and his father at the other, each had a fixed loop in hand, shaped to fit neat-

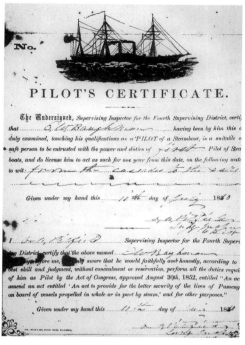

PILOT'S CERTIFICATE.

Nez Perce County Historical Society
River pilot's certificate

ly over a bollard aboard the boat or a rock ashore so that the boat could be snubbed off and kept afloat.

Unfortunately, both Willie and his father's loops at the line ends were ashore, for each had assumed that the other would drop *his* loop over the boat's bollard.

As events turned out, it did not matter, for even as they stared at each other with sheepish chagrin, Captain Stump worked the *Colonel Wright* free of the rocks in which she was entangled, moved her out into the main channel of the river, took her downstream a quarter mile, then, finding quieter water there, brought her bow into the current. Easing her into the shallows off the Idaho shore, he patiently waited for the line-carrying crew to walk down the bank and rejoin the boat.[5]

While Willie and his crew shame-facedly coiled and stowed the line aboard, Captain Stump and the master carpenter went below to appraise the damage done to the boat's side. The fifteen-foot-long rupture was well above the water line, it turned out, so an hour's labor by the carpenter and his helpers sufficed to make temporary repairs so that the hull would not leak and the boat could safely embark on its return trip to Lewiston. In his final report, Willie noted:

> *Covered the same distance it had taken us four and a half days to ascend the river in three and a half hours coming down.*

While the *Colonel Wright* was out of service undergoing permanent repairs, First Mate Willie Gray approached Captain Tom Stump and asked for a week's leave to undertake a private venture. When asked its nature, Willie said, "A man named Phil Atwood owns a sawmill above Clarkston on the Washington side of the river, sir. He says lumber there is worth only fifteen dollars a thousand board feet. But if he can get it down the Snake and Columbia to Umatilla, Oregon, which is booming, he can sell it for fifty-five dollars a thousand."

"Why doesn't he?"

"He's tried several times, he says, making up rafts of lumber and trying to float them down the river. But his luck so far has been bad. When the rafts hit the rapids, they break up, the lumber is scattered for miles along the banks, and before he can recover it, white settlers and Indians pick it up and carry it away."

"What does he want you to do?"

"I told him, sir, that if his lumber raft was put together right, and if he got the right man to take it downriver for him, it would get to Umatilla in two or three days."

Captain Stump smiled around his newly lighted cigar. "Then you told him you were the right man?"

"Yes, sir, I did. For ten dollars a day, I told him, I'd take on the job and guarantee to float his raft of lumber down to Umatilla within a week without a piece missing."

"Well, if anybody can do it, Willie, you can. Hop to it."

After supervising, assembling, and lashing together a raft containing fifty thousand board feet of lumber at Phil Atwood's mill just above Clarkston, Willie Gray brought it across the river to Lewiston, where Atwood added 10,000 feet more. A big, red-faced man in his early forties, Atwood hovered at Willie's side, nervously questioning him about every detail of the operation.

"Don't worry about a thing, Mr. Atwood," Willie reassured him. "I know every rock and rapid in the river. I won't lose a stick of your lumber."

"I'm going to be riding on the raft with you, Mr. Gray. I won't let you go without me."

"If you insist, sir. I'll carry a skiff amidships in case you decide to get off."

"How big a crew will you be hiring, Mr., Gray?"

"There'll be no crew, Mr. Atwood. Only me."

"How will you control, the raft?"

"With a single steering oar, sir, which I'll be holding at the stern."

"That sounds crazy to me. On the other rafts, we had three men, two with sweeps on each side and one steering in the stern, doing their best to keep the rafts out of the fast water. But they weren't enough. Once the rafts got into the rapids, they broke up and my lumber was scattered all over the river."

"Your men didn't know what they were doing, Mr. Atwood. I do."

"You *say* you do. But I'm not so sure."

"Relax, Mr. Atwood. Just sit back and enjoy the ride."

Between Lewiston, Idaho, and Umatilla, Oregon, lay 180 miles of the Snake and Columbia, with at least half a dozen major and two dozen minor rapids, Willie knew, in any one of which the raft could come to grief. During previous unsuccessful attempts to float lumber rafts downriver, crews had tried to manage them with side sweeps. All he planned to use was a steering oar at the rear. When approaching a rapid, his predecessors had made desperate efforts to keep to the edge of the rapid in order to avoid the faster water. In the same situation, he intended to steer the raft directly toward the center of the rapid, where the current's force would give the clumsy raft such impetus that it would quickly shoot through into slack water. If worst came to worst, Willie knew that for him all the rapids were swimmable—a piece of knowledge likely of small comfort to Mr. Atwood.

As they moved down the Snake at a brisk nine miles an hour, Willie cheerfully told his employer that they would get along all right until they came to Palouse Rapid.

"There we might have a serious time of it," he said, "for the water pours through a narrow chute and empties into an eddy, which boils back toward the current from the south shore."

"But you think you can get through?" Mr. Atwood demanded.

"Yes, sir. One way or another."

"What does that mean?"

Before Willie could answer, the front part of the raft entered the rapid and he was too busy to talk. The current proved to be so swift that it shot the raft into the eddy at breakneck speed. Before he and Atwood knew what was happening, the forward part of the raft went under water, then the current caught the back end of the raft and it went under, too.

"We're sinking, Mr. Gray!" Atwood screamed.

Indeed, that was exactly what was happening, Willie realized, for the raft was no longer in sight beneath them. Now the water covering it was up to their knees. Seeing the skiff about to float away, Willie grabbed its painter, told Atwood to get aboard, then joined him. Picking up the oars, Willie used them to keep the skiff pointed downstream in the same general direction the raft had been going when it disappeared.

"What happened to the raft?" Atwood shouted in bewilderment.

Too embarrassed to admit he did not know, Willie made no reply. Reaching down with an oar, he could feel only water beneath him, so he continued to concentrate on keeping the skiff in the middle of the main channel. Truth was, his confidence was badly shaken, for this had been his first command— and he had lost it. As for Mr. Atwood, his face, his voice, and his words were gloomy.

"I should have known you couldn't do it, Mr. Gray. Running a steamboat through a rapid like the Palouse is one thing. Taking a big, clumsy raft of lumber through it all by yourself is quite another. The raft will bust apart, I'm sure of that. If and when it does come up, my lumber will be scattered all over the river—"

By now, the skiff was half a mile downstream from Palouse

Rapid, where the water was deep and quiet. Suddenly Mr. Atwood broke off his angry tirade, then exclaimed, "Willie! Do you feel something coming up from underneath us?"

"Yes, sir! I do!"

What they both felt at the same time was the big, clumsy raft of lumber—still intact—rising out of the depths underneath, lifting the skiff—which was still positioned dead center on the raft—clear of the water. Not a single lashing was broken; not a stick of lumber was out of place.

Telling the story later to Captain Stump, Willie concluded, "You never saw a man more pleased than Mr. Atwood."

It was small wonder that Phil Atwood was pleased. For Willie's four days' work plus a day's bonus given out of the goodness of his heart, Phil Atwood had paid the nineteen-year-old riverman fifty dollars. For this sum, William Polk Gray had brought a raft of lumber worth $900 in Lewiston, Idaho, downriver to Umatilla, Oregon, where it sold for thirty-three hundred dollars—a net profit of slightly under $2,400. Not a bad return on a fifty-dollar investment.[6]

Chapter 6 footnotes

1. Re-created dialog.
2. Bernard DeVoto, Editor, *Lewis and Clark Journals*, op. cit., pg. 232.
3. During the early years of its existence, the Corps of Engineers was assigned the task of clearing obstructions from established harbors and navigable rivers. Gradually over the years, its duties were expanded to making harbors more usable and rivers more navigable when benefits could be shown to exceed costs.
4. Upon his return to the Wallowa country, Old Joseph set poles ten inches thick and ten feet long in cairns of rock along Minam Grade, telling a white man through an interpreter that they showed "where his line was to the Wallowa country. "
   Known as "Old Joseph's Deadline to early settlers in the area, the markers were maintained by the Nez Perces and seen, if not respected, by the whites for a number of years. Grace Bartlett, *The Wallowa Country, 1867-77*, Enterprise, Ore., 1976, p. 3.
5. "Reminiscences," Gray, op. cit..
6. Ibid.

Glory days on the river

A fter helping his father take the keelboat upriver through the rapids between the mouth of the Snake and Lewiston, William Polk Gray claimed, "There has never been any combination of wood, iron, or water that has ever scared me."

But what he called "narrow escapes" did frighten him, he admitted. In his youth, he certainly had his share of them.

"As a boy of four years of age," he wrote later, "I rolled down a sand bank on the ocean shore into a mass of drift logs, with an older brother hauling me out just as a returning wave would have ground me to pieces. As a boy of ten, I climbed the mast of a brig and was placing my hand on the masthead, when my foot slipped. I fell about twenty feet until my foot caught in the crotch of two ropes, leaving me hanging head down until a couple of sailors climbed up and rescued me."[1]

In July 1861, when he was sixteen years old and serving as captain of the *Sarah F. Gray*, which he had helped his father build, he nearly drowned when he miscalculated the depth of the water.

"We were tied to the bank in Umatilla Rapids, waiting for wind. The crew were all ashore. As it was a warm day, I stripped off for a swim. I knew that the water outside was not deep so I took a pole and sounded. Assured that it was all right, I drew a deep breath and leaped out, head first for a dive and a swim down the rapids."

Unfortunately, his sounding had missed a rock just under the surface, which his head did not. Though he was knocked unconscious, the air in his lungs kept his body afloat as it drifted 200 yards downriver, where it was seen by a crew member on the sloop *Mount Hood*, which was anchored there. Fishing him out of the river, the crew members laid him on the deck and started pumping his arms to get the water out of his lungs and revive him, which they soon did.

"In the spring of '63, my father had a row with a purser for stealing," Willie recalled later. "One day father was lying on some cord wood on the boat, dozing. When the purser saw him asleep, he stole aboard, seized an axe, and drew back to strike him in the head. Father didn't see him, but I did, catching the axe just before the man struck and jerking it out of his hands."

Thrown off balance, the man fell overboard into three feet of water. Wading ashore, he drew a gun described by Willie Gray as "a five-shooter," and began firing at the boat. The crew dodged for cover, but Willie, who had tried to shoot the same revolver before and thought it a poor excuse for a gun, ran down the gangplank, picked up a rock, and hit the man directly in the stomach, "which was a large target."

"One of his shots drew blood on my right hand," Willie said, "and another cut the shoe on my right little toe. But my rock in the stomach ended the fight."[2]

The next violent incident involving Gray occurred when he was captain of the *Almota*, a premier boat in the fabled "Wheat Fleet" carrying grain downriver to Portland.

Shortly after tying up in late afternoon on the north side of the Snake at Palouse Ferry, the boat was approached by a bedraggled man in an Army uniform, who asked for free passage downriver to Wallula. Gray told him the company had given him strict orders not to carry anyone without a ticket or a pass.

"I don't have any money for a ticket," the soldier said. "Can I at least sleep aboard?"

Running the Snake at night was considered too dangerous, so the boat would stay at the landing until daylight. Giving the soldier permission to sleep aboard, Gray told the watchman to make sure the man got off the boat early the next morning. Just

Columbia River Maritime Museum
The owners of the Shaver Trasportation Company in Portland took pride in their hard-
working stern-wheeler tugboats. Boats from the Shaver fleet line up for a publicity
photo.

after daylight, the watchman came up to the pilot house and
told Captain Gray that the man was still on board.

"Put him ashore," Gray said curtly.

But the man refused to leave the boat, again asking to be
taken to Wallula even though he could not buy a ticket. When
Gray blew the whistle signal to let go the lines and get under
way, the man still would not leave, so Gray came down to the
hurricane deck and confronted the soldier, who was trying to
climb the ladder leading up from the passenger deck.

"Get off the boat!"

"No! You've got to take me to Wallula!"

Putting a foot on the man's shoulder, Captain Gray tried to
force him down to the passenger deck. When that effort failed,
Gray jumped down to the lower deck, seized the soldier around
the waist, and tried to scuffle him to the ladder leading down to
the main deck. After resisting for a few moments, the man
appeared to surrender, saying,

"All right, I'll go. Just give me my blankets and I'll get off the
boat."

Getting the blankets, Gray handed them to the soldier, who
started to leave, then turned back, saying, "The hell with you! I
won't go ashore."

Exasperated with the obstinacy of the man, Gray crowded past him, grabbed him around the waist, pulled him down the stairs to the main deck, picked him up, and then threw him bodily ashore. Sure that the matter was settled, Gray turned away and was climbing the ladder to the hurricane deck when the man drew a revolver and started shooting at him, the first bullet from his gun singeing the shoulder of Gray's coat.

"How I had missed feeling the gun strapped to his waist when I scuffled with him, I don't know," Gray said, "but I had. My first thought was to get a weapon and shoot back. I rushed up to the officers' room, where I knew Van Pelt, the assistant pilot, and Charlie Benson, chief engineer, usually kept a pistol or two. But both weapons had been left ashore to be repaired, so I had to look around for some other kind of weapon."

With the gangplank pulled in but the boat still tied to the dock, the crazed soldier had scrambled back aboard the passenger deck, from which he was firing his revolver up at Captain Gray or anyone else in sight.

"Picking up a fire bucket full of water, I tried to drop it on his head," Gray said. "The bucket missed him but the water did not. When he lowered his gun to wipe the water out of his eyes, Lonnie Johnson, a big, tough fireman who was not afraid of anything, jumped out and knocked him down."

After the man had been tied up, Gray said, "Take his gun and throw him ashore. He hasn't hurt anybody."

"He nearly killed me," groaned the purser, who was doubled over and clutching his groin in excruciating pain. "One of the bullets hit me where I live."

Upon examination, it was found that a ricocheting bullet from the soldier's gun had struck the purser in the crotch, not breaking the skin but inflicting a grievous injury. So the man got free passage downriver to Wallula after all, being confined below decks for the trip. Turning him over to a deputy sheriff at Wallula Landing, Captain Gray requested that he be placed under arrest and charged with assault.

"But since the shooting had been done on the Whitman County side of the river, the Walla Walla County officials refused to take him," Gray said. "So we had to take him back to

Bill Gulick photo

A modern day stern-wheeler.

Palouse Ferry and give him over to Whitman County. He died a year later in jail at Colfax, a raving maniac."[3]

Some years afterwards in Wrangell, Alaska, Captain Gray experienced another "narrow escape" in a case of mistaken identity. While acting as captain of the stern-wheeler *Casca*, running between Fort Wrangell and Telegraph Creek on the Stikine, he was returning to the boat after attending a church social in Wrangell.

"While passing a place where bushes grew close to the board walk," he said, "a man jumped out and struck at me with a knife, aimed at my heart. The knife went through my coat and vest but was turned by my white starched bosom shirt. The stroke was so vicious the man lost his balance. Before he could recover, I had found his throat and knife hand."

The man was a Mexican, Gray learned, who apologetically explained that "he thought I was the man who had stolen his

Idaho Historical Society

Built by the Oregon Steam Navigation Company in 1876 the *Almota* had a large capacity for passengers and freight. On this trip, the boat was met in Lewiston by several Nez Perce Indians.

woman. The next day two ladies mended my coat and vest and warned me against Mexicans."[4]

Perhaps the best way to describe what must be called "glory days on the river" would be to embark on an imaginary trip from the mouth of the Columbia to Lewiston, Idaho Territory, at the height of the gold rush during the 1860s. The distance is 465 miles. People taking the trip could not sleep late. Historian Randall Mills writes:

> *The boats were good, but the passengers had to get up early to ride them. Those heading up the Columbia from Portland loaded all night; lines of drays strung out along Front Street for blocks waiting their turn to drive out on the big two-level company dock at Ash Street. By 4:30 in the morning the passengers began to arrive, and at a little*

before 5:00 the freight was stowed and the pilot climbed into the pilot house.

The wheel was lazily turning, but now black smoke began to roll from the tall stack. Late passengers rushed up the landing stage, and the lines were cast off. The big wheel threshed the water, moving the prow of the boat away from the dock, and a pillar of steam shot from the tall escape pipe. Then with a flurry of white foam the long white vessel turned into the current, pointed downstream and slipped past the town. It was five o'clock in the morning. One hour later the downstream boat for Kalama and Astoria would pull away, and then the dock would be quiet until eleven, when the boat from the Cascades came in.[5]

During the years when steamboat traffic flourished on the river, the whistles of more than 200 boats echoed off the cliffs rising above either shore. Most children learned to identify each whistle lest they be ridiculed by their peers, especially the boys. Many youngsters dreamed of growing up to be steamboat captains—and some of them did, earning such fabulous salaries as $500 a month for being the master of a boat that might pay for itself with one year's travel on the river, bringing cargoes of gold worth a $100,000 down from Idaho to Portland each trip.

As boat builders became more knowledgeable about the river, most of the steamboats plying the quiet, deep waters between Portland and Astoria were side-wheelers, while those running the middle river above the Cascades and upriver from Celilo Falls were stern-wheelers.

Accommodations and amenities on the boats ranged from adequate to luxurious. Usually passengers took breakfast from tables in the main saloon, paying "two-bits" for the meal at first, then later up to twice that price—fifty cents. By the time Portland passengers had finished breakfast on the upriver trip, the boat had run out of the Willamette and into the Columbia, and had stopped briefly on the north shore at Vancouver. If the weather was decent, the passengers gathered on deck to take in the spectacular scenery of the Gorge: Beacon Rock, Rooster Rock, Multnomah Falls.

At first, the Oregon Steam Navigation Company, which soon established a monopoly on river travel, was dead set against having bars aboard its boats. But because gentlemen in that place and time felt a great hardship in traveling dry, bars were soon opened and rented out to concessionaires. Their operations proved so profitable that the company raised no objection when the steamboat's head barkeeper was elevated to the honorary title of "captain," even though he was not licensed to pilot the boat.

At eleven o'clock, the boat docked at the Lower Cascades, where a train of portage cars waited. All the passengers went ashore. Because fast freight headed upriver had to be taken off the boat and transferred to railroad cars, a job that took an hour or so, there was no hurry. Once loaded, the small locomotive that had replaced mules as motive power tooted its whistle and began to move, with the passengers riding in elegant, light-colored coaches.

At the Upper Cascades, the passengers got off the train and ate lunch at a hotel next to the landing. While they waited for the freight to be transferred to the boat destined to take them to The Dalles, they could watch the churning rapids, gawk at the remains of the blockhouse attacked by Indians in 1856, or go to the bar for their second or third drink of the day.

In early afternoon, the stern-wheeler would pull out into the current, more noticeable here, and begin to chug the fifty-odd miles to The Dalles. During the four or five hours of this part of the trip, the scenery changed dramatically. The lush greenery and thick evergreen forest of the rainy region west of the Cascade Mountains gave way to the bleak, open, basalt-covered dry country east of the Cascades. Sated with viewing scenery by now, the lady passengers looked forward to the comfort of a bed in a good hotel (which they hoped would not be cursed with the bane of travelers of that day, fleas, lice, and bedbugs) while the men anticipated a hearty meal, a few drinks in a friendly bar, and a bed in a room shared with not more than three strangers.

"They had a choice," writes Randall Mills. "The Cosmopolitan Hotel or the Umatilla House, the former being somewhat smaller and less gaudy, but still popular, having seventy-five rooms with such luxurious touches as a billiard room and a ladies' par-

lor, with piano. The Umatilla House was said to be the best outside of Portland, in spite of its notoriously friendly fleas and
occasionally chummy bedbugs. Its fittings were elegant—the
only word that seems appropriate to describe them."6

The Umatilla House's 123 rooms and two baths, with a lava-
tory in the basement, made it the most luxurious hotel east of
the Cascades. Its dining room was large and a corps of cooks
and waiters served the crowds that moved through the hotel
every day. Passengers heading downriver were called at 4 a.m.
Those going upriver had to be aboard the portage train in front
of the hotel at five o'clock. If the ever-present wind had not
blown too much sand over the tracks, it took ninety minutes to
reach Celilo Falls. Below the mouth of the Deschutes, John Day,
and Umatilla rivers, tricky rapids challenged the pilots.

Normally, the 120-mile run to Wallula, where the Columbia
made its big bend to the north, took a full day, with the boat laying over there for the night and discharging passengers headed
inland for Walla Walla, thirty miles east by stage, wagon, or
horseback. Early the next morning, the boat would depart for
the mouth of the Snake, eleven miles to the north, then turn
east and prepare for a 140-mile battle with the fierce, treacherous rapids of the Snake, a journey which under the most favorable conditions would take only a day but, when battling late
spring flood waters and ice floes, might take three.

Though most of the steamboats built for the middle and
upper river were stern-wheelers, there were a few exceptions.
The most magnificent example was the Oregon Steam
Navigation Company's *Oneonta*, built in 1863 to serve on the
run from the Upper Cascades to The Dalles. Designed like a
Mississippi River steamboat, she had two tall stacks forward,
with the pilot house behind them and her side-wheels set well
back from center. Her enclosed freight deck extended over the
guards, as did her cabin deck, which stretched from stem to
stern. She was big for her day—182 feet long—and expensive to
operate.

As revenue dwindled along the middle river, the *Oneonta's*
owners asked master pilot Captain John C. Ainsworth to bring
her down through the six-mile stretch of wild rapids to the
lower river, where there was more traffic. Ainsworth decided to

wait until the river ran in full early summer flood, which smoothed out its hazards but picked up its rate of flow to almost thirty miles an hour. To maintain steering-way, the boat needed to cruise faster than the river. Under a full head of steam, the *Oneonta* could do a little better than thirty; coupled with the current, she'd be moving close to sixty miles an hour. Few railroad locomotives of that day could go as fast.

Captain Ainsworth brought the steamer through without so much as a scratch. Never mind that, after seven years of service on the lower river, the *Oneonta* was converted into a barge and ended her days ignonomiously. She'd had her day of glory as the first "mile-a-minute" steamboat to come booming through the Gorge.[7]

In that day of truly free enterprise, the Oregon Steam Navigation Company became sarcastically known as "the benevolent monopoly." Control of the river required ownership of the portages, since they represented bottlenecks in the flow of goods. Portage roads existed on both the Oregon and Washington sides of the river, so the O.S.N. paid the seller's price to buy one of the routes. It immediately reduced rates, bringing its competitor across the river to the verge of bankruptcy, then bought it, too. Not surprisingly, the portage rates went back up shortly thereafter. Applying the same strategy to competing steamboat lines, O.S.N. soon owned all of them. Within a few years, there was not a boat landing, a steamboat, a portage train, or a single facility along the 465 miles of the Columbia and Snake rivers from Astoria to Lewiston that was not stencilled "Property of O.S.N."

The "benevolent" part of the monopoly did not extend to commercial shippers, who screamed to high heaven over the rates they had to pay. For example, a ton of freight in this land of few scales was assumed to measure forty cubic feet. So, if a farmer from Walla Walla wanted to ship a wagon and a team of horses from Wallula Landing to Portland, the O.S.N. agent at Wallula measured the maximum length of the wagon with the team in harness, then measured the maximum height of the wagon unhitched from the team, with its tongue raised vertically, multiplied these figures by the width to determine the cubic

Columbia River Maritime Museum
Although the *Oneonta* was the first steamboat to boom through the Columbia River
Gorge at a mile-a-minute clip, other boats also ran the rapids. The stern-wheeler
Hassalo shoots the rapids while a crowd watches from shore.

footage, and then divided that figure by forty. Thus, the calcu-
lated tonnage far exceeded the real weight.

Of course, after the team and wagon were taken aboard, the
horses would be stalled below deck, the wheels and tongue of
the wagon would be removed and stacked inside the bed, other
wagons would be placed on top, and the load securely tied down.
But the tonnage figure remained the same.

The benevolence was applied to those folks down on their
luck, such as an unsuccessful gold miner, who would be given
passage and meals downriver "on the cuff", or a cash-poor merchant or farmer, who could put freight charges "on account" and
pay them if he became solvent. But when the traffic could bear
it, the O.S.N. Company charged the users of its services to the
limit.[8]

Once it had been established that a steamboat could not go
upstream through Hells Canyon, the Oregon Steam Navigation
Company began to consider the possibility of building and
launching a boat upriver from the obstacle. Owned by Portland
interests, the company had a profitable monopoly on the freight
and passenger traffic ascending the Columbia and Snake to the

north Idaho mines. But following the Boise Basin and Owyhee strikes in southern Idaho, passenger traffic from San Francisco began to favor the water route to Sacramento, thence by stage to Red Bluff, California, and northeast across the Nevada desert.

Over this route, the fare from San Francisco to Idaho City was only $66. By sea to Portland, up the Columbia to Umatilla Landing, then across the Blue Mountains by stage, the ticket price came to $123. Furthermore, since the ocean voyage was rough and disasters frequent, more and more people bound for the south Idaho mines were by-passing Portland. A Portland OSN official wrote:

> We must leave 'no stone unturned' to divert all the Boise and Owyhee trade this way. Hence the building of a steam-boat on Snake River to run from Olds Ferry to a point equi-distant from Owyhee and Boise City is not a matter of choice but necessity. . .[9]

Olds Ferry was located on the Idaho side of the Snake River opposite Farewell Bend. By building a steamer that would ply the relatively tranquil 125 miles between the eastern base of the Blue Mountains and the Boise City-Owyhee road, the OSN hoped to divert traffic back to Portland, cut into the revenues of the Oregon-Idaho stage companies, and give the owners of the San Francisco-Red Bluff route something to worry about. If the Snake proved navigable as far upriver as Shoshone Falls, a con-nection might even be made with Salt Lake City and the transcontinental railroad hopefully soon to come.

A shipyard was established near the mouth of the Boise River, and in late summer of 1865 freshly cut and milled lum-ber to be used in the steamer began to arrive. Her boilers, engines, and metal parts had to be transported up the Columbia to Umatilla Landing, then freighted across the Blue Mountains over often impassable roads. Since the Indian troubles of 1866-68 were beginning at this time, arrows and bullets fired by hos-tiles now and then made workmen scramble for cover. But on April 20, 1866, the *Shoshone*, as the steamer built on the western edge of the Idaho desert was named, was launched with enthusiastic ceremony.

On her maiden voyage, the *Shoshone* proved the Snake navigable between Olds Ferry and a point a few miles upstream from the mouth of the Bruneau River. During the summer of 1866, she made several runs from Olds Ferry to Owyhee Ferry, and though operating at a loss, did have an effect on the rate war. Coal deposits had been discovered along the banks of the Snake in this area, but the coal was of such low grade that it was useless as fuel. Like most of the country along the lower and middle Snake, the banks were treeless and the supply of firewood soon was exhausted. In August 1866, John C. Ainsworth of the OSN was forced to report:

> *Our Snake River boat is laid up for want of wood. We do not think of starting her again before next spring, at which time, if we succeed in getting wood and making the proper connections, she will do a fair business. . .*[10]

But the wood problem could not be solved. For three years the *Shoshone* lay idle at her moorings, then in 1869 the officials of OSN decided to take a risky gamble. The steamboat would be brought downriver through Hell's Canyon. An editor of the period wrote:

> *A more perilous and uncertain adventure has never been undertaken in these waters, and we shall watch its progress with interest. The canyon between Powder River and the mouth of the Salmon is said to be seventy miles long and supposed to be a continuous succession of rapids the whole way. . .River men have always considered it an impossibility to navigate the canyon even with a small boat. . .*[11]

The first problem faced by Captain Cy Smith was that the timbers of the boat, which had lain in shallow water and carried no load for three years, had warped and shrunk so badly in the dry desert air that great gaps let daylight though the planking. He solved that by activating the steam-powered pumps, filling the interior with water, then pumping it dry once the planking swelled and became watertight again. Under his skilled hands, the inland-built steamer was brought from Owyhee Landing into the upper reaches of Hell's Canyon in late June, 1869, where low water and desertion by crew members who thought the venture too dangerous forced her to tie up near a stream still known as Steamboat Creek until the following spring.

Then another OSN crew under experienced Captain Sebastian Miller, supplied with plenty of fuel and heavy rope, maneuvered her through the hazardous rocks and rapids of the canyon's depths and brought her badly battered hulk down to Lewiston in late April 1870.

Eventually, the *Shoshone* was taken through the tamer rapids of the lower Snake, over the Columbia's Celilo Falls, and through the Upper and Lower Cascades—white water that could be run downstream by a handful of daring pilots when the river was in flood. Later, the still restless steamboat was taken up the Willamette River, hauled around the Oregon City Falls, and plied the upper reaches of the river until wrecked near Salem in 1874. Next spring, when high water cast her hulk ashore, a farmer detached her pilot house and converted it into a chicken coop—the final ignominy for a well-traveled lady who never was really at home on any river.[12]

Chapter 7 footnotes

1. Gray, "Reminiscences, 1925," p. 1, Penrose Library Archives, Whitman College, Walla Walla.
2. Ibid, p. 2.
3. Ibid, p. 3.
4. Ibid, p. 4.
5. Randall Mills, op. cit., *Sternwheelers Up Columbia*, p. 43.
6. Ibid, p. 45.
7. Ibid, p. 46.
8. Ibid, p. 42.
9. "STEAMBOAT DOWN THE SNAKE," The early story of the Shoshone," *Idaho Yesterdays*, V. 5, No. 4, Winter Issue, 1961-62, p. 25.
10. Ibid, p. 31.
11. Ibid, p. 32.
12. Ibid, p. 33.

Doc Baker's Rawhide Railroad

As the mining boom in Idaho waned during the late 1860s, it became clear that the fertile, rolling hills and valleys of southeastern Washington Territory were producing a new kind of gold: wheat. Grown in such quantity that it became a glut on the local market, the high-quality grain was being exported to Portland, San Francisco, and Pacific Rim countries overseas, where it brought premium prices. Since the only means of transporting it was on boats owned by the Oregon Steam Navigation Company, the management of OSN was vitally interested in any project that would simplify carrying the wheat to the river landings where it could be taken aboard as revenue-earning cargo.

Also interested in shipping the grain was an eccentric pioneer banker in Walla Walla, Doctor Dorsey Syng Baker.[1]

A licensed physician who had graduated from Jefferson Medical College in Philadelphia in 1845, Doctor Baker had practiced in Des Moines, Iowa, for a couple of years, migrated to the Willamette Valley in 1848, then had forsaken medicine to engage in several business ventures. After marrying and fathering seven children, he had suffered an illness at the age of thirty-four that had crippled his left arm and leg. Refusing to recognize that he would be physically handicapped for the rest of his life, he had moved his family to Walla Walla in 1858 and expanded his activities into farming, ranching, and the mercantile business.

Going into partnership with a friend named John Boyer, Doctor Baker found their store besieged by requests from wintering miners to keep their pouches of gold dust in their big metal safe. Since the prospectors were glad to pay five dollars a month for the service, with the only record- keeping required a tag on each sack noting the amount of gold in the pouch and its owner's name, the partners at first called their establishment the "Bank Place." As the town grew and demand developed for the services of a real bank, the partners applied for and got a charter for the first bank to be established in Washington Territory. From that day forward, the Baker-Boyer Bank, as it was named, boasted that it had never closed its doors on a business day or lost a dollar of depositor money.

A cantankerous, not particularly religious man, Doctor Baker attributed his business success to the strict observance of two rules: (1) never risk deposited funds in questionable ventures, and (2) shun debt as you would the Devil.

Following the Civil War, three railroad companies—the Union Pacific, the Great Northern, and the Northern Pacific—had promoted grandiose schemes to build transcontinental lines across the country. By 1869, only the Union Pacific had laid any track, but their line connecting Omaha to San Francisco was a long way from southeastern Washington's grain-growing district. In the Walla Walla area, farmers wanting to transport their wheat to market either had to make the long haul to the river landings in their own wagons or pay professional teamsters as much as fifteen dollars a ton to take the sacked grain from their fields to the loading docks.

"It costs us thirty-three cents a bushel to put our wheat aboard the river boats," the exasperated farmers complained to Doctor Baker. "Adding freight charges to Portland, plus shipping costs along the coast or overseas, we have to pay close to a dollar a bushel to get our wheat to market. Something's got to be done."

"I agree," Baker said. "Let's begin by getting a railroad company to give us a cost estimate on building a branch line from Walla Walla to Wallula Landing."

At that time, the nearest existing rail connection was with the Union Pacific at Kelton, Utah, 600 miles away. Both the

Dorsey S. "Doc" Baker.

Great Northern and the Northern Pacific were lobbying Congress for forty-mile-wide grants of land across the continent against which they could issue bonds that would give them the millions of dollars they felt they would need before they could start laying track. If and when a transcontinental railroad passed through the Walla Walla area, it most likely would be the Northern Pacific. So it was that company Doctor Baker and the wheat-growing farmers pressured to give them a cost estimate of a feeder line from Walla Walla to Wallula Landing.

The news was not good. According to the Northern Pacific experts, thirty-two miles of narrow-gauge railroad would cost $673,000. Projected against anticipated freight revenue, which must be well under the rates charged by the Teamsters Association in order to attract business, there was simply no way the line could show a profit. Discouraged, the farmers gave up. But Doctor Baker did not.

"That's far too much," he snapped. "Give me a few days to do some figuring. I'm sure I can do better."[2]

He did. Alhough he knew nothing about railroad-building, he had designed, supervised, or built with his own hands such things as sawmills, gristmills, houses, and barns. If made of wood, metal, or any combination thereof, he was confident that he could build a railroad or hire men with the necessary skills to build it for him. With his usual thoroughness, he figured out every detail of the project before calling together twenty-four of his farmer, banker, and business friends.

"Acceding to my estimate, the railroad can be built for $330,000," he told them. "Half of what the Northern Pacific experts said it would cost. What I propose to do is form a company, with myself as president, that will sell stock and control every aspect of the project. That way, we can be sure not a single dollar is wasted."

"How much stock must we sell?" John Boyer asked.

"We'll begin with $30,000, subscribed to, I hope, by the men in this room."

"Where will the other $300,000 come from?"

"A public bond issue, sold county-wide. As I've worked out the figures, we can pay off the bonds at eight percent interest in twelve years, with freight charges not to exceed eight dollars a ton. If we put the bond issue on the ballot this September, we can start work at once, cutting timbers for the rails in the mountains and floating them down the Yakima River to Wallula."

"Timbers?" a farmer asked in a puzzled voice. "You're gonna use wooden rails?"

"That's one of the cost-savers I've worked out, Ralph. Instead of iron rails, we'll use four-by-six fir stringers topped with three-eights by two-inch strap iron on the straight stretches of track, with iron rails on the curves."

"Will that work?"

"It's worked on the portage railroads at the Cascades and The Dalles. I don't know why it won't work here."

"Won't you need heavier locomotives?"

"We'll see. What I plan to do after the bond issue passes is go East and see what locomotive factories in Pittsburgh can build for us. I'll get their price for thirty-pound rail, too, which we'll switch to later on. If it's too expensive in the United States, I'll check with mills in Wales, where I've heard there are good bargains."[3]

The Walla Walla and Columbia River Railroad Company was incorporated during the spring of 1871. Building got under way shortly thereafter. Soon, tales about "Doc Baker's Rawhide Railroad" that would become legend in the upriver country began to circulate. In order to save money on survey costs, one

First locomotive, Baker Railroad.

story went, Doc Baker hired an Irishman named Pat Pantry to determine the best grade across the hills and hollows between Walla Walla and Wallula. When the surveyor—who had a drinking problem—traded his instruments for booze, Doc Baker refused to replace them, forcing him to use a half-full bottle of whiskey for a transit level.

The grade Pat Pantry selected, railroad men reported later, was perfect.

Complaints about the quantity and quality of the food served in the Wallula boarding house where sawmill and railroad workmen ate were so loud and constant, rumor had it, that the laborers frequently threatened to go on strike. On one occasion, a story went, the cook was caught flavoring what was supposed to be duck soup by leading a live duck tied to a string through a pan of slightly salted warm water.

In order to save money, still another tale related, Doc Baker eliminated the cow-catcher on the locomotive he ordered from Pittsburgh, training a collie dog to walk along ahead of the locomotive, barking a warning to grazing livestock on the track. When a deaf or stubborn cow refused to move, the collie would raise his tail, to which a red flag was attached, in a signal for the train to stop.

Running short on strap iron, yet another story went, Doc Baker killed and skinned a bunch of scrawny cattle, cut rawhide strips—which *wore* like iron—out of their pelts, then used the strips to top the rails. This worked fine until an unusually cold winter, which drove starving wolves down out of the Blue Mountains, with the ravenous animals eating what they welcomed as frozen beef jerky, causing the rails to fall apart.[4]

Exaggerated as these stories undoubtedly were, the "Bedbugs That Cost an Election" tale was true, for years later Will Baker, Doctor Baker's son, told it himself. Concerned over the fate of the $300,000 bond issue, Dr. Baker embarked on a tour of the county ten days before the election, taking eleven-year-old Will along to drive the buggy as his father met and talked with businessmen whose votes were needed. In Dayton, thirty miles northeast of Walla Walla, the owner of a combined stage station, store, hotel, saloon, and eating house was a big, bluff, friendly man named Dewey Hollister.

"Everybody in the community liked Mr. Hollister," Will Baker recalled. "Father knew if we got him on our side, he could influence a lot of votes. By bedtime, we were sure that he and all his friends were for us and would vote for the bonds. Then, during the night, things started crawling over us."

"'Things'?" Will was asked.

"Bedbugs. Our beds, the sheets, the mattress, was full of them. So in the middle of the night, Father and I got up, went out to the barn behind the hotel where the stagecoach horses were kept, climbed up in the hay mow, and spent the rest of the night there. When we came into the eating house for breakfast the next morning, Mr. Hollister saw the sprigs of hay in our hair and asked Father why we had slept in the barn."

Penrose Library, Whitman College
Dorsey S. Baker near Wallula Gap

"And your father told him?"

"He sure did. Mr. Hollister got very mad, saying if there were bugs in the bed, Father and I must have brought then with us from some other hotel. Father tried to calm him down, saying no harm had been done and we'd gotten a good night's sleep in the barn. But it didn't do any good. When the election was held a week later, the railroad bond issue lost by eighteen votes. Twenty-eight of the 'No' votes were cast in Mr. Hollister's district."[5]

Despite the bond issue defeat, Doctor Baker insisted on going ahead with plans to build the railroad. With his wife, Caroline, and their six-month-old daughter, Henrietta, he left for the East by stagecoach on December 4, 1871, headed for Kelton, Utah, where he planned to catch the train to Pittsburgh and New York. The nine days spent bucking snowdrifts, enduring near-zero cold, and putting up with the discomforts of overnight stops at stage stations with few amenities would later be described by Mrs. Baker as "a pleasure trip."

Conferring with the locomotive building company of Porter and Bell in Pittsburgh in late December, Doctor Baker signed a contract for the building of a seven-and-one-half ton locomotive for $4,400, the shipping charges around the Horn and then up the Columbia River to Wallula Landing to be $1,424. Shortly thereafter, he ordered a second locomotive approximately the same size and price, one to be named *Walla Walla*, the other *Wallula*. Also ordered from the Pittsburgh company were several dozen sets of iron trucks and wheels to be fitted to wooden flatcars built at the site. Delivery was promised in early summer 1872, by which time Dr. Baker planned to have half a dozen miles of track completed from Wallula eastward so that the railroad could start earning money.

Going on to New York, where he hoped to sell stock in the railroad to Eastern bankers, he found then friendly and interested, but too cautious to invest at the present time, for several railroads much larger than his were rumored to be rushing toward financial disaster. Pricing thirty-pound rail, he found that the best he could do in the United States was seventy-one dollars a ton, with freight charges to Portland an additional ten dollars, raising the total price to eighty-one dollars a ton. Since Eastern bankers would extend him no credit, the price must be paid in gold—which he did not have.

Checking with British factory representatives in New York City, he got a much more friendly reception and price. Thirty-pound rail cast in Wales and shipped from Liverpool would cost him forty-four dollars a ton, to which an added twelve dollars freight and fourteen dollars duty would bring the total to seventy dollars, a savings of eleven dollars a ton.

As to terms of payment, that would be no problem, the British representative assured him, for England was used to "making liberal terms to customers in the far-off colonies of Her Majesty's Empire." Ten percent down, say, twenty on delivery, and the rest spread over a period of five years at twelve percent interest. Would that be satisfactory, old chap?

Resisting the impulse to tell the representative that Washington Territory was no longer a British colony, Doctor Baker said the terms would be fine.

When he returned home in the spring of 1872, building of the Walla Walla and Columbia River Railroad resumed in earnest.[6]

By late May, 1873 twelve miles of track had been laid between Wallula Landing and Frenchtown, over which the two locomotives, the locally built flatcars, and the single passenger car completed to date were making regular runs. Maybe *runs* was not the right word, for that was too fast a pace to describe the gait of the narrow-gauge train. Because the strap iron topping the wooden rails now and then came loose as the wheels passed over it, a "snakehead" occasionally pierced the floor of a car, causing the passengers to panic and the train to stop. Because of the slow speed of the train, no passengers ever were injured, but the experience was disconcerting.

In the desert-like region of low rainfall east of Wallula, sand drifts often buried the tracks, causing derailments. Like the snakeheads, these were not great problems, for with the help of crowbars, fence posts, and muscle power supplied by the backs of the train crew, passengers or pedestrians on the nearby road, the light engine and cars could easily be lifted back on the rails. On one occasion when a husky young pedestrian headed for Wallula came over and did yeoman work helping lift the train back onto its track, the conductor offered him a free ride the rest of the way as a reward for his services.

"No thanks, I'll walk," he replied. "I'm in a hurry."

Slow though the trains were, when the Walla Walla and Columbia River Railroad offered to carry sacked wheat over its twelve miles of completed track for half the rate the Teamsters Association was charging, it acquired most of the business, for the Oregon Steam Navigation Company shrewdly agreed to accept the grain at the end of track as if it were being loaded on the boats themselves. To the cries of "Foul!" by the Teamsters, the OSN replied,

"All we've done is declare the Touchet a navigable river, which moves our loading dock twelve miles east."

Never mind that at harvest time the Touchet River was only a few inches deep and barely capable of floating a small rowboat. It carried enough water to qualify for shippers, so a river loading port it became.[7]

Requiring two-and-a-half hours to travel the thirty-two miles from Walla Walla to Wallula Landing, the first train on the completed road made its run on October 23, 1875. With a monopoly on freight traffic from one of the most productive grain-growing regions in the West, the railroad was a money-maker from the start. Being a man who did not believe in borrowing funds unless it was absolutely necessary, Doctor Baker, as president of the company, made sure that construction costs and rolling stock were paid for within three years, for his shrewd banker's judgment told him that such transportation giants as the Oregon Rail Steam Navigation Company (as the O&N now called itself) and the Northern Pacific Railroad Company would move in and try to take over once they realized that his little railroad was a success. In a day when big corporations were unregulated, they would push him to the edge of bankruptcy, then buy him out for ten cents on the dollar.

Owning every boat landing and portage on the Snake and Columbia Rivers between Lewiston, Idaho, and the sea, the ORSN Company directors were fond of saying, "He who owns the shipping facilities, owns the river."

Doc Baker quietly disagreed. His view was that shipping facilities were worthless without freight revenue—which could only come from shippers of cargo such as wheat.

"He who owns the approaches to the river, controls it," he said.

Time proved him right. When he offered to sell his railroad to the ORSN for $1 million, the directors laughed at him. Very well, he said, he would build his own river boats and shipping facilities. Knowing that he had the resources to do it, the ORSN quit laughing, accepted his offer, and paid him a million dollars for his railroad. This was in 1878, only three years after its completion. On behalf of his stockholders, of whom he was the major one, he had made a 400 percent profit on their investment. As a tribute to what they called, "The stubbornest man in Washington Territory," the ORSN Company named its newest addition to the Columbia River grain fleet the *D.S. Baker*.[8]

Called by Captain William Polk Gray "the most beautiful boat on the river," the *D.S. Baker* normally carried 3,000 sacks of wheat from Wallula Landing downriver to Celilo Falls on each trip. Retaining a one-seventh interest in the railroad he had built for a few years after selling it, Doc Baker wanted

Penrose Library, Whitman College
Locomotive hauling logs on the Baker Railroad in the 1880s.

Captain Gray to be the master of his namesake boat on its maiden voyage. But it was not to be.

"A call was made for the *Baker*," Gray later wrote, "while I was on the *John Gates* up Snake River. But the water was very low and the time of arrival and departure from Wallula was uncertain, so another captain was detailed to make the trip on the *Baker*."

Who the other captain was, Gray did not say, but after taking 3,000 sacks of wheat downriver to Celilo Fall and being told that Gray would replace him from that time on, he behaved badly.

"He was ordered to wait for the *Gates* and change commands," Gray said. "He was jealous and loaded the *Baker* for me with 3,600 sacks of wheat."

When Gray took over the boat and found it seriously overloaded, he protested in writing to the local ORSN agent before starting downriver, but he did begin the trip.

"At Umatilla, the boat was so logy it took an hour to land her. Going through the rapids just downstream, the boat was hard to handle. When we reached John Day Rapids, she became unmanageable, striking the shore of the island head-on, knocking overboard about forty sacks of wheat which had been piled on the bow ten stacks high to make the overload for me."

After striking the island, the *D.S.Baker* swung around and hit a submerged reef, knocking holes in two compartments, which quickly filled with water. Working the boat off the reef, Captain Gray headed it on down the river.

But the assistant pilot, an excitable man named Pingston, usually known as "Captain Hatless," climbed the ladder to the upper deck and shouted,

"Beach her, Captain! She's sinking!"

"Go below," Gray ordered, "and shut your damned mouth!"

Filling with water, the two flooded compartments gave the boat a heavy list to port. Captain Gray told First Mate Martin Spelling, who he called "as good a steamboat man as ever trod a deck," to have crewmen carry sacks of wheat from port to starboard in an attempt to trim the boat as much as possible. As the boat moved on down the river toward Celilo Falls, which now was just sixteen miles away, Gray said,

"Captain Hatless, with his bushy hair floating in the breeze, would sneak up the pilot house ladder and inform me that she would sink before we could make shore. But the purser and steward, both good, level-headed men, would quiet the passengers by saying, 'The old man knows his business.' The old man wasn't so darn sure, but took the chance."

Though passengers wanting to go downriver were waiting at Columbia Landing, Captain Gray had more urgent business pending at the time, so he did not pull in to pick them up. Just ahead lay a rapid and trough called Hell Gate, described by Gray as "deep enough to sink the *Great Eastern*, which must be passed through very carefully and slowly, with every minute seeming an hour.

"But we swung around at Celilo and landed alongside the *Harvest Queen* with both our guards under water amidships. The crews of both steamers, forty-five men, didn't wait for wagons but carried the wheat sacks ashore on their backs, and the cargo was saved."[9]

Chapter 8 footnotes

1. The sources for this chapter are *Forty Years a Pioneer,* by W.W. Baker (a son), Lowman & Hanford Co., Seattle, 1934, and *Gold, Rawhide and Iron,* by Helen Baker Reynolds, a grand daughter, Pacific Books, Palo Alto, California, 1955. Before the latter book was published, its author asked me to read and criticize it in manuscript, her particular concern being putting dialog in scenes she had not actually witnessed. She was relieved when I told her that this was acceptable in a biography such as hers. While working on the book, she said that she understood that the original business letters, papers, and account books which her uncle, W. W. Baker, had used to write his 1934 biography, had been destroyed, for she could not find them. Many years later, this turned out to be not the case, for the material was found in the vault of the Baker Boyer Bank, which is still very much in business, and was deposited in the Archives at Penrose Library, Whitman College, where it now resides.
2. *Gold, Rawhide, and Iron,* op. cit., p. 114.
3. Ibid, p. 125.
4. In *Forty Years a Pioneer,* p. 129-154, W. W. Baker reprints the tall tale written by George Estes in 1916 which the author himself admitted was "fiction."
5. Ibid, op. cit.., p. 166.
6. Ibid, p. 182.
7. Ibid, p. 189.
8. Ibid, p. 199.
9. Gray, "Reminiscences."

CHAPTER NINE

Wreck of the *Daisy Ainsworth*
Suicide of the pony engine

B uilt and launched at The Dalles in 1873, the steamboat
Daisy Ainsworth had been named in honor of the
youngest daughter of OSN Company President John C.
Ainsworth, who had taken the wheel himself with his daughter
at his side when the boat made its first trial run. Designed by
master builder John Holland, the "Daisy," as she fondly was
called, was truly a palace boat, boasting all the luxuries of the
day. Cabin and stateroom floors were covered with deep-pile
Brussels carpets. Silver plate adorned dining saloon tables and
sideboards. Crystal chandeliers glittered with cheerful candle-
light.[1]

Called by Captain Gray "as good a steamboat man as ever
trod a deck," First Mate Martin Spelling felt responsible for the
loss of the elegant boat, though his fellow rivermen placed no
blame on him for the tragic wreck.

After making her usual daylight run from the Upper
Cascades to The Dalles with a full complement of passengers
under Captain John McNulty's command on November 22,
1876, the *Daisy Ainsworth* was turned over to Martin Spelling,
who recently had been transferred to the Middle River run by
the company. Having already put in a full day at the wheel,
Captain McNulty was not displeased to be replaced by First
Mate Spelling that night, for the "Daisy" was being turned into
a cattle boat.

Never one to decline paying cargo, the sharp-penciled local freight manager of the OSN Company had accepted a shipment of 210 live beef cattle to be transported from The Dalles down-river to the Upper Cascades Landing on the Washington shore, a forty-five mile trip that would take five or six hours.

"The boat usually scheduled for the night run was the *Idaho*," Captain Gray later explained, "but she was too small to handle that many cattle, so the *Daisy Ainsworth* was pressed into service."

The late November weather had turned stormy, with snow squalls howling through the Gorge. No moon shone to relieve the darkness. Looking down on the messy cattle-loading process as the nervous, bawling animals were driven aboard the freight deck, First Mate Martin Spelling watched critically from the pilot house high above, whose curtains had been drawn on three sides in order to shield the pilot's eyes from ambient sidelights that might interfere with his night vision directly ahead. A thin, stooped man in his late forties, Spelling was a sober, conscientious officer who knew the river just as well as Captains John McNulty and John Ainswoth did.

When the loading had been completed, Spelling reached for the speaking tube and whistled to the engine room, alerting Engineer William Doran to stand by, pulling the whistle cord in a signal to the deckhands to cast off fore and aft lines as the heavily laden *Daisy Ainsworth* prepared to pull out into the darkness-shrouded river. The proposed range markers and light buoys which the Corps of Engineers planned to install as aids to navigation had not yet been put in place, so only small circles of fitfully burning coal-oil running lights framed the outline of the boat. But First Mate Spelling knew the forty-five miles of broad, cliff-lined river ahead as well as he knew the lines in the palm of his hand. Furthermore, he remembered the exact location of shore lamps gleaming on the docks, landings, warehouses, and commercial buildings in the infrequent settlements along both the Oregon and Washington shores. Like all experienced river pilots, he knew how to take a fix on the position of his boat by blowing a few blasts with his steam whistle, then listening intently to returning echoes a few seconds later, giving him a reading on his whereabouts as precise as a sighting of a headland or a cliff top on a brilliant, sunny day.

After several hours of blind running through the snow-laced dark at medium speed, the *Daisy* passed Crates Point on the Oregon side of the river. Acting Captain Spelling put the wheel hard over, angling directly across to the Washington channel in order to avoid the sandbar opposite Cayuse Rock. With the wind howling up the Gorge against the boat's bow, the big stern-wheeler drove on into a nasty chop whose white-capped waves were beginning to smoke with streaks of foam. Passing long, low Memaloose Island, where the river Indians for untold genera-tions had placed their dead on raised platforms to await their journey to the spirit land, the boat skirted Mosier Rocks, then threaded her way through the treacherous channel between Eighteen Mile Island and the Oregon shore. Since it was now past midnight, the settlements of Hood River, on the Oregon shore, and White Salmon, on the Washington shore, showed few lights, for their occupants had gone to bed hours ago.

Knowing that he was near the end of his run, Captain Spelling called for half-speed as he stared intently into the darkens ahead, his eyes seeking the wharf lantern marking the end of the dock at the Upper Cascades, just upstream from which was a broad, low, gravel bank where the restless cattle, which had begun lowing nervously at the blast of the whistle over their heads, would be driven ashore. Having taken a bear-ing on a landing light on the Oregon shore directly across from which he knew the Upper Cascades wharf to be, Spelling was puzzled that the lantern he sought had not yet come into sight. A feeling that something was wrong grew in him. Intermittently through the snow squalls, he could see a light blinking ahead, but it appeared to be at least a quarter-mile upstream from where it *ought* to be. The echoes bouncing back from the boat's whistle sounded wrong, too. And was that low roaring sound he was hearing being made by rapids where he was positive no thundering white water existed?

Even as he reached for the speaking tube to order the engines stopped and reversed, the *Daisy Ainsworth* struck an underwater reef with a shuddering crash. Pitched forward against the wheel, Spelling realized too late that the boat was half a mile downriver from where he thought it to be, that the unyielding shoal of rocks upon which the craft had struck lay only 300 feet upstream from the powerful rapid called the Upper Cascades, and that the pride of the Middle River fleet had broken her back in a mortal blow from which she could not recover.

By putting out bow and stern anchors, Spelling managed to hold the boat steady in the stream for a while. But in the confusion the cattle stampeded, broke down the railings, and went overboard. Only a few of them managed to swim to shore.

As the boat settled on the reef, her main hog chains broke immediately, with some of the smaller ones snapping soon after. When daylight came, Spelling discovered that what he had taken to be a wharf light on the Oregon shore actually had been a lantern on a scow loaded with wood, which that afternoon had anchored a mile downstream from the permanent wharf. Now he and the crew aboard the *Daisy Ainsworth* found her situation extremely perilous, for the boat was perched on underwater rocks only 300 feet upstream from the falls.

During the day, salvage experts employed by the OSN Company and the Corps of Engineers brought a large work-barge downriver from The Dalles, from which they managed to get long lines on the wreck, holding it in place while her cabin, saloon furnishings, and engines were removed, later to be installed on other boats. As the most expensive stern-wheeler ever built for the Middle River run, the hull and equipment had cost sixty thousand dollars, the engines twenty-five thousand more.

"Insurance will cover part of the loss," President John Ainsworth told Captain Gray, "but the Company will pay for that later in the form of increased rates."

"How is Martin Spelling taking it?"

"Badly, I'm afraid. Given the circumstances, it's the kind of accident that could have happened to even the best of pilots. But he insists on taking all the blame."

Indeed, even though John Ainsworth spoke no word of criticism and assigned him a first mate's berth on the Lower River run a couple of weeks later, Martin Spelling fell ill after working a month or so and was put on paid sick leave until he recovered. But he never did. Grief-stricken, broken in spirit as well as health, he died a few months later.

"Tuberculosis," said the medical report. But his rivermen friends knew that Martin Spelling died from a broken heart.[2]

Soon after Doctor Baker sold his narrow-gauge railroad to the Oregon Steam & Rail Navigation Company, the decision was made to widen the track to standard gauge, purchase new, more powerful locomotives to replace the tiny *Walla Walla* and *Wallula*, and merge the company with financier Henry Villard's Northern Pacific, which, backed by $35 million in paper assets, was in the process of building a transcontinental line westward from Minneapolis-St. Paul through Spokane, then down the Snake and Columbia to Portland.

The track-widening process consisted of laying a third rail a foot or so outside the second rail of the narrow-gauge track so that the wheels of the older locomotives and flatcars could run on the older tracks until the wider gauge was in place. Beginning at the railroad yard in Walla Walla, then proceeding thirty-two miles west to the turnaround and unloading incline at Wallula Landing, this method made possible the construction of the new gauge and the destruction of the old at the same time.[3]

With his usual frugality, Doctor Baker had managed to find a buyer for the two narrow-gauge locomotives and strings of flatcars—a logging company in western Oregon—to whom all the outmoded equipment except the Pony engine, *Wallula*, had been sold and shipped prior to the memorable night on which the locomotive decided to drown itself rather than be carried off into the tall timber of the Siskiyou Mountains.

According to local legend, the only person in position to witness the swan dive of the *Wallula* was a dim-witted drunk named Bunky Burger, who was currently employed as a laborer on the relocation project. How he happened to be where he was at that particular time, he could not say, which was not an unusual circumstance, for at ten o'clock of a hot summer night, Bunky's mind and memory usually were so hazed by alcohol that he could not recall why he happened to be anyplace. The important point was, he was where he happened to be at that particular time, thus, had an unimpeded view of what he thought he saw occur, which could not be contradicted by any other witness.

As he later testified, what he thought he saw was this:

The little Pony engine, *Wallula*, parked on a flat stretch of narrow-gauge track 200 yards from the river in the warm darkness, panting like a tired, winded old man who has just run a long way. Soon after the locomotive stopped, its engineer, whom Bunky knew as Mac, and its fireman, Pat, climbed down out of the cab and headed up the hill toward the Wallula Palace Bar where, Bunky guessed, they would have a few cold beers. Which struck Bunky as a sensible thing to do, for the day had been very hot, firing the locomotive must have raised a tremendous thirst, and their day's work was done.

Having already consumed half a dozen beers himself, with a fresh one in his hand, Bunky was content to remain seated on a stack of railroad ties fifty feet away from the panting Pony engine, which to Bunky looked like it could use a few beers itself. From the talk he had heard on the job, the *Wallula* was scheduled to be fired up one last time tomorrow morning, then would chug slowly down the incline and be taken aboard the freight deck of the *Inland Queen*, which was due to arrive at ten o'clock downriver-bound for Celilo.

How did the little engine feel about leaving home? Bunky wondered. Would it like working in the woods? Would it miss seeing and whistling at all the cows, horses, sheep, dogs, coyotes, and people it had come to know in the years it had carried passengers and freight between Walla Walla and the steamboat landing? Would the high trestles, steep grades and frequent curves of the Siskiyou country make it nervous and afraid it might slip and fall off the rain-slick track? Or did little pony engines even *have* feelings?

Musing on these questions as he took another swallow of beer, Bunky heard—or *thought* he heard—two short toots of the *Wallula's* whistle, a signal that it was about to move. Ordinarily, it was the engineer or the fireman who pulled the cord that activated the whistle. But as Bunky recalled—or *thought* he recalled—both Mac and Pat had climbed down out of the cab a few minutes ago and gone up the hill to the Wallula Palace Bar to have themselves a few beers.

Still, he had heard the whistle toot.

The next thing he heard—or *thought* he heard—was the hiss of steam, the clank of the drawbar being engaged, and the squeal of drive wheels turning. Slowly at first, then, following a metallic clashing of gears, the locomotive slammed into what Bunky supposed Mac or Pat would call "full-throttle balling the jack" speed.

This struck Bunky as very odd. What was the little engine's hurry? Beyond the short stretch of level track on which the *Wallula* was parked, the incline leading down to the steamboat landing was steep and rather short. Furthermore, a derail device was clamped to the river end of the track in order to prevent a runaway flatcar or locomotive from rolling into the river when no steamboat was anchored there. And the *Inland Queen* was not due to dock for another twelve hours.

Nevertheless, the little pony engine *Wallula* was headed down the incline toward the unoccupied landing as fast as it could go.

Because Bunky's experience working on the railroad had not included witnessing what happened when a runaway locomotive going down a steep incline hit a derail device, he watched with considerable interest as what might be called an "irresistible force" met an "immovable object." Curiously enough, what happened was a kind of Mexican standoff in which neither the irresistible force nor the immovable object won or lost.

Instead, without budging an inch, the immovable object deflected the irresistible force up and out over the dark surface of the river in as graceful a swan dive as Bunky had ever seen a little Pony engine make. As the locomotive struck the water, its boiler fire was extinguished in a massive hiss, then it sank out of sight into deep water, leaving only a large, spreading circle on the surface for a time to show where it had vanished.

Interesting, Bunky mused as he took another swallow of beer. *Very interesting indeed*.

How long an interval of time passed between the *Wallula's* swan dive into the river and the return of Mac and Pat to the spot where they had left the engine parked, Bunky could not say. But he had finished the beer by then, had let the empty bottle fall to the ground, and had closed his eyes and taken a little nap. Next thing he knew, Mac grabbed him by one shoulder, Pat by the other, and shook him, shouting angrily,

"Where'd it go, Bunky?"

"What'd you do with it, Bunky?"

Even when cold sober, Bunky often found it difficult to describe events he had witnessed—or *thought* he had witnessed—in a way people could understand. When roused from a nap with seven beers in him, he found it impossible to say anything that made sense. The best thing he could do was pantomime what he *thought* he had seen happen.

Reaching up to pull an imaginary whistle cord, he went *toot-toot* to illustrate what the engine had sounded like when it gave warning it was about to move. Puffing out his cheeks, he went *hiss-hiss* to denote the sound it had made as it fed steam to its drive wheels. Doing a *clank-clank* and a *chug-chug*, he audibly imitated the sounds it had made as it got under way. To conclude the explanation, he extended his arms over his head, put his hands together, then pantomimed the arc of a swan dive as the speeding locomotive struck the derail, vaulted into the air, then descended with a final hiss beneath the dark surface of the river.

At first, Mac and Pat did not believe him. But faced with the indisputable facts that (1) the locomotive was gone, and (2) Bunky never lied about what he *thought* he saw, the bewildered engineer and fireman went back to the Wallula Palace Bar, organized a search party equipped with pine-knot torches, long poles, and rowboats, and soon located the spot where the *Wallula* had made its dive, identifying it beyond all doubt by a pair of Mac's gloves, Pat's lunch box, and half a dozen loose sticks of cordwood that had been in the cab and now were floating on the surface of the river.

"Blamed old engine was gettin' mighty cranky," Mac muttered as he tried to explain the loss of the *Wallula* to the OSN agent, Clem Purdy. "If I told Doc Baker once, I told him a dozen times that them drive-wheel brake shoes were wearin' out and ought to be replaced. But he was too tight to spend the money."

Bill Lilley photo
Lyon's Ferry, ca 1955.

"Drawbar was shot, too," Pat agreed. "Bump it the wrong way, it'd slip into gear on its own 'fore you knew it and the fool engine would start to roll."

"So it could of took off by itself, just like Bunky claimed it did," Mac added, nodding in agreement.

"Well, now, that may be true," Clem Purdy said, scratching his head in puzzlement. "But how did it blow its own whistle?"

"What's a toot or two to Bunky, Clem? With a few beers in him, he's apt to hear a whole brass band."

Probing around by torchlight thirty feet offshore, the search party soon located the exact position of the sunken locomotive, finding it lying in the dark brown silt in quiet water just downstream from the mouth of the Walla Walla River, sitting upright, with its bell-shaped smokestack ten feet under the surface. When the *Inland Queen* arrived from Lewiston at ten o'clock the next morning, already well laden with a cargo of sacked wheat collected at landings along the 140-mile length of the Snake River, it had no trouble steering clear of the sunken locomotive as it docked. After being told what had happened, Captain Lars Warren rejected the suggestion that he try to raise the locomotive and bring it aboard.

"That's a job for a salvage boat, not the *Queen*" he told Agent Purdy. "Make a report to the company, Clem. Maybe insurance will cover it."

Since Doc Baker considered insurance a form of gambling, in which pastime he never indulged, there turned out to be no insurance on the rolling stock of the Rawhide Railroad. So the locomotive that had drowned itself rather than leave home remained in its watery grave while buyer and seller bickered over the question of legal ownership.

Learning that the cost of raising the pony engine would far exceed its salvage value, the concerned parties tried to persuade the Corps of Engineers to declare it a hazard to navigation and remove it at government expense. But the request was denied, a Corps official curtly saying,

"You put it there; you fish it out."

Because converting from narrow to standard gauge and expanding the loading facilities at Wallula Landing required extensive rebuilding anyway, the OSN Company, which was being taken over by the Northern Pacific, found it easier to build a new dock and rail incline a hundred feet to the north of the little Pony engine's watery grave where it would not be a hazard to navigation no matter what the level of the river.

In time to come, projects would be proposed to raise the locomotive, but all would be abandoned because of physical or funding difficulties. To this day, the little Pony engine *Wallula* lies buried in the dark brown silt near the juncture of the Walla Walla River with the Columbia where it makes its westward bend toward the Pacific Ocean. [3]

In order to fill the need for the transport of grain and passengers down the Snake and Columbia, the OSN Company by 1878 had built and launched seven big steamboats: the *Harvest Queen, John Gates, Spokane,* and *Annie Faxon* at Celilo; the *Mountain Queen* and *R. R. Thompson* at The Dalles; and the *Wide West* at Portland.

Slated to run on the upper river between Celilo and Lewiston, the *Harvest Queen* was a veritable palace of a boat, the finest and fastest on that sector of the river. Two hundred feet long, with a thirty-seven foot beam and a seven-and-a-half-foot-deep hold, she could carry 500 tons of freight, had luxury quarters for 100 cabin passengers, with dining and bar facilities for twice that number. Under a full head of steam, she could do thirty miles an hour. She had a shallow enough draft to navigate the Snake all the way up to Lewiston at most stages of water and could be docked at all the river and beach landings for easy loading.[4]

Though there now were enough boats on the Snake and Columbia to handle the grain and passengers being moved downriver, the captains and crews of the newly launched craft were keeping a wary eye on a mode of transportation that could greatly affect their livelihood—the railroads. In February 1878, Doctor Baker sold six-sevenths of his stock in his narrow-gauge line to the Oregon Steam Navigation Company, with himself remaining as president. A year later, in May 1878, he sold his remaining stock to Henry Villard, who had bought the OSN Company and was beginning his spectacular career as a transportation king.

A man of vision, Henry Villard played the empire-building game with million-dollar chips. His grand scheme was to establish a great commercial kingdom in the Pacific Northwest by building a network of rail, river, and ocean steamer lines that would bring in new settlers by the hundreds of thousands. For a while, every hand he played was a winner.

First, he realized, he must control access to the region, which meant the Columbia River. By building along its banks, he would be in a position to meet and beat any westward-bound railroad, whether it be the Northern Pacific, now struggling across Montana, or the so-called Oregon Short Line, proposed from Salt Lake northwest across Idaho, the Snake River, and the Blue Mountains.

Like Doc Baker, Villard at first favored the three-foot narrow gauge, which was practical and cheap; he ordered grading to begin for a line along the Columbia from Wallula to Celilo. Because the fourteen-mile portage road from Celilo Falls to The Dalles and the six-mile portage track around the Cascades were also narrow gauge and had been acquired by his purchase of the OSN Company, he knew that gauge would be compatible with the line being laid west along the Columbia from Wallula. But there was a flaw in the plan, which he quickly saw.

Both the Northern Pacific and the Union Pacific were standard gauge—four feet eight and one-half inches—which would require the transfer of freight between the cars of their lines and his. This would be a major obstacle, he knew, discouraging through movements of freight. Very likely, either or both companies would decide to build their own lines along routes he could not control. For example, the Northern Pacific might build across the Grand Coulee country and the Cascades directly to Puget Sound, as Everett, Seattle, and Tacoma were urging it to do. Or the Oregon Pacific, which had formed a company headquarter in the Willamette Valley, might strike a deal with the Union Pacific, bypassing the Columbia River route, build east across the Oregon Cascades and high desert country, then effect a meeting with the Union Pacific somewhere around Farewell Bend.

Not wanting to risk that, Villard changed his plans, ordered the right-of-way survey crew to widen the grade and prepare for the laying of standard-gauge rail. With his usual luck, the financier guessed right on both scores, managing by some fancy financial footwork to stay a step ahead of the wolf pack of promoters trying to bring him down. By 1883, he had joined his now standard-gauge Columbia River line upriver from Portland to Wallula to the Northern Pacific, which had built southwest from Montana to Spokane, and with the Oregon Short Line built by the Union Pacific to Snake River, across the Blue Mountains, and down the south bank of the Columbia at Umatilla Landing.

For the time being, at least, the transportation empire being created by Henry Villard had two transcontinental connections.[5]

Chapter 9 footnotes

1. *Blow For the Landing*, by Fritz Timmen, Caxton, 1973, pp. 77, 78.
2. Ibid.
3. Other than the fact that the Little Pony Engine did roll off the end of the track and has never been recovered, nothing is known about its disappearance, so any story told by legend relaters cannot be disputed.
4. *Blow For the Landing*, op. cit., p. 28.
5. Ibid, p. 29.

Running the rapids

A nticipating the completion of rail lines along the Columbia and Snake, Henry Villard instructed his chief of operations for the steamboat branch of the OSN Company "to effect a redistribution of carriers" along the river route between Lewiston and Portland.

"We've got too many boats on the upper river," Villard said. "Unless we move some of them to where they're needed on the middle and lower river, we'll have choke points at the portages that will make our farmer-shippers scream. See to it, will you?"

As the chief of operations had quickly learned, the humorless, short-tempered, blunt-spoken Henry Villard never softened an order with a question mark. Move the boats, he said. How they were to be moved was the problem of the chief of operations.

With its 500-ton carrying capacity, the *Harvest Queen*, which had been making the run from Celilo to Lewiston for three years, was first on the list of boats to be moved from the upper to the middle river. This was the favorite boat of Captain William Polk Gray, now a senior pilot with the OSN Company, who had often served as its captain. He later recalled:

> *In July, 1880, I was on furlough in Portland when I received orders to go to Celilo and take command of the Harvest Queen, the pick of the upper Columbia, relieving Capt. J. W. Troup, who was to be married to Miss Fannie*

Stump. We left Portland at five in the morning on the L. J.
Potter, *loaded with 600 tons of merchandise and under the
command of Capt. John Wolf. Arriving at the Lower
Cascades, we transferred by the portage railroad to the* R.
R. Thompson. *This boat was loaded to the guards with
merchandise and under the command of Capt. McNulty.*

*Arriving at The Dalles at about five p.m., we transferred
passengers, baggage, fast freight, and express to the train
for Celilo Falls, where the Harvest Queen was loaded and
waiting with steam up. Her load consisted of about 500
tons of assorted freight, merchandise, and farm equipment. Every available foot of space was occupied, there
being two "setup separators" on the bow. There were six "set
up" wagons and four "set up" buggies on the hurricane
deck and 45 cords of wood for fuel.*

*We left Celilo at 6:15 p.m., stopping night or day only to
deliver freight or passengers at way landings, Umatilla,
and Wallula, entering the Snake River with about 300 tons
of freight. About ten o'clock the second night I was steering
through a shallow rapid, known as the false Palouse
rapids. These are abreast of the present Ayers Junction.*

*The night was dark, with no moon. A following wind
carried the smoke from the stack over the bow, shutting out
my view of the water. I knew I was close to a reef when
Bang! The boat had struck the reef and my heart went in
my mouth. I rang the gong instantly to stop. Passengers
crowded onto the "tooth pick" or forward deck, asking what
was the matter.*

*Can you imagine the thoughts of a man proud of his
record as a swift water pilot in charge of the "Pride of the
river" and striking his boat on a measly little rapids like
the false Palouse! Just at that moment, a voice came up
from the forward deck, "It's all right, Captain, we just
dumped a truck load of wood on back!"*

*Proceeding on up the river, we continued loading
freight and passengers and arrived at Lewiston without
accident or trouble. Leaving Lewiston at 8 o'clock Monday
morning, we picked up 250 tons of wheat on the Snake
River, more at Wallula and Umatilla, and arrived at Celilo*

with 450 tons of wheat at 6 o'clock Monday evening. The large loads of freight on the different steamboats along the river as mentioned is accounted for by the fact that the Oregon Steamship & Navigation Co. had a double standard of measurement. If freight measured more than it weighed, it was measured at 40 feet to the ton. If it weighed the mark, it was taken at 2000 pounds to the ton. A story was current in the early sixties that the steamer Colonel Wright, *whose extreme carrying capacity in dead weight was about 80 tons, had carried on one trip from Deschutes Landing to Old Fort Walla Walla more than 1000 tons of freight for the government, consisting of wagons and camp equipment.*

The wagons were knocked down and hauled from The Dalles to Deschutes, where they were set up and measured from the front end of the tongue to the back end of the wagon and from the top of the cover bands to the ground and from inside to outside hub. They were then knocked down again and stored aboard the Colonel Wright. *One man reported that they set up the folded tents and measured them, but I don't believe it.*[1]

The captain selected to command the *Harvest Queen* during its hazardous journey from the upper to the middle river was twenty-six-year-old James W. Troup. A protege of Captain Gray, he knew the perils of the river almost as well as his mentor did, for in the course of several sessions with the older man, he had been well schooled in the principles of running wild waters. For instance, Gray told him, it was useless to fight the power of the current when moving downriver. Unless your stern-wheel was turning at full speed to give you steering-way, you had no rudder control in a forward direction. With the wheel turning full speed astern, you could get enough lateral steering-way to keep your boat in the main channel, but if a sharp rock jutting above the surface split the main channel in two, it became a by-guess or by-God gamble as to which was the best choice to take, with only a few seconds to make up your mind.

"So far as I know," Captain Gray told him, "no one has ever tried to take a steamboat as big as the *Harvest Queen* over

Celilo Falls and down through The Dalles Rapids before. Farther downriver, a smaller boat went through the Cascades by accident back in '58. It was called the *Venture*."

"Did it survive?"

"Oddly enough, it did."

Built by R. R. Thompson and Laurence Coe, who were captains and stockholders in the OSN Company, the *Venture* had been launched just above the Upper Cascades. It was to be put into service on the middle river run to The Dalles. With forty passengers aboard for the trial trip, Captains Thompson and Coe pulled out from the Upper Cascades dock before the *Venture's* boilers could supply the engine with a full head of steam. Sucked into the rapids and completely out of control, she went over the turbulent boil of the Upper Cascades, a fall of five feet, stern first, bounced merrily along through three miles of white, surging, rock-strewn water, stayed upright as she tumbled over the four-foot-high falls of the Middle Cascades, then tossed and heaved through three more miles of angry water until finally lurching over the five-foot drop of the Lower Cascades. Striking a rock ledge just under the surface of the quiet water there, she stranded until her passengers were rescued by a sailing schooner.

"The only person lost," Captain Gray said, "was a man who panicked and dove overboard when the *Venture* went down the first waterfall. Apparently he thought he could swim better than the boat could. His body was never found."[2]

"Well, that's one mistake I'll never make," Captain Troup said, shaking his head. "When I go over the falls, I want all the wood and iron the boat's got between me and the water."

Called "Celilo" by the local Indians or "Tumwater Falls" by the lower river tribes, the great Columbia River fishery was a series of chutes, channels, and tumbling rapids that extended some fourteen miles from head to foot. Their earliest and best description was published in the *Lewis and Clark Journals*. Clark wrote:

> *The first pitch of the falls is 20 feet perpendicular, then passing thro' a narrow channel for 1 mile to a rapid of*

about 8 feet fall below which the water has no perceptible fall but is very rapid. Capt. Lewis and three men crossed the river to the opposite Side to view the falls which he had not yet taken a full view of. At 9:00 A.M. I set out with the party and proceeded on down a rapid Stream of about 400 yards wide. At 2 1/2 miles the river ran into a large basin to the Stard. Side on which there is five lodges of Indians; here a tremendous black rock Presented itself high and Steep appearing to choke up the river; the current was drawn with great velocity to the Lard. Side of this rock at which place I heard a great roreing. I landed at the Lodges and the natives went with me to the top of the rock which makes from the Stard. Side, from the top of which I could see the difficulties we had to pass for several miles below; at this place the great river is compressed into a channel between two rocks not exceeding forty-five yards wide and continues for 1/4 of a mile when it again widens to 200 yards and continues this width for about 2 miles when it is again interspersed by rocks. The whole of the Current of this great river must at all Stages pass thro' this narrow channel of 45 yards wide.[3]

Above and below this fourteen-mile section of turbulent river, the Columbia was half a mile wide and relatively tranquil, Clark wrote, but here—where the river literally turned on edge—he estimated the current to be thirty miles an hour.

The description of Celilo Falls by William Clark had been written in late October, Captain Troup knew, when the volume of water in the river was at its lowest point and the twenty-foot vertical falls higher than at any other time of year. During the peak spring runoff in late May, snowmelt over the headwaters of the Snake and Columbia supplied such a tremendous volume of water that Celilo Falls and the fourteen miles of rapids immediately downstream leveled out into a broad, tumbling, roaring chute of white water on the surface of which any object that floated was impelled down river at breakneck speed.

"Ideally, late May would be the best time to take the *Harvest Queen* down to the middle river," Gray told Captain Troup. "Can you wait until then?"

"I'm afraid not. The chief of operations says Mr. Villard wants the middle river boats in place by the first of March. I told him if we get some heavy rains and a sizable runoff in late winter, as we usually do, I'd be willing to give it a try."

Busy on the Celilo-Lewiston run, Captain Gray saw the rains come and the runoff begin in late January 1881. He heard that Captain Troup had decided to make the dangerous run in early February. As a matter of curiosity and an opportunity to take part in a new river-running experience, Captain Gray would have been glad to go along, if invited, but he was not in the least surprised that an invitation to be a guest pilot was not forthcoming. At best, a captain as skilled as Jim Troup needed no advice when running a river; at worst, the OSN Company would not risk losing two seasoned steamboat captains in a single accident if a disaster did occur.

Because this was the first time such a big stern-wheeler had been taken over Celilo Falls and down through what Lewis and Clark called the "Long Narrows," details of the run of the *Harvest Queen* soon became part of the legend of the river.

Leaving Celilo Landing a quarter-mile above the falls the morning of February 4, 1881, the *Queen* carried a large load of pitch-filled cordwood for the boiler furnaces, as well as a good supply of dimension lumber for repairs and bracing. Four carpenters, three mechanics, and half a dozen deckhands were aboard in case emergency repairs must be made. Though the maximum October drop of twenty feet had been smoothed out by the runoff to six, plunging over the brink, Captain Troup later told Gray, was like landing on concrete after falling off a building.

"When she struck the water below the falls, both rudders were ripped away. More than half the slats in the stern-wheel were so badly damaged the wheel fouled before we could stop the engines."

Lurching sideways completely out of control, the *Harvest Queen* broke a drive rod on her starboard engine, slewed across the channel into a rock, knocked a gaping hole in her hull, and filled two below-decks compartments with water. As she glanced off the rock, she shot across a sharp lava reef and smashed away a large section of her bow housing,

"I ordered an anchor dropped," Captain Troup said, "but the rush of the current parted the chain. Fortunately, the crew managed to rig a kedge, which held till the engineer could get the engine running on the pillow blocks. With it working, we limped into an eddy where we could secure lines ashore, tie up, and make repairs."

The patching process took a week. With the worst of the hazards behind him now, Captain Troup resumed his record-setting trip through the turbulent waters of the Big and Little Dalles, at last reaching the broad, tranquil sector of the middle river on which the *Harvest Queen* was slated to serve.[4]

Though running a big river steamer down both Celilo Falls and Cascades Rapids, as was later done by Captain James Troup and other pilots, never became a routine event without danger or risk, it did develop into something of an exact scientific operation which only a few qualified river pilots were allowed to perform. One of the best of these practitioners was Captain James McNulty, who, a year after Captain Troup's run, set a record that would never be equaled.

Built at The Dalles in 1878 for the middle river run, the elegant *R. R. Thompson* was a big, luxurious boat designed to serve passengers who insisted on the best accommodations. Two hundred and fifteen feet in length, with a thirty-eight-foot beam and a large freight deck, the *Thompson* boasted nicely fitted-out passenger facilities and a ladies' cabin furnished with quality carpeting, plush settees, and polished wood-paneled walls. Though not the fastest boat on the river, she was built for comfort and was described by travel agents as a "palace boat" with the "finest cuisine afloat."

For four years, she proved herself to be the most popular boat on the middle river. But the 1882 completion of the south bank railroad east from Portland to Umatilla spelled doom for the luxury steamboat fleet, so one by one the stern-wheelers were brought down over the Cascades to the lower river.

By all odds, the rapids-running trip of the *R. R. Thompson* provided the most excitement. On June 3, 1882, under the command of Captain John McNulty, she left The Dalles at six-thirty in the morning. Running at full speed to the Upper Cascades, she reached the landing there in 121 minutes. This was an average of twenty-three miles an hour, quite respectable for a stern-wheeler designed for comfort and luxury rather than speed.

Pausing only briefly to survey the route ahead and alert the chief engineer that he intended to take the boat through the rapids as fast as it would go, Captain McNulty pointed the *Thompson's* bow into the boiling current and rang for full speed ahead. Because the river was running in full summer flood, the rocks, ledges, and other navigational hazards were buried under heaving mountains of foam. Tearing through the six miles of rapids in six minutes and forty seconds the *Thompson's* speed for the run was just under sixty miles an hour.

That record would never be matched.

A week later, when Captain James Troup was asked to bring another OSN boat, the *Mountain Queen*, down through the Cascades Rapids, a locomotive pulling half a dozen passenger-filled cars along the south bank track was given a running start so that it could attempt to keep up with the speeding steamer. Even though the boat's time of eleven minutes was much slower than the run of the *Thompson*, the locomotive lost the race by three hundred yards.

Still later, in 1888, Captain Troup again was in the pilot house when the *Hassalo* made a serious attempt to beat the record set by the *R. R. Thompson*. Running the Cascades in late summer when the water was low, the channel narrow, and the rocks more dangerous, Captain Troup took the boat through the six-mile run in a flat seven minutes, only forty seconds short of the record set by the *R. R. Thompson*.[5]

"When a railroad bridges a river," veteran pilots began to say in the mid-1880s, "it's time for us to look for another line of work. Our day is almost done."

By 1885, two bridges had been completed across the Snake River, one at Ainsworth, just above its juncture with the Columbia, another at Riparia, halfway between its mouth and Lewiston. The Oregon Rail & Navigation Company, which had maintained its separate identity, did not go out of business in the upper river country. But it came perilously close. Instead of constructing solid, low-level spans across the Snake, which would have blocked upstream navigation to Lewiston permanently, the railroads put in place swing-spans, which could be opened to permit the passage of steamboats and then closed for travel by trains.

How the Navigation Company managed to persuade Henry Villard to keep a few stern-wheelers such as the *Annie Faxon, Spokane,* and *John Gates* on the Celilo-Lewiston run even after the completion of the rail lines and their bridges, is not known. But it was fortunate he did, for on this stretch of river it soon was proved that the railroads could not replace water transport for either passengers or freight.

So far as passengers traveling west from Salt Lake were concerned, the change of trains at Umatilla could be endured if the traveler were headed for Spokane and points east. But if he were going to Lewiston, traveling on a clean, well-appointed stern-wheeler with an excellent dining room and bar, as well as a comfortable stateroom, was much more pleasant than riding on a jolting, cinder-choked, smelly day coach.

As for the movement of freight, wheat farmers in the Walla Walla Valley and the Palouse Hills found the railroads to be long on promise but short on fulfillment. Though a freight train could move wheat to market well enough when it got the empty cars to the right place at the right time, the two needs were seldom met. To their great annoyance, the farmer-shippers often found their sacks of grain piled in twelve-foot-high, quarter-mile-long rows at the railroad sidings, waiting in the sun, wind, and weather for the trains to haul them downriver to Portland. Since the farmer received no payment for his crop until it reached the marketplace, he was not happy with the delay.

As a consequence, every downriver-bound boat was laden with all the sacked wheat it could carry, with the farmer-shippers paying premium rates to put it aboard. Howls of protest from the inland country carried on down the Snake and Columbia, through the Gorge, and were heard loud and clear in the Portland office of the O.R.N. Company.

"We need more railroad cars in the Snake River country, Mr. Villard," Company executives told him, "And more boats."

"I know! I know! Bringing so many boats downriver was a mistake. I admit that. Fix it."

"Boats don't run rapids upriver, sir."

"So build new ones where we need them. I'll see what I can do about getting more railroad cars."

What really was needed so far as transport on the Columbia-Snake River system was concerned, Company executives agreed, was implementation of an "Open River" policy by the federal government, an improvement long advocated by farmers and businessmen living east of the mountains. Since this would mean building locks and canals around both the Cascades and Celilo Falls, the project was so vast it could be undertaken only by the federal government. Busy with railroad-building at the moment, Henry Villard refused to get involved in it.

"It's too political for me," he told the executives. "But if you want to develop it, go ahead."

"The first thing we'll need to do," the executives agreed, after discussing the problem, "is start the process by getting one foot in the door. Maybe a modest appropriation for a feasibility study by the Corps of Engineers would be the way to begin. Let's take a couple of Oregon Congressmen to dinner. . . "[6]

Chapter 10 footnotes

1. Gray, "Reminiscences," pp. 1,2.
2. Ibid.
3. De Voto, *Lewis and Clark Journals,* op. cit., p. 264.
4. *Blow For the Landing*, op. cit., p. 32.
5. Ibid, p. 101.
6. Ibid, p. 27.

The ice-breaker and fixing the Creator's mistakes

Senior Captain Thomas Warren, one of the lower river pilots who had agreed that the days of steamboat men were almost done, had reason to modify his opinion during the bitter-cold month of January 1886. His attitude change was caused by a request that he assist Captain Kenneth Manning, master of the iron-hulled side-wheeler *Olympian*, in rescuing passengers on a snowbound train marooned in the Columbia River Gorge near Hood River.

"When Henry Villard makes a mistake," the public relations people in the Portland office of the O.R. & N. Company told Captain Warren, "it's never a small one. For two years those iron-hulled boats he had built back in Delaware and put in service on the West Coast have been white elephants. Now maybe one of them can redeem herself."

The two craft conceived by Villard in what most steamboat men declared a complete lapse of common sense were the *Olympian* and her sister ship, the *Alaskan*. Both were iron-hulled side-wheelers of magnificent proportions. The *Olympian* was 262 feet long and forty feet wide, while the *Alaskan* was fourteen feet longer. The *Olympian* arrived in Puget Sound in 1884 and was put in service on the Tacoma-Victoria run under the Oregon Rail & Navigation flag.

The *Olympian* had incandescent lights, mahogany tables in a 220-foot long main saloon, plush furniture, and the finest Wilton velvet carpet money can buy. All of her fifty staterooms

Building the Columbia River Jetty.

had brass bedsteads instead of berths. She displaced 1,400 tons. Her dining saloon could seat 130 people and she had fancy glass chandeliers and an ebony-trimmed grand staircase.

The *Olympian* lost money on Puget Sound. Villard sent her to the Columbia River to see if she coul do better there. Since she drew nine feet of water, the only place she could be used was on the Portland-Astoria run.

On January 22, 1886, a massive blizzard struck the Columbia Gorge just west of Hood River, paralyzing both rail and boat traffic. Because of unusually low temperatures earlier in the month, the Columbia River had been frozen solid from bank to bank during the past two weeks, making the river impassable to wooden-hulled boats. Massive snowdrifts covered the O.R.& N. tracks along the south bank, bringing all traffic to a standstill.

Upon reaching the vicinity of Hood River two mornings earlier, the westbound Pacific Express had been halted and ordered to remain there while means were sought to rescue her passengers and those expected on the following trains.[1]

"Captain Manning has plenty of experience piloting the *Olympian*," the public relations people told Captain Warren.

"But he doesn't know the river between Portland and Hood River nearly as well as you do. With his boat's iron hull and power, she ought to be able to break through the ice if you can guide her into a channel more than nine feet deep so she won't run aground."

"That I can do."

Since it was past noon on the cold, cloudy, late January day before Captain Warren went aboard the boat and it got under way from the Portland dock, darkness was falling by the time the *Olympian* had moved down the Willamette to its mouth, then turned east and started fighting its way up the ice-choked channel of the Columbia. Tying up for the night just below Vancouver, the *Olympian* resumed its rescue attempt at seven-thirty the next morning, finding the river frozen over so solidly from its surface to its bottom that it was forced to act like a gigantic ice chisel, running its sharp, iron-clad bow into the unyielding pack ice time and again until its forward progress was halted, backing up, then charging and forcing itself atop the ice until its weight broke it apart and opened a narrow channel up which it could steam.

As they stood in the pilot house while the big metal buckets of the side-wheels churned fragmented chunks of ice astern with a deafening roar, Captain Manning shouted to Captain Warren, "It's like chopping up blocks for an icehouse with a fourteen-hundred ton wedge! How far upriver do we have to go?"

"Forty miles!" Captain Warren shouted back. "Do you think she'll hold together that long?"

"God knows! But we'll keep trying till she rams her way through or falls apart!"

Hour by hour, the big iron-hulled *Olympian* made slow progress, the chopping action of her side-wheel buckets breaking up the floes so that the sluggish current could carry the shards of ice downstream. Ten miles above Vancouver, the boat met disaster when a huge section of what appeared to be solid ice suddenly broke loose and started floating downstream, taking the boat with it.

"It was like the whole surface length of the Gorge had given way," Captain Warren said later, "with the boat caught in the

middle, leaving her helpless. For nearly an hour and a half she
was carried back downriver until she was thrown into an eddy
below the sandbar upstream from Vancouver, where she lodged
against solid ice."

Though both bow and stern anchors were put out, they failed
to hold, with the eddy itself finally keeping the boat in place,
where it remained during the night. By morning, the bulk of the
loosened ice floe had moved on downriver to such an extent that
Captain Manning judged it safe to try again.[2]

By mid-afternoon, the *Olympian* had managed to buck her
way through ice jams at Fisher's Landing, Rooster Rock, and
Cape Horn. By evening, she had made it to Dodson's Fish Wheel
Landing, four miles below Bonneville, which was where the
Lower Cascades Rapids began. Learning that a short distance
upstream, the ice was piled up twenty feet above the surface of
the river, Captain Warren told Captain Manning it was useless
to attempt going any farther.

"We're about ten miles west of where the train is stalled," he
said. "One way or another, the marooned passengers will have
to find their way to us. There's no way we can go to them."

"The railroad superintendent has sixty-five laborers aboard
the boat," Captain Manning said, nodding agreement. "I'll tell
him it's time to put them to work."

On the morning of January 28, the trains stalled at Hood
River and The Dalles were ordered to try to reach Dodson's Fish
Wheel Landing. Working feverishly in the bitter cold, the sixty-
five husky axemen, whose usual task was clearing brush for
right-of-way, slashed a path through the tangle of bushes and
trees from the river bank where the side-wheeler lay to the railroad track. By ten o'clock the next morning, 175 grateful passengers along with mail and freight, had been transferred to the
Olympian.

Taking on food and drink in the toasty-warm comfort of the
dining room and bar, the men and women rescued from the
snowbound train vied with one another in telling blizzard and
ice stories that in time to come would take their place among
the legends of the river. Along the quiet stretches of the
Columbia between Hood River and The Dalles, one passenger
said, the ice had been eleven feet thick, capable of supporting

Columbia River Maritime Museum
Tug *Daniel Kern* hauling rock for river mouth jetties.

heavily laden wagons and teams of horses as they crossed back and forth between Oregon and Washington Territory.

In the heart of the Gorge, another traveler related, Bridal Veil, Horse Tail, and Multnomah Falls, whose 2,000-foot drop off the sheer lava bluffs lining the Oregon side of the river never before had been stilled, were all unmoving, massive icicles. Even the oldest of the local Indians, the passenger claimed, had never seen that sight before.

Adding spice to an experience none of the passengers would ever forget was the fact that they had been rescued and now were completing their journey on one of the most luxurious river boats they had ever seen, courtesy of the O. R.& N. Company.

Now that a channel through the ice floes had been broken by the iron-hulled *Olympian*, enough open water ran in the center of the river to let the boat steam at flank speed down to the mouth of the Willamette, then back upstream to Portland. Pulling in to the Ash Street dock at 3:30 p.m., Captain Manning discharged the boat's grateful passengers, then got into a row-boat and circled the craft to see how much damage had been done to it during the rescue effort. So far as he could tell, the *Olympian* had lost a little paint during its ordeal, nothing more.

Next day, the iron-hulled craft returned upriver with passengers and mail for the East. On January 30, the weather moderated, snowplows cleared the tracks through the Gorge, and normal rail service was resumed. By the time the boat docked at the Portland wharf, newspapers of the day had ample time to make a big story of the luxury boat's rescue of the 175 passengers on the snowbound train.

If the public relations people employed by the O. R.& N. Company had been on the ball, they could have run a big ad stating in large type:

NEXT TRIP, TAKE A BOAT!

Because there is no evidence that they did so, the rescue produced more praise than profit for Mr. Villard's white elephant. Anxious to make something out of the *Olympian*, Villard chartered her out to a company in the Alaska trade, where her experience as an ice-breaker might be of some value. Again a money-loser, she soon was back in his hands. Having no other use for her, he sent her to the Portland boneyard for abandoned ships, where she languished for several years. Finally, the bedraggled old queen was sold for a meager sum to a company which decided to take her back around the Horn and put her in service as a resort boat on the East Coast.

Exactly what happened to her during the trip is not clear. But by some misfortune or other she ran aground in the Strait of Magellan, the land of perpetual snow and ice, and was heard from no more.

Ever since *Speelyi*, the Coyote Spirit who had created this part of the world 10,000 snows ago, laid out the course of what the Indians called the *Chiawana* and the whites the Columbia, the 1,250-mile-long river had flowed without hindrance from its source high in the Canadian Rockies to its six-mile-wide mouth between the states of Oregon and Washington, where it melded its waters with those of the Pacific Ocean. Although the natives of this vast watershed would never have dreamed of altering the flow of the great river, the brash white newcomers to the

Bill Gulick photo
Rockwork on South Jetty at the mouth of the Columbia River.

Pacific Northwest had no compunctions whatsoever against changing what *Speelyi* had wrought.

Washington became a state in 1889, joining the Union of which Oregon had been a member for thirty years. Flexing their joint muscles, the two states immediately set in motion measures aimed at improving on what until then the natives of the region had accepted as a perfectly satisfactory river. During the next few years, three major projects aimed at enhancing what *Speelyi* had designed got under way: an improved ship channel across the bar outside the mouth of the river; locks and a ship canal in the Columbia River Gorge; a river shortcut near the headwaters.

Of the three projects, most river captains approved of the first and second, which were being funded by the federal government, while they considered the third one, which was being undertaken by private capital, a piece of utter nonsense.[3]

Near the headwaters of the Columbia at the base of the spectacular Selkirk Mountains up in Canada, proponents of the third project claimed *Speelyi* had made a horrendous mistake by allowing the Columbia to flow north, then west, and then

Columbia River Maritime Museum
Bailey Gatzert crossing the Cascade Rapids.

south again in an elongated oval 300 miles long. The river's only reason for doing this was that its waters were obeying the law of gravity, the would-be improvers said, but they could correct that. By cutting directly west across a mile-and-a-half-wide hump of land, the river could save itself 300 miles of pointless travel through useless, uninhabited mountain wilderness, which would allow it to reach the United States much sooner than it did now.

"What the company plans to do," Captain William Polk Gray was told, "is dig a canal that will connect the Kootenai River east of the divide with Columbia Lake west of the mountains. Once the project is finished, they say, boats can operate on whichever sector of river offers the most freight traffic."

"How many boats are running up there now?"

"So far as I can tell, the number fluctuates between two and none. But the developers say that if they dig the canal, traffic will come."

As time passed, tales drifting down from Canada ranged from odd to incredible. During the next few years, two steamboats—the *Duchess* and the *Clive*—were built at Golden,

British Columbia, on the east side of the divide, though steamboat men doubted that either was worthy of the name. Put together of scraps left over from an abandoned Canadian Pacific sawmill, no two boards in the *Duchess* were the same thickness, travelers who saw the vessel reported.

Her cabin looked like an enlarged privy, with the captain and steering apparatus of the boat sitting in a small penthouse on top. Propulsion was supplied by an undersized paddle-wheel turned by an engine salvaged from a St. Lawrence River ferryboat originally built in 1840.

But ugly as she was, the *Duchess* reigned alone on the upper Columbia for two years until the even less handsome *Clive* arrived to provide competition. Originally built as a pile-driving scow, the *Clive's* hull was a square, flat-bottomed barge which had been abandoned by the railroad. The same sawmill that had provided parts for the *Duchess* had been picked over for equipment installed in the engine room. Steam was produced by an upright boiler from a Manitoba corn-cob-fired steam plough, while the engine had been salvaged from a long-defunct river tug.

"So far as the paddle-wheel goes," one critic commented, "it's more useful in identifying the stern of the boat than in driving it through the water. On one trip, the *Clive* took twenty-three days to travel 100 miles between Golden and Columbia Lake—a lot of it sideways before a strong wind."

Nevertheless, the Canal Flats Company managed to obtain the necessary government permits, form a syndicate in England, sell stock, and raise enough money to start moving dirt. Completed in 1889, what was called the Baille-Grohman Canal, in honor of its builder, was 6,700 feet long and forty-five feet wide, with a ten-foot-high wooden lift lock 100 by thirty feet. But for four years following the canal's completion, the only thing that moved between the two sectors of now-connected river was a small amount of seepage water.

Finally, in 1893, a boat named the *Gwendoline* did use the canal, though from what Captain Gray heard of its first trip it was truly a "dry run." Built on the Kootenani River on the east side of the divide, the boat steamed to Canal Flats, found the locks in such a state of disrepair that they could not be used, then decided to cross the isthmus anyway, even if by traveling on dry land. After being partially dismantled, the boat was put on rollers and dragged over an improvised road to the lower sector of the river. This feat impressed the Canadian government so favorably that it agreed to spend enough money to put the canal and locks back in working condition. When this task had been done, the *Gwendoline* fired up her boilers, entered the east end of the canal, and then steamed triumphantly through to the east, theoretically saving herself a journey of 300 miles.

Dramatic though the two-way trip had been, it did not stimulate steamboat travel on the upper Columbia or increase use of the canal. In fact, eight years passed before the canal carried a steamboat on its surface again. But that passage was a spectacular one.

Built in Jennings, Montana, in 1897 for the Kootenai River trade, the *North Star* was purchased by Captain Frank Armstrong, who planned to put her in service on the Columbia near Trail, British Columbia, as an ore-hauling boat. With good and sufficient reasons to try the shortcut, he decided to take the canal. But when he and his boat reached its eastern entrance, he was chagrined to find it badly silted in. Going ashore and pacing off the length of the old wooden locks, he found them to be thirty feet shorter than his boat. As a further complication to his using the canal, he discovered that a low-level bridge with no draw span had been built across the midpoint of the canal at Dutch Creek for the benefit of local road travel.

No matter. He would use the canal anyway.

"What Captain Armstrong did," a steamboat man who had witnessed the incredible operation told Captain Gray, "was dig out the entrance to the canal and work his boat in as far as the locks. Since the wood was pretty rotten anyway, he had no trouble tearing out the lower gates, which he replaced with enough sand-filled ore sacks to create a pond that would float the *North Star*.

"Getting up a good head of steam, Captain Armstrong had his crew fire off a dynamite charge just before the boat reached the dam, letting it dive through on the crest. At Dutch Creek, a little farther on, he rigged a derrick on the bow of the boat,

Penrose Library, Whitman College
A tug and barge pass through Cascade Locks, which lifts vessels nearly 100 feet.

hoisted the bridge out of the way, passed through, then carefully replaced it."

Sad to say, despite all his ingenuity and labor, Captain Armstrong saw his plans come to naught, for the *North Star* had too deep a draft to operate on the lower sector of the Columbia except in high water. Furthermore, Canadian Customs officials decreed that since the boat had been built in the United States and no duty had been paid on its importation, it must be laid up until the appropriate taxes were paid. Feeling no taxes were due on a boat producing no revenue, Captain Armstrong took it out of service. For some years thereafter, when the would-be tax collectors were not looking, he stripped it of usable parts which he transferred to his other boats. Eventually, nothing remained of the original *North Star* except its hull, which he converted into two unnamed, untaxed barges.

Though the silt-and-weed-filled scar across what came to be known as Canal Flats would remain for many years as physical evidence of man's futile efforts to correct a mistake made by *Speelyi*, the upper Columbia boat canal would be used no more . . .[4]

So far as the second river improvement project was concerned—locks and a ship canal in the Columbia Gorge—it moved by fits and starts as funds became available. Pressured by river shippers who had long resented the extra freight charges they must pay to have their products portaged fourteen miles at Celilo Falls and six miles at the Cascades, the Corps of Engineers in 1875 had surveyed the rapids in the Gorge and recommended that a canal be built around them.

Soon thereafter, Congress approved $90,000 to get the work started. When it was discovered that this amount would not be nearly enough to complete the project, work slowed but enough money was added each year to keep hopes up and crews digging for the next ten years.

When the south bank railroad was completed by the O.R.& N. Company in 1883, interest in the canal dwindled to almost nothing. A further blow was struck against shippers when stern-wheelers working the middle river were taken over the Cascades Rapids during high-water periods and put into service on the lower river, leaving shippers no choice except to use the railroads. Not surprisingly, rail rates went up. But the outraged cries by aggrieved wheat men in eastern Oregon and Washington rose to such a pitch that they soon were heard in the halls of Congress.

As a result, an appropriation of $1,239,000 was approved by Congress as an earnest payment against whatever amount might be required to complete the project, whose cost likely would run in the neighborhood of $8 million.

When work got under way at the Cascades, swarms of laborers, masons, carpenters, and equipment operators moved in with digging equipment, piles of dark volcanic rock, timbers, and lumber for concrete forms cluttering the six-mile-length of the project. The locks would be in two steps, with the lower chamber having a lift of twenty feet and a length of 490, while the upper chamber had a lift of eighteen feet and was 402 feet long. In between the two locks, a ninety-foot-wide ship canal would be able to handle any boat on the river at that time, as well as ocean-going ships in the future.

The piles of lava rocks were for the sides of the ship channel, curious visitors were told, which would be laid by stone masons

Columbia River Maritime Museum
A twentieth century stern-wheeler, the *Bailey Gatzert*, moves through the Cascade locks on an upriver journey.

brought over from Italy. These men were so skilled in their trade, it was said, that they could lay a dry wall twenty-five feet high without mortar or sealer of any kind, which would stand for a thousand years without leaking a drop of water.

Combined, the two locks would lift a boat forty-two vertical feet, an indication of why this six-mile-stretch of river had been such an obstacle to navigation. Completion date for the project was to be the fall of 1896, if the Corps of Engineers did not run out of money, which was not likely for congressmen and engineers knew that an unfinished project would be a black eye for them both.

"Come the fall of '96," shippers predicted, "we'll see boats passing through the locks to the middle river."[5]

Meanwhile, work was getting under way on the third project—improving navigation over the bar at the mouth of the river.

From the time of its discovery by Captain Robert Gray in 1792, the Columbia River Bar had been a graveyard for ships. In the 100 years that had passed, the number of vessels lost or destroyed in the area—fishing boats, harbor craft, and seagoing vessels—had exceeded 2,000. Marine historians estimated, at least 1,500 lives had been lost.[5]

Because winds, tides, and currents brought air and water of varying temperatures and velocities into constant contact, changes in the weather near the river's mouth could be sudden and extreme. From April until August, the prevailing winds in the vicinity of Astoria blew from the northwest; for the rest of the year, southwesterly winds dominated. On the coast during the summer months, northwest winds now and then became gales, which sometimes lasted for several days. In winter, southerly winds could rage at any time, bringing with them heavy southwest swells and monstrous seas.

Fog frequently shrouded the mouth of the Columbia during July, August, and September, but it could roll in at any time. Often extending many miles out to sea, it could be very dense and last for days, stopping all traffic in and out of the river. The average annual rainfall at Astoria was seventy-seven inches; the velocity of the current at the entrance to the river was two-and-a-half knots at its peak; and the range between high and low tides was seven and a half feet.

"What the Corps of Engineers plans to do," Captain Gray was told, "is cut the channels of the river down from several into only one. This will hurry it up, they think, so that the one channel will flow fast and deep."

"Do you think it will work?"

"They say it worked at the mouth of the Mississippi. But here, who knows?"

Back in 1841, Captain Gray knew, Lieutenant Charles Wilkes of the United States Navy had made a disastrous attempt to survey the river's mouth. Complaining that the bar's constantly shifting sands made it difficult to draw reliable charts, he proved his point the hard way when a unit of his squadron, the USS Peacock, grounded on the north shore of the river entrance and became a total loss. In remembrance of that unhappy event, the spot had been christened "Peacock Spit," a name it still bore.

Lieutenant Wilkes expressed puzzlement that so knowledgeable a navigator and explorer as George Vancouver had failed to discover the mouth of the River of the West. "I found breakers extending from Cape Disappointment to Point Adams in one unbroken line," Wilkes wrote in 1845. "I am at a loss to conceive how any doubt should have ever existed that here was the mouth of the mighty river, whose existence was reported so long."[6]

From an early time, reasonable ship captains accepted the necessity of employing local pilots with knowledge of the sandbar's changing channels before attempting to take their vessels into or out of the river. Impatient captains wishing to save money or time often took chances piloting their own ships—then regretted doing so. In 1840, for example, four ships were wrecked on the bar: the *Aurora*, the *Morning Star*, the *Sylvia de Grasse*, and the *Josephine*. In 1852, five ships were wrecked: the *Dolphin*, the *General Warren*, the *Machigone*, the *Marie*, and the *Potomac*.

After Captain George Flavel established his bar pilot association in 1850 and the State of Oregon began issuing licenses to Columbia River Bar pilots, wrecks became less frequent. But recently, a surprising number of sailing ships that had seen their day and no longer were able to compete with steam-propelled craft were attempting to enter the river without going to the expense of employing a pilot—and coming to grief. Part of this could be ascribed to the fact that the sailing ships were being staffed by inexperienced or over-the-hill officers and crews. A more important cause for the wrecks may have been the fact that, if a master wanted to ground his ship for the insurance money, the sand spit guarding the south entrance was an ideal place to do it.

"This is the only coast where a captain and his crew can walk ashore from a shipwreck," underwriters said cynically. "These days, a lot of them do."[7]

As aids to navigation, a lighthouse had been built in 1856 atop Cape Disappointment 220 feet above the sea on the north side of the river, shooting its 700,000 candlepower on the white flash and 160,000 on the red twenty-one miles out to sea. On the south side, the Point Adams Lighthouse with similar beams had been built in 1875. As a further aid to navigation beginning in 1892, a lightship equipped with a foghorn went on station five miles at sea outside the entrance to the Columbia, where it was manned year-round by a Coast Guard crew. Since the vessel stationed there was out of touch with land and had to endure all extremes of wind and weather, the sailors were forced to live aboard for six-week stints without relief. It was the worst kind of sea duty imaginable.

But whatever price paid in boredom and discomfort by men tendering warnings to ocean-going craft, it paled to insignificance when compared to the terrible loss of life by those who made their living going to sea in small boats. Legendary among the disasters that occurred between Tillamook Head to the south and Willapa Bay to the north was the unexpected storm that struck on May 4, 1880.

On that bright, sunny, mild spring morning, virtually every boat in the area was at sea trolling for salmon or bottom fish. Unknown to the fishermen in the 250 vessels working offshore, a phenomenal freak of weather was in the making. A local historian later wrote:

> Without forewarning, a powerful wind of hurricane force suddenly came out of nowhere, changing the peaceful ocean waves into massive, seething billows. Showing no mercy, winds of more than one hundred miles per hour contorted the sea's face and made playthings of the small fishboats. Pummeled, tossed, turned, capsized, and swamped, one by one they disappeared from view, the terrified fishermen thinking the end of the world had come. Thrown into the mass of liquid fury to fend for themselves, death to most came quickly.[8]

The uncommon local squall, which roared in from the northwest, lasted only thirty minutes. By the time it ended, more than 240 vessels had been destroyed and over 300 lives were lost.

Crossing the bar and entering the river had been a high-risk adventure during the age of sail. With the advent of steamboats, it became only slightly less dangerous. At low tide, the river meandered through channels cut in the constantly shifting sand. A pilot coming through deep water one day was never sure what he might find the next. "Two problems faced the Corps of Engineers," a report written in 1875 stated. "First, to find a way to make the channel deep enough at low tide to permit ships of ordinary draft to enter; second, to keep the channel open once it has been dredged."

In their search for a solution to the river's sandbar problem, the Corps called on Colonel James Eads, who had encountered a similar difficulty at the mouth of the Mississippi.

> *On first glance there seemed to be little similarity between the clear Columbia and the muddy Mississippi endlessly dumping silt into the Gulf,* (the report continued), *but the effect was the same. The ocean kept pushing sand up toward the mouth of the Columbia and building bars that the river had to cut through. Surveys in 1878 showed that an application of the methods Eads had used just below New Orleans would be effective. In 1884 the first appropriation for construction was made. Soon thereafter, work on the project began.*[8]

In principle, the solution was simple enough, although its accomplishment was going to be expensive and prolonged. The river had to be compressed between two dikes or jetties of stone. One would be built out from the north shore, Cape Disappointment, and the other from the south, where there was a low projection called Clatsop Spit. Narrowing the passage between the two jetties would increase the river's velocity naturally, scouring the channel in a continual process, thus maintaining a safe depth for ocean-going ships.

Railroad tracks were built atop the jetties where pile drivers pounded timbers into the sands to form trestles for extending more rails toward the Columbia's central channel. Engines pushed strings of cars loaded with rocks to be dumped into the water. Gradually, as more and more rocks went into the water beside the trestles, they packed and merged as long ridges or dams against which the waves piled sand to make the whole thing an extension of the spit or jetty itself. Where the bottom seemed unstable, trainloads of brush or small trees with their branches left on were dumped to form a mat that held the rock in place until the waves did their work of scooping sand.

Much of the rock came from a hundred miles upriver, transported there by a specially built stern-wheeler, the *Cascades*, a large vessel able to push or pull alongside five huge barges filled with tons of rock. By the time the engineers finished their work, the river had gouged out a thirty-foot-deep channel.

> *The jetties grew from the first thousand feet built in 1894* (a report stated) *until the south jetty reached out seven miles from its beginnings at Fort Stevens. Toward it from Cape Disappointment the north jetty stretched four-and-one-half miles and gathered itself behind a shoal that enlarged Peacock Spit.*[9]

In truth, modifying the channel of a large river is a project that never ends. As long as water runs downhill, ocean tides ebb and rise, and winds move waves toward or away from shore, the river bottom will change and the depths of ship channels must be closely monitored, as they still are at the mouth of the Columbia River.[10]

Chapter 11 footnotes

1. *Blow For the Landing*, op. cit., p. 147.
2. Ibid.
3. Ibid, p. 87.
4. Ibid, p. 88.
5. James Gibbs, *Shipwrecks of the Pacific Coast,* Binfords & Mort, Portland, 1957, p. 98.
6. During the age of sail, exploring an unknown coast with a following wind and tide was a risky business, so most prudent captains stood well out to sea when approaching the mouth of the Columbia.
7. After the Peter Iredale went aground on Clatsop Spit in 1906, Captain Lawrence and his crew walked ashore, celebrated their survival with a drink of whiskey, then turned the shipwreck over to the underwriters, who eventually paid off in full. *Roadside History of Oregon*, by Bill Gulick, Mountain Press, Missoula, Montana, 1991, pp. 87, 88.
8. *Oregon's Salty Coast,* by James Gibbs, Superior, Seattle, 1978.
9. Blow For the Landing, op. cit., p. 186.
10. Ibid.

Shipwrecks and river disasters

In the late 1870s, the spectacular wreck of a large steamship with many lives at risk took place just inside the mouth of the Columbia River. With a licensed, experienced pilot aboard, the *Great Republic* grounded the night of April 18, 1879. Built in 1866 at Greenport, Long Island, New York, she had served in the China trade for several years, then in the 1870s began carrying freight and passengers between San Francisco and Portland. A big side-wheeler measuring 378 feet in length, she was registered at 4,750 tons. She was also fast, once making the 100-mile run from Portland to Astoria in five hours and fifteen minutes.[1]

Departing San Francisco in the spring of 1879, she was carrying 896 passengers and more than 100 crew members when she arrived at the mouth of the Columbia at midnight on April 18. The pilot boat was waiting for her and pulled alongside, putting Pilot Thomas Doig aboard.

"He was a good man," his peers said, "and not one to make mistakes. But that night, according to the Court of Inquiry which was held later, he made a bad one."

There was not a ripple on the water, (Captain James Carroll, the ship's master, told the Court of Inquiry), *and we came over the bar on a slow bell all the way, crossing safely and reaching the inside buoy. The first and third*

officers were on the lookout with me. I had a pair of glass-
es and was the first to discover Sand Island, and found the
bearings all right. I reported to the pilot, who had not yet
seen it. We ran along probably two minutes, and I then told
the pilot I thought we were getting too close to the island
and that he had better haul her up. He replied, "I do not
think we are in far enough." A minute later I said, "Port
your helm and put it hard over, as I think you are getting
too near the island." He made no reply, but ran along for
about five minutes and then put the helm hard aport, and
the vessel swung up, heading toward Astoria. But the ebb
tide caught her on the starboard bow, and being so near
the island sent her on the spit.[2]

Grounding so lightly that few of the people aboard knew she
had struck, the *Great Republic* found herself stranded, for the
tide was ebbing and she had no chance to get off the sandbar
that night. Aware of the fact that the barometer was falling,
indicating an impending storm, Captain Carroll appealed to
Fort Canby for assistance. The tugs *Benham* and *Canby* soon
arrived, followed by the *Shubrick* and the *Columbia*. With the
aid of these and a number of small boats, the passengers were
taken off the ship and transported to Astoria, while the crew
remained on board to off-load cargo and coal in an attempt to
lighten ship and float her off the sandbar on the next high tide.
Captain Carroll later told a court of inquiry what followed:

At 8 p.m. a southwest gale started in making a heavy
sea, chopping to the southeast about midnight. Up to this
time the ship was lying easy and taking no water, but the
heavy sea prevented the tugs from rendering assistance
and also drove her higher on the spit, and shortly after
midnight she began to work, breaking the steampipes and
disabling the engines. A few remaining passengers were
put ashore on Sand Island at 6 a.m. on Sunday and were
followed by the crew, the ship beginning to break up so that
it was dangerous to remain aboard. The last boat left the
ship at 10:30 a.m., and in getting away, the steering oar

A brass band entertains *Annie Faxon* passengers at a stop during an excursion trip.

broke and the boat capsized, drowning eleven of the four-teen men it contained.

At about this time a heavy sea boarded the ship and carried away the staterooms on the starboard side, gutted the dining room, broke up the floor of the social hall and carried away the piano. Several seas afterward boarded her forward and carried away the starboard guard, offi-cers' room and steerage deck, also a number of horses. I remained aboard until 5:00 P.M., when the pilot and I low-ered a lifeboat and came ashore.[3]

Despite the efforts to save her, the *Great Republic* was des-tined never to get off the bar intact. After the underwriters had settled with her owners, a salvage firm paid $3,780 for the stranded vessel and its cargo and went to work reclaiming what it could, which wasn't much. A month later the hull aft of the walking beam crumbled into the sea and the fore and aft main-masts went over the side. In another ten days the walking beam and the two large paddle-wheels alone remained intact. Part of the wreckage could be seen at low tide as late as 1891, with the steamer's grave then marked on the charts as "Republic Spit."

Many stories which may or may not have been true later were told about the wreck. A local favorite was the one about the fat Chinaman who didn't float.

Among the crew members leaving the ship before the seas became too rough, so the story went, was a plump, jolly, round-faced Chinese cook named Ah Ling. The rope ladder down which the other crew members had climbed had become dislodged and fallen into the sea by the time Ah Ling came on deck. But that posed no problem. All he needed to do, his shipmates called up from the lifeboat being held in quiet water in the ship's lee, was jump into the water and be picked up after he came to the surface. The fact that he could not swim was of no concern, for, wearing a voluminous, black quilted jacket and being as fat as he was, there would be enough air pockets in the jacket and enough fat in his body for him to pop to the surface like a cork.

Though it took a lot of back-and-forth jabbering between him and several of his Chinese assistants who were already in the boat to convince him to jump, Ah Ling finally did so, splashing into the water only a few feet from the boat. Moving to the spot, his shipmates waited for his corpulent body to come up, as they knew it must do.

And waited. . . and waited. . . and waited. . .

But Ah Ling never came to the surface.

Not until weeks later, when an unusually high tide washed his body ashore, did his shipmates learn why Ah Ling's body had been far less buoyant than they had thought it would be.

Before leaving the kitchen and coming to the side of the boat, he had filled the pockets of his jacket with the ship's silverware.

One of the oddest river accidents occurred in downtown Portland on a frosty November morning in 1891. Involving a steamer, a drawbridge, and a streetcar, it was reported in the *Oregonian*:

> *Groping her way up the Willamette River toward Portland's Madison Street Bridge through a heavy, pea-soup fog at 8:15 yesterday morning, the little steamer*

Washington State Library
Annie Faxon at Snake River Landing.

Elwood *was making its usual run to Oregon City. Shivering against the morning frost, the pilot pulled the whistle cord, blowing a long and three shorts for the drawspan, at the same time ringing down to the engine room for a full stop.*

In response, the bridge tender acknowledged the whistle, swung the bridge gate shut against electric streetcar and horse-drawn vehicle traffic, then opened the span to let the Elwood *through.*

At the throttle of the town-bound Hawthorne trolley, the motorman eased back a few notches to check the speed his car had picked up on the downgrade to the bridge. As he peered through the fog, he saw the barrier and the open draw. He pushed the control lever to full off and wound on the hand brake to stop the car. The wheels locked, then slid like sled runners on the frosty rails.

As the streetcar struck it, the barrier's wood shattered; for an instant of time, the car hung on the edge, then it slipped slowly over into the river. It narrowly missed the steamer.

There was nothing the pilot of the Elwood could do as his boat drifted over the circle of bubbles where the streetcar had fallen in. He could not start his engines, for the paddewheel would strike survivors struggling in the water. He could only wait until he was clear of the bridge before he could turn back to help. By then, rowboats had been launched, rescuing twenty survivors who had struggled free from the sunken streetcar. Seven people did not make it. [4]

A light draft boat built specifically for the Portland-to-Oregon City run so that she could pass over the rapids at the mouth of the Clackamas River, the *Elwood* had been carrying a maximum load of passengers that morning. If the streetcar had slid through the barrier a few seconds later, it would have dropped squarely on top of the stern-wheeler, causing a much greater loss of life.

On the Snake River between its mouth and Lewiston, a tragic accident occurred in the spring of 1893 when a steamboat's boiler exploded. One of four boats built at Celilo in 1878, the *Annie Faxon* was the best of the grain and passenger haulers on the upper river, a vessel whose engines and propulsion machinery always had been scrupulously maintained. Captain Harry Baughman, her master, was an experienced senior pilot with the O.R.& N. Company; her officers were well qualified for their jobs. On this trip, the likable, handsome young purser, Harold Tappan, was celebrating his marriage in Lewiston the afternoon before by bringing his beautiful bride, Susan, along on a company-approved honeymoon voyage downriver to Celilo, The Dalles, and Portland.

After slowing the engines at Wade's Bar, Captain Baughman pulled the whistle cord and eased the boat in toward the landing, where a lone passenger and a few packages of freight were waiting to be taken aboard. Leaving his wife in the office, Purser Tappan came out on deck to collect the dollar fare from the passenger and check the manifest for the freight. As the *Annie Faxon* neared the dock, Captain Baughman rang down to the engine room for a full stop.

Nez Perce County Historical Society
Remains of the *Annie Faxon,* after the explosion.

Suddenly from below decks came a low rumble, followed immediately by a terrific explosion. The force was so great that the steamboat literally was blown to bits.

Turning to speak to a deckhand standing nearby, Purser Tappan was stunned to see a man's body sailing over the railing, while just beyond him, flying debris decapitated another crew member. Thrown overboard by the force of the explosion, both Purser Tappan and Captain Baughman survived. Eight crew members and passengers did not. Among the casualties was Susan Tappan, the purser's bride of less than twenty-four hours, whose body was never found.[5]

What justly was called a "miracle" by the Nez Perce Indians of the region occurred soon after the explosion when the lifetime work of two lady missionaries was rescued from the deep, cold waters of the Snake River. A carefully wrapped package entrusted to the express company and shipped aboard the *Annie Faxon* by Miss Kate McBeth had been addressed to the Indian Office of the Smithsonian Institution in Washington,

D.C. Contained in the box, which had a waterproof, red oilskin wrapper, was the most complete dictionary of the Nez Perce language ever compiled. The material was painstakingly assembled word by word during the twenty years that Sue McBeth, who had died a month earlier, and her younger sister, Kate, had lived with the Nez Perces. The 15,000-word dictionary of Nez Perce words and their English meanings was a one-of-a-kind volume so precious that, when it was offered as a gift to the Smithsonian, the director of that esteemed repository of national treasures was so delighted that he had given detailed instructions as to how the package should be wrapped and shipped.

No matter what local white people might have thought of missionaries in general and spinster ladies in particular, to the Christianized Nez Perces living on the reservation near Lapwai and Kamiah, the McBeth sisters were holy people. Devastated by the death of her older sister, Sue, the slightly younger sister, Kate, was ending her mission and returning to her home in Indiana. Deeply religious Indians, such as Elder Billy Williams, took some consolation in the fact that the words they had spoken in their own tongue, which the McBeth sisters had translated into English, were being sent east to a repository maintained by the Great White Father.

"Are you traveling on the *Annie Faxon*, too, Miss Kate?" the express agent for the O.R. & N. Company in Lewiston asked as he accepted and registered the package.

"No, I'm not," Kate McBeth answered, shaking her head. "The half-price vouchers sent me by the Missionary Society call for transportation by stagecoach north to Spokane, then east on the Northern Pacific through Butte, Bismarck, and Chicago, with a change there to the Ohio and Eastern."

"You've got a long ride ahead of you, Ma'am. Do you have a sleeper berth?"

"Heavens, no! A half-fare day coach is all the Missionary Society can afford. But I won't mind. Are you sure the package for the Smithsonian will go through without difficulty?"

"Don't worry about it, Miss Kate. It's registered for special handling all the way."

Thanks to the telegraph lines paralleling the Northern Pacific tracks, Kate McBeth read a newspaper account of the *Annie Faxon* disaster when her train stopped in Butte, Montana, late the next afternoon. Concerned about her precious package, she wired an inquiry to the express company agent in Lewiston, asking if the manuscript had survived. Yes, he replied, it had been recovered and sent on to the Smithsonian, but he did not know how much damage had been done to it. Kate later recounted the details:

> *All the time I had lived at Fort Lapwai, the clerk at the sutler's store, with his young wife, had been on the best of terms with me. Two years before, he had bought a farm on Snake River, but moved to it only last spring. He understands and talks Nez Perce quite well.*
>
> *That morning he was on the shore of the river and saw much stuff floating down. His eye was caught by a red box. He mounted his horse and waded out as far as he could. He had a long rope tied to the saddle. He made a noose upon it—threw it out just as the box was going over some rapids, and caught it. He drew it to shore, opened it, and recognized the Nez Perce script. He said at once, "This must be Kate's writing."*[6]

Despite its protective wrapping, the pages of the notebook were soaking wet, so the young clerk—whose name was King—opened it up and stood it on end to dry. A couple of days later an agent from the express company arrived and took it back to Portland, where the drying process was completed before the dictionary was forwarded to the Smithsonian, whose experts were pleased to find the entries so painstakingly recorded by Sue and Kate McBeth still perfectly legible.

Elder Billy Williams, a Christianized Nez Perce who had become a preacher, called the recovery of the dictionary a miracle, saying, "It seems as if that box were a living thing, that the Lord was caring for it."

Author's note: In the spring of 1994 when my wife and I spent five weeks doing research at the Smithsonian and the Library of Congress, Archivist Paula Fleming found the dictionary for me and put in my hands. Other than a few waterstains on the cover, it was in good condition. Containing 435 pages of penned entries, it had never been copied, I learned. Paula Fleming said she would copy it for me at thirty-five cents a page, which I was willing to pay, until she said, "We might have it on microfilm. Let me take a look."

They did have it; she made me a copy for twenty-five dollars, which I brought home and donated to Penrose Library at Whitman College in Walla Walla.

Like the *Shoshone* back in the 1860s, which had been built and launched in the Idaho desert near Farewell Bend by the Oregon Steam Navigation Company in an attempt to make money out of the gold and silver boom in southwestern Idaho Territory, the stern-wheeler *Norma* was built and launched in the same area in hopes of bringing in revenue from a copper discovery in Hell's Canyon in 1891. Called the Seven Devils boom because of its proximity to the Idaho mountain range nearby, the flurry of mining excitement was said to be the "biggest ever," with fortunes to be made by all parties concerned.

Rails had moved into the Snake River country by then, the Union Pacific having built what was called the Short Line to Portland along the route of the Oregon Trail. The run of the *Norma,* which was built on the banks of the Snake near Huntington, Oregon, was to be from the railroad connection downriver to Seven Devils Landing, a distance of sixty miles. If traffic warranted, she would also run upriver to Weiser or beyond—providing draws were put into the three bridges which the Union Pacific had built across the Snake without stopping to consider that steamboats might wish to use the river.

The *Norma* was 160 feet long, thirty-two feet wide, six feet deep in the hold, and drew forty inches of water under her normal load of 200 tons. Soon after her launching in the spring of 1891, she proved she could run downriver to Seven Devils Landing and back by making a successful trip. But when she attempted to steam upriver, neither pleas, threats, nor lawsuits aimed at the Union Pacific, the Corps of Engineers, the War Department or anyone else the O.R & N. could think of to sue could remove the inconsiderately built bridges. After several

Oregon Historical Society photo
Built above Hell's Canyon in 1891, the *Norma* was brought through the canyon to Lewiston by Captain William Polk Gray in 1895.

years of unprofitable traffic on a limited stretch of river, the company decided to do as it had done earlier with the *Shoshone*—bring her downriver.

The man chosen to accomplish the feat was Captain William Polk Gray, now fifty years old, with most of those years spent on Pacific Northwest rivers. When Willie Gray finally got around to writing his account of the trip, his prose was as colorful and vivid as his first hand verbal account.[7]

> *We left the Union Pacific bridge across Snake River near Huntington at 2:00 p.m., May 17, 1895. At Bay Horse Rapids, three miles down, while drifting in a channel improved by Government engineers, we touched on what afterward proved to be a piece of two-inch steel drill which had been broken off and left when the engineers were working there some years before. The drill ripped several holes through the bottom and the boat swung around and damaged the stern-wheel badly. Working the boat clear with*

spars and lines, we went down to J. A. Gray's Landing and repaired the wheel and patched the holes in the bottom.

Left Gray's Landing on the 18th, no wind. I was steering, my brother, the mate, was watching the Government chart. I saw indications of reefs or shoals and remarked: "It don't look good, what does the chart say?" He replied: "All clear—there is a black rock marked on the shore." But I was not satisfied and rung the bell to stop. Almost immediately she struck the starboard knuckle, making a hole forty feet long and four feet wide. I grabbed the chart and flung it out the window and we touched no reefs or rocks afterwards except at Copper Creek Falls. We had struck the edge of a reef about a foot under the muddy water which the Snake carries while in flood.

We were drifting while the mate inspected the damages. I knew they were bad but the crew had been discouraged at the Bay Horse trouble and I was afraid they would jump the job if we landed above Sturgill Rapids, three miles below us. From where we were the boat could easily steam back to the Bridge. I heard that Sturgill Rapids were very swift and it would be almost impossible to bring the boat back over them with our damaged side, so I kept on down slowly. The men gathered on the forward deck and one man asked if I was going to land. I made no reply and soon we were below the rapids, where we landed. There was some talk and I told them we would repair damages as much as possible. We had plenty of lumber and forty cords of wood in the hull. The boat had bulkheads all through her. We built a bulkhead as close as we could to the hole in the side and pumped out the six bulkheads that had been flooded. The men had understood that we would go back over the rapids and the evening before we were ready to start I had sounded the men out as to going on or going back. Every man wanted to go back.

Approaching the engineer, I said, "Charlie, this boat is worthless up here. What do you think of going back?" He replied: "We came up to get her. I say go on or put her where they can't find her." I replied: "Charlie, you're my man. The

Franklin County Historical Society
Stern-wheeler *Lewiston* load cargo.

*boys think I'm going to make a short trip down a few miles
to test our new bulkhead. But we will forget to come back."*

*We left Sturgill May 21st, and after we had gone down-
stream about ten miles the boys accepted their fate. About
5:00 P.M. we came around a short point and there was a
steel cable ferry across the river and less than eight feet
above the water. I stopped and backed the boat instantly. A
strong current was carrying us down to certain decapita-
tion of everything above the main deck, but the boat was a
good backer and Charlie answered nobly. I managed to
land her, head down, against a rocky cliff and the men
wound several ropes around rocks enough to hold her with
the engines working.*

*I whistled several times for the ferryman to lower the
wire. but no one moved, so I sent the mate and two men
across the river to lower the wire. When the mate asked the
ferryman, whose name was Brownlee, why he had delayed
lowering the wire, Brownlee replied: "I am doing it to pro-
long your lives. You have a bullheaded fool running that*

White sand beach, now under backwaters of Lower Granite Dam.

boat and not a soul of you will live to go through that canyon. I have been on top of those cliffs and I could jump across that canyon. I saw a drift log a hundred feet long up-end under one cliff and it never came up."

The ferryman was slow in lowering the wire and it was dark when we hunted a landing below. I wonder if you can imagine the strain on a pilot on a strange river known to be swift and treacherous, on a dark night, over-shadowing mountains throwing impenetrable gloom over all, and no searchlight.

About noon the next day we reached the landing above Copper Creek Falls and everyone walked down on the Oregon side to see them. They are more of a pour than a fall. From the brink of a cliff which jutted out into the still water at the foot of the cliff I measured the drop at eight- een feet. For an hour I watched and studied the currents, eddies and back-lash of the water, and decided that the least damage to the boat would be done by dropping over the fall on the Idaho side and let the back-lash hold me from the cliff as much as possible. The water pours over the fall and the current at about three hundred feet below the summit of the fall. The underside of the point of this cliff has been worn away until the over-hang extends over the water a good many feet and a considerable amount of the current passed under the cliff.

When I returned to the boat I called the carpenter, who had been foreman of Construction for years with the Oregon Steam Navigation Company and had asked to go with me for the excitement of this trip. Putting my foot on the starboard guard about ten feet aft of the stem, I said: "She will strike about here. I want you to run in a bulk-head six feet back of that to the midship keelson, then have the mate back it up with cordwood in case the water should rush in hard enough to tear away your bulkhead."

He examined the falls and replied: "You ain't intending to go over that place, are you? You will drown us all." I looked at him a moment and then asked: "Tom, you never had much notoriety, did you?" "No, why?" "They have all our names that are on this boat, and if you should be drowned your name will be in every paper in the United States and Europe."

His reply: "Oh, go to hell!" sounded like the decree of fate. I replied: "Put in the bulkhead, Tom, and we will chance the other place." An hour later the sounds of his hammer ceased and I heard a mumbling. Walking softly to the bulkhead hatch, I heard: "Damned old fool going to be drowned for excitement because a damned fool wants noto-riety." But the bulkhead went in good.

The next morning I made the only quarter-deck speech of my life. Calling the crew together, I said: "Boys, you have persuaded yourselves that there is danger to your lives in going over those falls, but there is not a particle of danger to your lives. The boat is built of wood enough to float her machinery and there is forty cords of wood in the hold. We could knock the bow and side in and while the wreck is floating we have boats enough to carry us all ashore. There are life preservers enough for three apiece if you want them, but don't get excited and jump overboard. Snake River never gives up her dead. Now get ready to go."

When we dropped over the fall we seemed to be facing certain destruction on the cliff below, but I knew my engineer was "all there" and would answer promptly. We backed slowly and within ten feet of the rocks to starboard her bow passed the mouth of Copper Creek, where an eddy emptying gave her a slight swing out and I backed strong with helm hard to starboard—the bow must take its chances now, the stern must not.

Almost before one could speak the bow touched the point of the cliff just hard enough to break those guard timbers without touching the hull, and we bounded into the still water below. The carpenter who had stationed himself on the hurricane deck outside of the pilot house with two life preservers around him stepped in front of the pilot house and shouted: "Hurrah, Cap! "You start her for hell and I'll go with you from this on!"

A little below Copper Creek Falls we entered the canyon and although a bright sun was shining outside, in the canyon it was twilight. I was too busy watching the surface of the river but the men on deck said they saw stars through the gloom. Shortly after coming out of the canyon we passed down a slight cataract that has cut its way through a plateau of blue clay and granite boulders. The channel was not over sixty feet wide and a mile or two long, with a drop estimated at one hundred feet to the mile. We tied up on account of wind the rest of the day at Johnson Creek, which is now the head of navigation, and reached Lewiston May 24th. . ."

From time to time in years to come, small stern-wheelers and screw-propeller boats would venture upriver into the white-water rapids of Hell's Canyon, assisted through the worst ones by ringbolts buried in the rocks of the cliff walls from which a quarter-mile of stranded steel cable would be carried downstream into quiet water below the rapid in a water-proof barrel. There, an ascending boat would pick up the cable, detach the barrel, then hook the cable onto a power winch aboard, following which it would literally haul itself up through the rapid by tightening the boat's winch foot by foot while the stern-wheel or screw-propeller pushed the craft from behind.

But the creek at Johnson Bar would remain the head of navigation, just as it was in the days of the Snake River's veteran pilot, Captain William Polk Gray.

Chapter 12 footnotes

1. Lewis & Dryden, *Marine History of the Pacific Northwest,* edited by E.W. Wright, Antiquarian Press, New York, 1961, p. 256.
2. Ibid, p. 266.
3. Ibid.
4. *Blow For the Landing*, op cit., p. 57.
5. *Marine History,* op. cit., p. 410.
6. *Roll On, Columbia*, by Bill Gulick, University Press of Colorado, 1998, V. Three, pp. 186-189.
7. *Idaho Yesterdays*, Vol. 1, #2, Summer, 1957, pp. 7-9.

Cascade Locks and the Eureka Mine

C eremonies celebrating the opening of Cascades Locks and the six-mile boat canal around the rapids were held on a crisp, clear day, November 15, 1896. By now, the "benevolent monopoly," established by the O.S.N. Company and its successor the O.R. & N. Company had given way to an era of "reasonable accomodation". Which was a nice way of saying it was better to achieve corporate peace by paying a rival not to duplicate services than to compete with him.

Operating on the river now were the boats of three companies: Shaver Transportation; the O.R. & N.; and The Dalles, Portland, & Astoria Navigation Company.[1] As the oldest pilot on the river, Capain William Polk Gray was invited to be an honored guest aboard the first boat to enter the locks, the *Sarah Dixon*, which was commanded by the owner of the company, Captain James W. Shaver. Standing beside Captain Shaver in the pilot house as the lower lock gate was closed and the boat was smoothly lifted twenty-four feet, Captain Gray felt distinctly uncomfortable gazing out at the white-water rapids rolling past. Floating serenely around a rapid by diverting a portion of the river's own water to defy the law of gravity seemed like cheating, in a way. Sooner or later, he feared, Mother Nature would take her revenge.

Directly behind the *Sarah Dixon* in the 490-foot-long lock was the *Regulator*, while behind it was the *Dalles City*, each vessel loaded to capacity with dignitaries and deck passengers going along for the historic ride. Aboard all three boats, the dining saloons and bars had been open for the past two hours, with bands playing dance music and patriotic airs as the boats moved up the six-mile-long ship canal on the Oregon side of the river. When the *Sarah Dixon* reached the upper lock and sat waiting for the eighteen-foot lift to fill, Captain Shaver gave Captain Gray a sidelong look and a sly grin.

"I suppose you plan to be on board the first boat to reach The Dalles?"

"Why, yes, Jim, I do. Since the dedication committee turned down the three-boat-race idea as too dangerous and settled for a coin flip, I understand that your boat will be the first one through the locks, there will be a few more speeches and toasts, then the *Regulator* will lead the way on upriver to The Dalles."

"That was the order decided by the coin flip, yes. But while the coin was in the air, I put my hands behind my back and crossed my fingers—"

"—so I accepted the invitation of Captain Walter Snow to transfer to the *Regulator* above Cascade Locks—" What Jim Shaver had just said suddenly registered on Captain Gray. "Crossed your fingers, you say? Why did you do that?"

"Because I believe in free competition, Captain Gray. If things work out the way I've planned, the *Regulator* will be wallowing in the *Sarah Dixon's* wake all the way to The Dalles. I advise you to stay aboard."

How the matter had been arranged, Captain Gray never knew, but somehow during the speeches and festivities at the Upper Cascades several attractive, friendly young ladies lured Captain Walter Snow into the ladies' saloon, where champagne was flowing freely amid song, laughter, and high-spirited conversation around the piano. Meanwhile, Captain James Shaver instructed his chief engineer to stoke the fire under the boilers with pitch-filled wood. When the speeches were finished and the three boats headed upriver at what was supposed to be a safe, sane pace, the safety valve aboard the *Sarah Dixon* somehow got stuck in the closed position, with the result that both the *Regulator* and the *The Dalles City* were left far behind, while the *Sarah Dixon* and Captain Shaver's guest, Captain Gray, arrived in The Dalles a full half hour ahead of the other two boats.

Though the owners of the losing steamboats were irate and threatened dire revenge against the captain who had crossed his fingers during the coin flip and left them in his wake, all parties concerned were soon mollified when agreements were made to divide potential revenue on the middle and lower river.

"As I understand it," Captain Gray later told his upriver friends, "The Dalles, Portland, & Astoria Company will pay Shafer two hundred and fifty dollars a month to stay off the middle river. The O.R. & N. Company has offered Shafer the same amount if his company will quit competing with their fast night boat, the *T. J. Potter*, on the Portland-Astoria run. In return, the *Sarah Dixon* will retain its monopoly on the Clatskanie and short-haul routes on the lower river as long as Shaver wants them. That way, everybody can stay alive."[2]

Truth was, "staying alive" was about all the steamboat companies managed to do for the next few years, despite the expensive improvements that had been made to river navigation. Their chief competitor was the railroad, for long-haul shippers preferred rail because of its speed and convenience. So far as passenger traffic was concerned, most people along the banks of the Columbia and Snake favored traveling the leisurely, comfortable, scenic way—by boat—despite the fact that it took them longer to get where they wanted to go. Since passenger traffic alone could not pay a profit to steamboat companies, more and more boats were taken out of service, brought downriver, or junked. Left with little or no competition in the freight-carrying field, the railroad companies raised their rates higher and higher. In response, grain growers and bulk shippers living east of the Cascades screamed their demands for government lock-and-canal projects that would give them the "open river" they felt they needed to bring down the exorbitant rail freight rates. As one of the few captains still working the Celilo-Lewiston run on a regular schedule, Captain William Polk Gray watched developments with considerable interest.

The last great barrier to free and open navigation of the Columbia River now lay between The Dalles and Celilo Falls. For more than eight miles the river churned and boiled through one impassable rapid after another. As far back as 1858, a nine-teen-mile-long wagon road had been scraped through the sage-brush, over which freight bound for the interior could be hauled. In 1863, this was replaced by the O.S.N. Company's portage railroad at a cost of $650,000. After operating until 1882, this south bank line became a link in what would eventually become the Union Pacific to Portland.

In an attempt to quiet the increasingly angry demands of shippers for river improvements at Celilo, the Corps of Engineers set forth a number of ingenious proposals. The most imaginative of these was an elaborate boat-railway that would hydraulically hoist steamboats from the river at the foot of Five-Mile Rapids and transport them eight miles to Celilo Falls.

As Captain Gray understood it, the way this would work was that a steamboat would pull into a partially filled lock with flat-cars parked below. Draining the lock would lower the vessel onto the cars, which then would be towed by four locomotives pulling side by side to another lock above the rapids, where the process would be reversed. Though Congress appropriated $250,000 for planning and right-of-way purchase in 1896, only $30,000 had been spent by the end of the 1900 fiscal year. By then, the folly of the scheme had become clear, so Congress ordered all work halted while a study was made of the feasibil-ity and cost of a more conventional ship canal.[3]

"Which is a shame in a way," Captain Gray told his friends. "Now we'll always wonder if such a cockamanie scheme would have worked. I've seen trains ride on ferryboats, but never a boat on a train."

An 1879 survey recommended a canal on the Washington side of the river at a cost of $7.6 million, but nothing came of it. In 1888, another called for one on the Oregon shore at a cost of $3.7 million. Again, the idea was shelved. By 1900 a new plan was ready, suggesting two locks and a three-thousand-foot-long canal around Celilo Falls; a thirty-three-foot lift lock there; a nine-thousand-foot canal around Five Mile Rapids, with a sub-merged dam at the head of the rapids; and navigational improvements at Three Mile Rapids. The whole project was esti-mated to cost around $4 million. By fits and starts, the work progressed as administrations and economic conditions

Nez Perce County Historical Society
Steamboats at the Lewiston, Idaho, docks on the Snake River.

changed from year to year, but it never totally stopped. The completion date was estimated to be ten to fifteen years away.[4]

Meanwhile, a mining boom in the lower portion of Hell's Canyon drew the attention of the O.R. & N. Company when the promoters of the Eureka Mining Company came to them and asked if they could give boat service for hauling mining equipment in and precious metal out of the remote, inaccessible district, which had few roads or trails. Making an exploratory trip upriver from Lewiston in a small company stern-wheeler piloted by veteran riverman Captain Harry Baughman, an executive of the steamboat company told the managers of the Eureka Mining & Smelting Company that, while the O.R. & N. Company did not own the kind of boat required to navigate the fifty-five miles of rapids and white water between Lewiston and the site of the mine, it would be glad to help design and build one to fit the needs of the mining company. Furthermore, the O.R. & N. Company would give Captain Baughman a leave of absence so that he could operate it, as well as contract to transship the refined ore produced by the mine downriver to Lewiston at favorable rates. The mining company agreed to the terms.

The history of mining in the Hell's Canyon region of the Snake went back many years, for the walls on either side of the river had been riddled with "gopher hole" mines ever since the Idaho boom days of the 1860s. So far, nobody had struck a bonanza. Because each spring's flood in the high country to the east and south washed down deposits of "flour" gold that settled along the sandbars as the river level subsided, a prospector working with a shovel, pan, rocker, or sluice box could recover eight to ten dollars' worth of gold a day, if he worked hard enough. But only a handful of Chinese miners willing to move in and take the white man's leavings were industrious enough to do that.

Back in 1886, there had been a scandal that reached international levels when thirty-three Chinamen working a sandbar sixty miles above Lewiston had been brutally murdered and their bodies thrown into the river by half a dozen white roughs who had seen them working and thought they had made a big strike. In the newspaper accounts Captain Gray had read, the amount of gold allegedly stolen ranged from five to fifty thousand dollars, according to whom you believed. Eventually, four of the suspected murderes were brought to trial, but were acquitted because of "lack of evidence"—a euphemistic way of saying no white jury in that place and time considered killing Chinamen much of a crime.

Even so, the United States eventually paid China $276,619.75 in damages "out of humane consideration" for all the Chinese killed in the West over a period of ten years. But none of the stolen gold was ever found.[5]

Having bought the undeveloped claim at the mouth of the Imnaha River from its discovers for $15,000, the developers named it "Eureka!" (Greek for "I've found it!"), then organized a company and sold $3 million dollars worth of stock to optimistic buyers, who believed the promoters' promise that the three-foot wide vein of copper running through the base of the mountain was so pure and easy to mine that it alone would pay development costs, leaving the millions of dollars worth of gold to be found in the same tunnel pure profit.

Though the vein had been found, developing it posed many problems. No wagon roads came within twenty-five miles of the

Nez Perce County Historical Society
A stern-wheeler noses into the bank at an isolated Snake River landing.

site, and the pack trails were steep and dangerous. At river level, no trees grew—a serious handicap in the days when it was was axiomatic that "it takes a forest to support a mine." Lumber was needed for buildings and for shoring tunnels, while a great deal of firewood was required to stoke the steam boilers in the stamp mill and the smelter.

For forty years, Lewiston, Idaho, fifty-five miles down the Snake River, had been the supply center for north-central Idaho mines. Waterways normally offered the natural and logical avenues for transportation, but the Snake ran downhill in such a hurry in this area that no regular boat service had ever been established on its turbulent, surging course. In this stretch of river, no less than thirty-two rapids were distinctive enough to have names—and several of them were killers.

But the lure of precious metal in Hell's Canyon prompted the Eureka Mining & Smelting Company, with the help of Captain Harry Baughman and the O.R. & N. Company, to build a boat suitable for transporting men, animals, and supplies between Lewiston and the site on a regular schedule. It would be called

Mountan Gem at Eureka Bar, 52 miles south of Lewiston.

the *Imnaha*. While its keel was being laid and its hull began to take shape in Lewiston, work went on at a feverish pace upriver. On Febrary 27, 1903, a reporter for the Lewiston *Tribune* wrote:

> At their Imnaha camp, a force of thirty men are now driving extensive tunnels into the bowells of the mountains. Forty more are working on a wagon road leading to the timber supply, where a sawmill will operate. W. E. Adams, the engineer, is now engaged in surveying a townsite at the mouth of Deer Creek, about a mile and a half from the smelter. Eureka has been selected as the name of the new twn, which ought to become a place of considerable importance in the near future.[6]

Far from being a homemade boat, the *Imnaha's* boilers came from Portland, her engines from Wisconsin, and some of the machine parts from Pennsylvania. Several special features enabled her to cope with the wildest river in the Pacific Northwest. Sturdily built and heavily cross-braced in the bow, she stretched 125 feet, with a twenty-six-foot beam. Able to carry 100 passengers and a large cargo of freight, she drew only twelve inches of water when fully loaded. It was estimated that on trips upriver, she could handle fifty tons of freight; coming downriver, 125 tons. To breast the heavy current of the Snake, her steam boiler operated at pressures up to 250 pounds per square inch.

If the power of her engines proved unequal to the task of driving the boat through the rapids, she carried 1,500 feet of steel cable wound around a power capstan in her bow with which she could pull herself through the white water. After making a trial run to Riparia, seventy miles below Lewiston, Captain Harry Baughman pronounced the *Imnaha* ready to tackle the job for which she had been built.

Carrying only its crew, a few passengers, and a reporter for the Lewiston *Tribune*, the new stern-wheeler left its dock Tuesday afternoon, June 30, 1903, cheered on by several hundred spectators.

For the first twenty miles, the rapids were mild, the *Tribune* reporter wrote later, giving the boat little trouble. Reaching what was known as the Earl Place a mile below Buffalo Rock, the *Imnaha* tied up for the night.

The next day, she resumed her journey, passing through rapids every mile or so as the riverside bluffs rose higher and higher above either shore. Pulling in to the mouth of the Grande Ronde on the Washington side of the river, the boat paused long enough to take on a supply of fuel and water, then made ready for the three-mile run to the foot of Wild Goose Rapids, long regarded as a major obstacle to navigation upriver. The *Tribune* reporter gave a graphic description of its nature:

> *The rocks in fact unnaturally force an immense volume of water against the natural flow of the river and a wall of seething, swirling water results. At the right of this channel the bluff extends almost perpendicular to the waterline and a boat is forced to the left and into the face of a steep, rough climb. The* Imnaha *crept along the right bank of the island slowly and then plunged into the rapid.*

The steam gauge showed 210 pounds and the boat steadily crowded forward, while the water dashed in roils to the rim of the lower deck. In two minutes the crest of the rapid had been reached. Cheers were heard above the rush of the waters and the din of the heavy engines. Then the steam gauge began to fall, and slowly, inch by inch, the boat was carried back. Bad coal had defeated the noble craft, and when she drifted into the lee of the island the gauge registered but 160 pounds.

The bells in an instant rang ahead, the boat was pointed to the left channel, and in just three minutes Wild Goose had been conquered and the boat nestled calmly in peaceful waters above.[7]

When questioned about the loss of power, Captain Baughman told the reporter: "The coal is inferior and the boiler fouled. With a few more pounds of steam, we could run the main channel. In fact with good fuel, the *Imnaha* could climb a tree."

Poor or scarce fuel long had been the curse of steamboat operations on Snake River, Captain Baughman said, both below and above Hell's Canyon. Pitch-filled wood burned better than low-grade coal, but no pine forests grew at river level. Cordwood cut at higher elevations, as it would have to be at the Eureka mine site, and then hauled by wagon eight or more miles down to the river over narrow, twisting roads, was both expensive and scarce.

Leaving her moorings above Wild Goose, the *Imnaha* spent more than three hours fighting her way twelve miles upstream to the mouth of the Salmon River. Two strong rapids—Cougar and Coon Hollow—were negotiated with no more than 182 pounds of steam pressure. Above the Salmon the craft entered waters traveled only once before by an upriver-bound steamboat—the *Colonel Wright* back in 1864, when it had gone twenty-five miles on up the river on an exploratory trip.

Here, narrowing channel walls pinched the river in so tightly that it was less than 100 feet wide. Directly ahead lay Mountain Sheep Rapids, Captain Baughman said, with the Eureka mine site just two miles beyond. But in those next two miles, the *Imnaha* encountered serious problems. The reporter described them to *Tribune* readers:

> *On the right hand bank for a distance of several hundred feet, huge boulders have rolled into the channel, forming innumerable cross-currents and swirls. Then the roils from the upper rapids are met, which leads to "The Narrows." The latter, as the name suggests, comprises a chute of water that pours down with a steep fall between a long ledge of rocks and an immense rock that has fallen from the mountains above into the stream.*
>
> *Directly back of the rock lies an eddy which forms a back current of perhaps five miles an hour. The water presented an innocent appearance to the passengers. But Captain Baughman saw trouble ahead. A driving rainstorm with a strong wind was prevailing when the boat shot into the race of the narrows. The* Imnaha *made a game fight for a minute and poked her nose beyond the point to the left. But a swirl from the current veered her to the right and she was crowded back. Captain Baughman rang to go ahead, but like a flash the stern-wheel was caught in the back current and the boat shot to the opposite shore, turning completely around. She then faced downstream and a landing was made beneath the right bank.*
>
> *It was decided to put out a line and the cable was strung for a distance of a quarter of a mile along the right hand shore. The boat again shot out into the stream and tackled the strong current, but she had approached to a point within only ten feet of the rock when the heavy current of the eddy caught her.*
>
> *Straight toward the bluffs on the right bank she darted, and as the bow turned with the current the cable "deadman" gave way. Captain Baughman signaled for a back wheel, but the bow grazed the bluff. The bow then swung back across the stream and the hull slid on a sloping rock, where the craft was temporarily lodged. She was soon, however, backed off the rock and the run to the opposite shore was made, where the craft was tied up for the night.*[8]

Captain Baughman directed a deckhand to take a two-mile hike along the narrow beach on the right hand shore to the Eureka mine site, requesting that a crew and explosives to blast away the obstructing rock be sent downriver. In response, mining engineer W. C. Adams came down to the spot where the *Imnaha* was moored, examined the rock, and estimated that the task of removing it would take several days. After a full day of drilling, setting charges, and blasting out ledges on the Oregon side of the canyon, he decided that the big rock on the Idaho side of the channel must be pulverized, too. Impatient with the delay, Captain Baughman went ashore and hiked up to the head of Mountain Sheep Rapids to give it a closer evaluation. After contemplating the wild, tumbling, tossing water for a few minutes, he told First Mate Blum, who had accompanied him,

"If the *Colonel Wright* could run it, so can I. Tomorrow is the Fourth of July. We'll celebrate it by running Mountain Sheep without waiting for the rock to be blasted."

Shortly after daylight the next morning a six-man crew went ashore on the Oregon side of the river, dragging with them 1,500 feet of steel cable carried aboard the boat, managing to manhandle it over the rocks, through the shallows, and past several projecting lava bluffs to a spot above Mountain Sheep Rapids, where they secured a loop in its upper end around the base of a massive granite boulder. Because the downstream end of the cable did not quite reach the spot where the *Imnaha* was moored, a three-quarter-inch-thick rope line was tied to the lower end of the cable, with a workman taking a station atop a flat rock, prepared to heave the rope end aboard the boat when and if the *Imnaha* managed to churn her way that far into the surging white water. The *Tribune* reporter detailed what followed:

> At exactly 10 o'clock the Imnaha *left the bank and tackled the current for the fourth time. She "walked" up to the crest between the two rocks where she was held for fully three minutes. The man on the rock made an unsuccessful throw with the light line; there followed two unsuccessful casts by deckhands on the boat, and then Mate Blum shot out a line that reached the goal.*

Nez Perce County Historical Society
The *Lewiston* keeps steam up while iced in.

In a minute the cable was pulled aboard, the line tight-
ened, and the wiry craft crept inch by inch over the top of
the current to smooth waters. From the time the Imnaha
left the rapid until the cable was slacked and taken
aboard, only fifteen minutes had elapsed. The run to
Eureka was then made in forty-five minutes and the boat
tied up at exactly 11 o'clock. She had made the run from
Lewiston to Mountain Sheep Rapid in ten hours.

A wild demostration occurred at Eureka when the boat
was seen in the canyon below. On the highest peaks, the
miners could be seen waving their hats with enthusiasm,
and loud blasts resounded through the valley.[9]

As the boat pulled into the sandbar on the Oregon side of the
river, where the dock that would serve the new town of Eureka
soon would be built, Captain Baughman explained to the newspaper reporter that the continuing explosions echoing and re-
echoing off the three-thousand-foot-high walls of the canyon
were the hardrock miners and "powder monkeys" exuberantly
celebrating both the arrival of the *Imnaha* and the Fourth of
July by "shooting off anvils."

"What they do," the captain said, "is cap a stick of dynamite and lay it on an anvil or some other hard surface, then put a big empty tin or iron can on top and light the fuse. It makes the loudest firecracker you ever heard."

"Well, you certainly deserve a twenty-one-anvil salute yourself, Captain Baughman!" the reporter exclaimed. "Your feat in establishing the first boat service between Lewiston and Eureka is an event that will be long remembered."

"Thank you, sir. But I'm not the first pilot to come this far upriver. As a nineteen-year-old first mate aboard the *Colonel Wright,* Captain William Polk Gray did that in 1864. Be sure to mention him in your story."

Given a tour of the works by the chief mining engineer, W. C. Adams, the reporter collected a gunny sack full of mineral samples and learned a great deal about the operation.

"We suffered some minor hull damage when we scraped against a couple of rock ledges," Captain Baughman told the reporter and, later, Captain Gray. "But overall, the first trip worked out fine. Even after lining a couple of rapids, we made the upriver trip in ten hours. Coming downriver took just three-and-a half hours."

"You've asked the Corps of Engineers to do some channel work upriver, I understand," Captain Gray said, "before you establish a regular run to Eureka."

"That's right. The mine manager tells me it'll be a couple of months before the smelter can produce enough refined ore to give us a load coming downriver. The Corps plans to lease the *Imnaha* as a work boat while they blast out the hazards I've marked on their charts. They've also agreed to set ringbolts in the cliff walls above two rapids."

"Which two?"

"Wild Goose and Mountain Sheep. In both places, the Corps plans to embed heavy iron rings in the rock walls on the Oregon side of the river, with fifteen hundred feet of steel cable and a waterproof barrel that we can fish out of the water below the rapid, bring the cable aboard, hook it to the steam-powered capstan in the bow, then pull ourselves up through the rapid while the stern-wheel pushes from behind."

"Sounds like a time-saver to me."

"It will be. Since we won't have to send a crew of deckhands ashore to do our cable-stringing each trip, it'll be a labor-saver, too."

After completing her channel improvement work with the Corps of Engineers during the next two months, the *Imnaha* began regular runs upriver in September. In early October, she suffered her first serious accident when the current threw her against a rock that punched a hole in her hull. Dropping downriver to Riparia, she was patched up and declared as good as new. Returning to Eureka with a load of half a dozen horses for the mine, she carried forty tons of granite from the newly opened Lime Point quarry back downriver to Lewiston.

Because the flow of the Snake had become so low downstream from the mouth of the Salmon that navigation was dangerous, additional trips in late October were postponed until autumn rains raised the level of the river.

By November 8, 1903, the rains had come, the Snake began to rise, and the *Imnaha* embarked on her fourteenth trip to Eureka.

It proved to be her last one.

Chapter 13 footnotes

1. *Blow For the Landing*, op. cit., p. 33.
2. Ibid, p. 34.
3. Ibid, p. 37.
4. Ibid, p. 37. The Celilo Canal was finished in 1915.
5. The settlement was made on October 19, 1888. In 1902, the Lewiston, Idaho, *Tribune* reported that two young men had appeared in Joseph, Oregon, with $700 in gold dust they claimed they had found in a flask they had dug up in the vicinity of the old Chinese gold camps.
6. Lewiston, Idaho, *Tribune*, Jan. 28, 1903.
7. Ibid, July 4, 1903.
8. Ibid.
9. Ibid.

The wreck of the *Imnaha*

L eaving the Lewiston dock Sunday morning, November 8, 1903, the first part of the *Imnaha's* trip went smoothly. But a few minutes before pulling into the landing at Eureka, above Mountain Sheep Rapids, disaster struck without warning. Captain Baughman later told what happened:

> We had successfully ascended the rapid and cast off the line when in some manner the wheel picked up the bight of the line, which caught in the eccentric rods. As a result, the rods were bent, the rock shaft broken, and the engines rendered useless. At the time this occurred, the boat was about four hundred yards above Mountain Sheep Rapids, and the helpless steamer drifted stern-on onto the sharp rock that has been a menace to navigation since the boat was first placed in commission.
>
> The wheel struck the rock squarely and was doubled back over the boat. The bow then swung to the Oregon shore where it remained but a moment when the stern slipped from the rock and swung to the Oregon side while the bow turned against the big rock, completely filling the channel.[1]

Because the Snake River was only sixty-two feet wide at that point, the 125-foot-long boat now was turned broadside to the tremendous force of the current. Fortunately, it hung there long enough for the fifteen crew members and twenty-five passengers to scramble ashore. Quick thinking by Chief Engineer L. H. Campbell prevented what could have been a murderous explosion. He later said:

> *Knowing that great danger existed from escaping steam in case the boat was badly injured by striking the rock, my first move was to start the pumps and open the siphons. By the time the boat commenced to go to pieces the steam was so reduced that no danger of an explosion existed. As the boat struck the rock, I swung out of the engine room at the side door, but as the jar was not sufficient to break the pipes the dangerous period had passed and I returned to the engine room to find the entire stern had been stove in and that the abandonment of the boat was sure to follow.*[2]

Only seconds after the last of the crew and passengers got safely ashore, the bow of the disabled boat dipped. The *Imnaha* slipped off the rock upon which she had lodged and drifted into deep water downstream. Taking water rapidly now, the hull tilted and the boiler tore loose from its supports and rolled into the water, carrying a large portion of the pilot house with it.

The *Imnaha* was finished.

Though no human lives were lost, several horses tied to stanchions on the freight deck were forgotten by the crewmen scurrying ashore. Their whinnies of terror as the boat sank were pathetic to hear, said the survivors, but nothing could be done to save them.

As in all such disasters on the river, rumors, guesses, and attempts to place blame lasted for months, with no conclusive results. Had an inexperienced deckhand thrown the barrel attached to the slack cable into the river on the wrong side of the boat? Had the helmsman turned the boat the wrong way, making the stern-wheel hook into rather than avoid the looped winching line? Had an order been carelessly given, not heard, or recklessly disobeyed? No one could say.

Ultimately, the blame was placed on Captain Baughman, of course, for the *Imnaha* was under his command. But knowing the man as he did, Captain Gray could not believe that the accident had been entirely his fault.

Nez Perce County Historical Society
The steamer *Lewiston* on what appears to be an excursion.

"When a boat is running a white-water rapid, things can happen awfully fast," he said. "A crew member gets distracted and forgets what he's doing, an unexpected swirl passes under the boat, a back-eddy caused by an underwater slide lifts the stern-wheel out of the water for a few seconds—and *wham!*— you're in big trouble. But whatever happens, the captain has to accept the blame."

The O.R. & N. Company did not own the boat, so had no insurance on it. Neither did the Eureka Mining & Smelting Company, writing off its $35,000 cost as a total loss. As well capitalized as the company was supposed to be, it refused to build a new boat itself.

"How will you get your refined ore downriver if you don't have a boat?" local people asked.

"A good question," company officials replied. "But since we're putting three million dollars into developing the mine, building a boat to transport our refined ore downriver and the supplies and equipment you Lewiston merchants will be selling us back upriver seems a small thing to ask of you."

After the Lewiston businessmen had subscribed $22,000 for the building of a new stern-wheeler called the *Mountain Gem* to ply the upper river, the O.R. & N. Company selected William Polk Gray to be its skipper, feeling that if any man knew that stretch of wild water, he did. But by the time the new boat was launched in September, 1904, the Hell's Canyon mining boom bubble had burst.

Angry investors who had purchased millions of dollars' worth of stock began filing lawsuits against the corporation directors because their money was going into the ground with no profits coming out. The digging stopped.

With no ore to bring downriver, the *Mountain Gem* ceased runs to Eureka and began hauling freight and passengers on the Snake River below Lewiston. Eventually, smaller boats would be built to carry mail, groceries, farm and ranch supplies, fishermen, hunters, and sightseers to remote cabins and camps in the upper reaches of Hells Canyon.

Prospectors would continue to pan for gold on the sandbars of the Snake, occasionally exposing a vein that merited drilling, blasting, and excavating in "gopher hole" mines. But the bonanza promised at Eureka never was realized. The tunnel between the mouth of the Imnaha and the Snake would remain there for years to be explored by the curious and eventually by mining experts who would re-assess its mineral potential more scientifically than its discoverers and promoters had done.

Not surprisingly, their verdict was that the copper vein's width should have been measured in inches, not feet, and that the potential wealth of the mines in the area should have been stated in thousands rather than in millions of dollars. Like so many boom-and-bust mines, Eureka's real value may well have been more in exploiting its stock-holders than in extracting its copper, silver, and gold from the native rock. . . [3]

On their way down the Columbia to the Pacific in the fall of 1805, the Lewis and Clark party had missed seeing the future site of Portland because the mouth of the Willamette River had been hidden behind fog, rain, and a tree-shrouded island.

Penrose Library, Whitman College
Boardwalk and pool at the 1905 Lewis and Clark Centennial Expo in Portland.

Traveling east the next spring, they would have missed it again if a "Cashook" Indian had not escorted Captain Clark and a party of seven men back to the lower valley of what the local Indians called the Multnomah River for a brief look around, accepting the payment of "a birning glass" for his services.[4]

But on the 100th anniversary of the Lewis and Clark Expedition in 1905, the movers and shakers of Portland had no intention of having their city overlooked again. As a birthday gift, local promoters meant to call the attention of the nation and the world to their growing metropolis by putting on a Centennial Exposition.

Plans for the "Great Extravaganza," as the celebration came to be called, began before the turn of the century. By then, world's fairs were widely accepted as "schools of progress," attracting investors and newcomers to the host city. It would be, boosters claimed, the greatest exposition ever staged on the West Coast, one that would put Portland on the national map once and for all. If one of the two cities bearing the Portland name should be called a backwoods hamlet, the backers asserted, it must be the one in Maine.

Pointing out that Americans had flocked to the Centennial

Exposition in Philadelphia in 1876, to the Columbian Exposition at Chicago in 1893, and to Omaha's Trans Mississippi Exposition in 1898, the local exposition promoters noted that St. Louis was planning a real humdinger for its Louisiana Purchase Exposition in 1904 to celebrate the beginning of the Lewis and Clark journey west. Therefore, would it not be eminently fitting, proper, and rewarding for the great state of Oregon in general and for Portland in particular to tell the nation about the Promised Land lying at the end of the Lewis and Clark Trail?

Though Portland's population was barely 100,000 souls, the city's movers and shakers were thinking big. Businessmen asked to put up $300,000 to get the project rolling pledged that amount within ten days. Dispatching five special agents to stalk the corridors of western capitols and cadge votes in the nearby barrooms, the exposition's "con" men showed their supporters they were excellent salesmen. By the end of 1903, sixteen states came through with appropriations for exhibits; ten would construct special buildings. Prompted by the fact that the exhibition would promote and benefit the entire state, the legislature authorized $450,000 for exhibits emphasizing "the development of our material resources and manufacturing interests."

In lobbying for money in Washington, D.C., the Portland promoters soon found that nobody in Congress cared about historical heroes and their 2,000-mile trek. But they did share the same vision of the Pacific trade that had motivated the exploration and settlement of the Oregon Country.

With congressional delegations from California and Washington supporting the claim that the exposition was a Pacific Coast enterprise supported by chambers of commerce from San Diego to Spokane, it was not difficult to sell the slogan: "The railroads opened the door and laid the region's resources open for development. The only remaining need is for enough people to break the soil and fall the trees."

When it was pointed out that ocean-going sailing ships and river-plying steamboats had played an important role in laying the region's resources open for development, the promoters wisely added shipping and the potential of Pacific Rim markets to the region's assets.

"China alone offers a tremendous market for American grain," one imaginative publicist declared. "Why, if every Chinaman would eat one pancake a month, it would require all the flour ground from all the wheat raised west of the Mississippi to satisfy the demand. And that flour would have to be carried in ships sailing from West Coast ports."

How the wheat-raisers west of the Mississippi would go about persuading the Chinese to eat, let alone pay for, a pancake a month, was a question neither asked nor answered.

One of the best chunks of money spent on publicity was the $50,000 appropriated by the Oregon State Legislature in 1903 for the state's participation in the St. Louis Lewis and Clark Centennial Exposition in 1904. Among many other products donated, displayed, or given away at St. Louis were six tons—a freight car load—of Oregon prunes.

From the central business district, fair-goers could catch the Portland Railway streetcars for a twenty-minute ride for a nickel to fairgrounds built on reclaimed swampland in northwest Portland. For a dime, they could board a steamer for a ride down the Willamete to the U.S. Government Building on the fairgrounds. For $1.50 they could take an eight-hour ride upriver to Cascade Locks and back aboard the newest, fastest, most luxuriously furnished stern-wheeler currently operating on the lower Columbia, the *Bailey Gatzert*, with lunch or supper included, according to which of the twice-daily round-trips was taken.

Most of the people visiting the region for the first time took the boat leaving Portland at eight-thirty in the morning, for the daylight hours were the best time to see the scenic wonders of the Gorge. Older people familiar with river travel preferred the trip leaving Portland at five-thirty in the afternoon, for this was a more romantic twilight and night cruise, with the river to be viewed by moonlight while couples danced to an orchestra playing such recently composed hits as "The Bailey Gatzert March."

If the clumsy, overweight, retired businessman dancing with his lovely, silver-haired wife was trying to waltz in step to march time, it was not likely anybody in that crowd noticed.[5]

Meanwhile, as traffic increased on the Columbia from Astoria to Portland and on upriver through the Cascades Locks and the ship canal to The Dalles, tug and barge companies located in Portland and Vancouver, Washington, on the north side of the river found their location ideal. By transferring freight carried on seagoing vessels to barges at the Port of Astoria, masters who did not want to navigate the intricacies of channels upriver could save their vessels considerable turn-around time, an important factor these days for increasingly bigger ocean-going ships.

These days, most newly built tugs were screw-propelled, diesel-fueled, highly maneuverable, low-in-the-water craft which could pull or push three large barges scaled to fit with only a few inches to spare within the two sets of locks now in operation at the Cascades and those in the process of being built between The Dalles and Celilo.

One notable exception was the radically different, steel-hulled, stern-wheel tug, the *Jean*, which was built and launched in a Portland shipyard in 1910. By then, Captain William Polk Gray was sixty-five years old and living in Pasco, Washington, spending most of his time as a pilot on the Snake River and sel-dom visiting Portland. But he did keep up with what was going on downriver through captain friends who now and then came to call.

"She's got four diesel engines that can operate independent-ly," one of them told him. "Her twin stacks are set just aft of the pilot house. She has three rudders and the stern-wheel is in three sections, each one capable of turning backward or forward independently or at the same time."

"Sounds like she'd have good maneuverability."

"Her captain says he can spin the *Jean* in a circle within her own length. Which ought to make her a great harbor tug for tight spots like the Portland docks along the Willamette River."

In national circles these days, New York and San Francisco shipping interests were buzzing with news of two impending events which they were convinced would drastically change the commercial world: completion of the Panama Canal and the probability of another European war. That either happening would effect traffic on the Columbia and Snake Rivers was a matter neither Captain Gray nor the tug and barge companies took seriously.

"Opening the Panama Canal will lower shipping costs to the West Coast," Captain Gray conceded. "But I doubt if it will increase our business much. Foreign squabbles have never been the concern of the United States in general or the Pacific Northwest in particular—and never will be."

Although the Panama Canal was opened and war did start in Europe in 1914, a much bigger event insofar as the upriver country was concerned was the completion of the Celilo locks and ship canal a year later. Though not asked to make a formal speech at the dedication ceremonies, Captain Gray, now in his seventies and looking like an Old Testament prophet with his white hair and beard, had plenty to say to any reporters who cared to listen.

Leading a steamboat fleet that had come downriver from Lewiston, Pasco, Wallula, Umatilla, and Arlington, Captain Gray declared that people who believed that the Columbia and Snake Rivers had only recently been made navigable by the Corps of Engineers were "know-nothings," as far as the history of those rivers was concerned.

"As soon as railroads were built along the banks of the river thirty years ago, the numbskulls started saying the rivers were too dangerous to navigate because of rapids and rocks. The idea was so prevalent that in 1903, when I was preparing to take Idaho Senator Heyburn and a party of excursionists from Lewiston to The Dalles on the *Mountain Gem* for the opening of the portage road, the senator asked me if it would be safe for his wife to make the trip. He was surprised when I told him that the river had been navigated for forty years and at one time carried all the traffic between Portland and Lewiston."[6]

As the climax to a week of festivities which drew an estimated twenty thousand people to Celilo, the official program distributed to the enthusiastic participants declared:

> *To the Inland Empire, the Celilo Canal is relatively of as much importance as is the Panama Canal to the nation as a whole. It will re-establish trade lines; it will mean the revision of railroad tariffs; it will bring new development to the great valley of the Columbia, a territory rich with latent possibilities.*

> *This may come about slowly and by gradual degrees,
> but it will come, and the present celebration commemorat-
> ing the completion of the Celilo Canal marks the com-
> mencement of a new era of commerce and industry for this
> section of the great Northwest.*[7]

The sheer magnitude of the amount of earth moved during the digging of the canal and the construction of the locks was impressive.

"Next to the Panama Canal, it's the biggest earth-moving project ever undertaken by the federal government," the statistician said. "One million, four hundred thousand cubic yards of granite had to be excavated, while 800,000 cubic yards of gravel had to be removed. A million pounds of dynamite were used to blast out the channel."

With a final price of $4,850,000, the Celilo Locks and Ship Canal was considered a bargain by the Inland Empire farmers and businessmen who had lobbied for it so long. Eight-and-a-half miles long, sixty-five feet wide, and eight feet deep, the canal had numerous passing turnouts so that traffic would not be delayed. Now that it had been put in service, it allowed the largest steamboat operating on the river to travel from Astoria, Oregon, to the Snake River port of Lewiston, Idaho, 465 miles inland, without a single portage.

At long last, the advocates of an "Open River" had achieved their dream.

Chapter 14 footnotes

1. *Lewiston Tribune*, op. cit., Nov. 11, 1903.
2. Ibid.
3. *Roadside History of Oregon*, op. cit., p. 394.
4. *Lewis and Clark Journals*, op. cit., p. 339.
5. *Roadside History of Oregon*, op. cit., pp. 168-172.
6. Gray, "Reminiscences," op. cit.
7. Marshal N. Dana, "The Celilo Canal—its origin—It's Building and Meaning," *Oregon Historical Quarterly,* 1915, pp. 109-124.

Upper river survey, 1891

From time to time during his long career, Captain William Polk Gray worked for the Corps of Engineers as master of a specially equipped boat which removed boulders, underwater ledges, and other obstructions to navigation. Usually this work consisted of blasting a dangerous rock, installing a ringbolt to which a quarter-mile of steel cable could be attached above a rapid, or dredging an accumulation of sand or gravel that was impeding the passage of boats. Larger, long-term projects such as building levees at the mouth of the river or locks and ship canals at the Cascades and Celilo Falls were handled by full-time employees working under longer contracts. But when the question of navigability of rapids in the Snake or upper Columbia arose, he was usually consulted.

In 1881, Colonel Thomas William Symons, Corps of Engineers, headed an expedition which floated the Columbia River from the Canadian border to its juncture with the Snake in order to check the feasibility of establishing commercial navigation on that sector of river.[1] In the course of the job, Colonel Symons hired a river guide named Pierre Agarre, who was said to be the last of the Iroquois *voyageurs* brought out by the Hudson's Bay Company from Montreal in 1812. Now called "Old Pierre" because of his age, he had been made famous in a gruesome sort of way by Alexander Ross in his book *Fur Hunters of the Far West*, published in 1855:[2]

At a distance of seventy miles from Boat Encampment, (Ross wrote) *there is a very bad system of rapids, known to the voyageurs as the Dalles des Morts. They are about two miles long from end to end. Many a poor fellow has closed his earthly career by entrusting himself to their treacherous waters, and a number of solitary graves are here to be seen, and the names of victims never found are carved on the surrounding rocks.*

Along this portion of the river there occurred in the year 1817 one of those terrible episodes of frontier life, at the thought of which the heart turns sick. On April 16 of that year, a party of twenty-three men left Fort George, now Astoria, to ascend the Columbia and cross the Rocky Mountains by the Athabasca Pass. On May 27 they arrived at the mouth of Portage River, or Boat Encampment, after the most severe labors and exposure in dragging their canoes up the rapids and making their way along the river shores.

Seven men of the party were so weak, sick and worn out that they were unable to proceed across the mountains, so they were given the best canoe and sent back down the river to Spokane House. After leaving the Rocky Mountains they went rapidly down the river until the Dalles des Morts were reached. Here, in passing their boat over the rapids by a line, it was caught in a whirlpool, the line snapped, and the boat and all its contents of provisions, blankets, &c, was irrevocably lost.

Here the poor fellows found themselves utterly destitute, and at a season of the year when it was impossible to procure any wild fruit or roots. The continual rushing of the water completely inundated the beach, which compelled them to force their way through a dense forest, rendered almost impervious by a thick growth of prickly underbrush. Their only nourishment was water. On the third day, Macon died, and his surviving comrades, though unconscious how soon they might be called upon to follow him, divided his remains into equal parts, on which they subsisted for several days.

From the sore and swollen state of their feet, their daily

Skagit Chief in freight service on Puget Sound, 1952.

progress did not exceed two or three miles. Holmes, the tai-
lor, shortly followed Macon, and they continued for some
time to sustain life on his emaciated body. In a little while
of the seven men only two remained alive, Dubois and La
Pierre. La Pierre was subsequently found on the borders of
the Upper Lake of the Columbia by two Indians who were
coasting it in a canoe. They took him on board to Kettle
Falls, from whence he was conducted to Spokane House.

He stated that after the death of the fifth man of the
party, Dubois and he continued for some days at the spot
where he had ended his sufferings, and on quitting it they
loaded themselves with as much of his flesh as they could
carry; that with this they succeeded in reaching the Upper
Lake, around the shores of which they wandered for some
time in search of Indians; that their horrid food at last
became exhausted, and they were again reduced to the
prospect of starvation; that on the second night after their
last meal, he (La Pierre) observed something suspicious in

the conduct of Dubois, which induced him to be on his guard; and that shortly after they had lain down for the night, and while he feigned sleep, he observed Dubois cautiously opening his clasp knife, with which he sprang on him, and inflicted on his hand the blow which was evidently intended for his neck.

A silent and desperate conflict followed, in which, after severe struggling, La Pierre succeeded in wrestling the knife from his antagonist, and having no other resources left, he was obliged in self defense to cut Dubois's throat, and that a few days afterward he was discovered by the Indians as above mentioned.

In his late seventies when hired by Colonel Symons in an Indian village near Fort Colville, Old Pierre was still hale and hearty in spite of being almost deaf, nearly blind, and just about out of teeth. He had outlived several Indian wives, and had more sons, grandsons, and great-grandsons than he could count. Living in a sprawling, ramshackle log cabin on the east side of the Columbia a few miles upstream from a turbulent stretch of water called Rock Island Rapids, the rawboned, stoop-shouldered, cantankerous French-Canadian bargained for two hours before reaching an agreement.

With the financial details settled at long last, Old Pierre selected four paddlers from among the grandsons who were living in skin tepees and driftwood shacks adjacent to his cabin. At least Colonel Symons assumed they were direct descendants, for their names were Big Pierre, Little Pierre, *Pen-waw* (which he was told meant "Pierre" in the local Indian tongue), and a stray named Joseph. All the paddlers were swarthy, black-eyed, well-muscled men, just as Old Pierre must have been in his younger days. Watching them load the *bateau* under the critical eye of Old Pierre, Colonel Symons probably thought,

"Bad as his teeth are these days, Old Pierre will have to gum us to death if he turns cannibal. But those paddlers of his look mean enough to take mighty big bites, should they get hungry."

Whatever seeing, hearing, or chewing infirmities he suffered, it was clear to the colonel that Old Pierre knew exactly what he was doing when it came to running a river in a native canoe. His station would be standing at the steering oar in the stern of the craft. Directly ahead of him a part-Indian-member of the survey party who could act as an interpreter sat cross-legged in the bottom of the canoe, facing forward, holding a sounding pole with which he would measure the depth of the water and test the condition of the bottom of the channel.

Stowed amidships under tautly lashed canvas tarpaulins was the party's supply of food, drink, blankets, surveying instruments, and camping gear which they wanted to keep dry. Also seated facing forward and using the relatively level surface of the canvas-covered supplies as a work table, an assistant to Colonel Symons would record distances, chart rocks and hazards, and map the river in as much detail as possible.

The four paddlers would sit facing backwards at oarlocks on alternate sides, so that they could see the steersman and carry out his commands, ready to pull ahead or back water as ordered. In the bow of the boat, Old Pierre grudgingly permitted Colonel Symons to kneel, sit, or stand, as he wished, so that he could read and memorize the river for future reference.

As the lines securing the *bateau* to the bank were cast off and the boat pulled out into the river, several of the women being left behind in the village cried, wailed, and howled in such apparent anguish that Colonel Symons began to think they all believed that the crew of the boat was doomed to perish in the waters ahead. The prospect did look menacing, for the Columbia was running in full early summer flood, icy snowmelt water coming off mountain glaciers upstream was frigid to the hand, and the rumble of the rapids ahead had an increasingly ominous tone.

Unable to make sense of the raucous bantering going back and forth between the wailing women on the bank, the half-blood paddlers, and Old Pierre, the colonel asked the interpreter if he had any idea what they were saying.

"The women are calling Old Pierre all kinds of names, saying he's a stupid, evil old man, hell-bent on drowning their husbands or sons. Apparently only one of the paddlers has ever gone down this stretch of river before. They say he's going to make them all widows. He laughs at them and says as long as the paddlers do what he tells them to, they'll be safe. If not, they

Northern Pacific train ferry *Tacoma*.

can drown, for all he cares. He says he'll be glad to take the widows into his bed."

"Is Rock Island a bad rapid?"

"It can be, he says. Once, years ago, when he ran it in an overloaded Hudson's Bay Company canoe, the *bourgeois* in charge
refused to take his advice as to which channel to run, picked the
wrong one, split the canoe on a rock, and drowned eight of the
sixteen men aboard—including the *bourgeois* himself."

"Well, I hope Old Pierre remembers which channel to take
today—and can see well enough to find it."

"He hasn't drowned yet, he says. He doesn't intend to drown
now."

Despite his outwardly cavalier attitude toward the hazards
of the river, it soon became apparent that Old Pierre was basi-
cally a cautious man. As the river narrowed and the current
quickened a mile upstream from Rock Island Rapids, he steered
the *bateau* into an eddy on the east bank, ordered fore and aft
lines secured around black boulders lying above the high-water
mark, then invited Colonel Symons and his assistant ashore
with him for the purpose of making a careful inspection of the

dangers ahead. Taking his clipboard and pencil along, the assistant spent the next two hours drawing a detailed sketch of Rock Island Rapids as they examined it foot by foot.

Returning to the *bateau* after the inspection had been completed, Colonel Symons and his assistant resumed their positions aboard, while Old Pierre harangued the four half-blood paddlers in their own tongue and gave them detailed instructions as to what he expected them to do. His first order seemed to be for them to strip off all their superfluous clothing, for each man took off his jacket, shirt, trousers, and moccasins, leaving their dark, muscular bodies clad only in skimpy, dirt-stained, gray-white loincloths. To keep the hair out of their eyes, each man pushed his braids and forelock up under a bright-colored handkerchief, which he then tied tightly around his head, appearing to get ready either to work up a sweat or take a swim.

In addition to long oars extended from locks on alternate sides of the boat, each paddler placed beside his feet a shorter paddle and a stout pole with which he could fend off rocks, if need be. As the fore and aft lines were cast off and Old Pierre steered the *bateau* out into the strong current of the river, he startled the survey party members by throwing back his head and letting out a blood-curdling howl.

"*Klooshe nanitch! Sagahalie Tyee skookum chuck! Chako, chako!*"

As the four half-blood paddlers bent to their oars with long, powerful strokes that increased the speed of the already swiftly moving *bateau*, they began chanting the same words in unison. When Colonel Symons asked the interpreter what the chant meant, he answered,

"It loses something in the translation. But roughly they're yelling, '*Look out, God of the Big River Rapids! Here we come!*"

From his experiences making downriver runs through rapids aboard a stern-wheeler, Colonel Symons knew the importance of traveling faster than the current in order to maintain steering-way. But until now he had not realized that the same principle might hold true in a dugout canoe. Well into the speeding race of the upper reach of the rapids now, the *bateau* was traveling so fast that he shuddered at the thought of striking one of the huge black rocks that were passing by on either side. Still, Old Pierre and the half-blood paddlers continued to shout their challenge to the Big River God.

Directly ahead loomed an immense black rock toward which the boat was being carried at tremendous speed. Did Old Pierre see it? the colonel wondered. Half-blind as he was, probably not. But even as Colonel Symons turned to shout a warning to the steersman, Old Pierre gave an abrupt hand-signal to the paddlers. Their reaction was instantaneous.

With one pair taking two deep pulls on the right-hand oars, the other pair pushing strong back-water thrusts on the left-hand oars, then Old Pierre adding a quick sideways stroke with the steering oar, the rock that a moment ago had appeared to be directly ahead suddenly was passing an arm's length away on the right-hand side.

Old Pierre issued another command. Again, the paddlers responded instantly. With the deep-thrust oars bending like willows, the *bateau* spun around for two complete turns in the eddy into which Old Pierre had steered it. Then it broke clear and was heading downriver again.

Engulfed now in the tumbling, roaring waters of the main channel of the rapids, which extended through just under a mile of wild water, the *bateau* experienced no difficulty in staying afloat, though it gave its passengers an extremely rough ride. Reaching a quiet stretch of river just below the rapids where a sandy beach on the right-hand shore offered a good camping spot, Old Pierre steered the canoe to the bank and the crew went ashore. Though several hours of daylight still remained, Colonel Symons agreed with Old Pierre that a good day's work had been done and they might as well camp here.

After camp had been made, a fire built, and everyone changed into dry clothes, the assistant set up his drawing table and laid out a rough sketch of the area to be mapped, using a scale of two thousand feet to the inch. After setting down what he himself had seen of Rock Island Rapids, he and Colonel Symons conferred with Old Pierre, who not only had taken the boat through them under today's conditions but possessed an intimate knowledge of what the rapids were like at all seasons of the year. Even though the ancient *voyageur's* eyesight was so

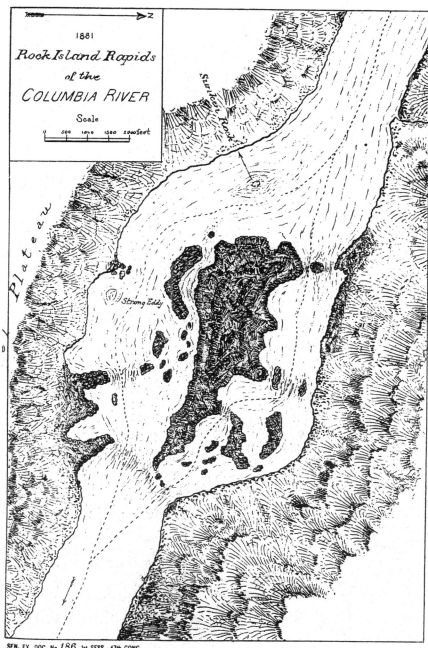

1881

Rock Island Rapids

of the

COLUMBIA RIVER

Scale

0   500   1000   1500   2000 feet

Plateau

Strong Eddy

Slacker Tide

SEN. EX. DOC. No. 186, 1st SESS., 47th CONG.

bad he could barely see the mapping sheet and his hearing so poor that they doubted that he heard much of the questions he was asked, he understood so exactly what was wanted of him that all the assistant had to do was set the information down as it was given to him. According to Colonel Symons' report, this is the gist of what Old Pierre said:[3]

> *There are two channels, the east and the west. We used the west channel today. At this stage of water, I am sure that a good, powerful steamer, properly handled, could go up it. In extreme low water, the west channel becomes nearly dry, thus is unnavigable. The west channel is considerably wider than the east one, and is quite straight at the lower end, where it is made crooked by dangerous rocks just beneath the surface.*
>
> *The east channel is deeper, and is the better one in low water. In extremely high water, it is also better, though in ordinary floodwater like today, the east channel is the best for boats.*

Looking over his assistant's shoulder as he sketched, Colonel Symons listened to Old Pierre's description of varying water conditions, then said,

"Looks to me like the west channel would be the best for year-round navigation. We'd need to blast out a few rocks, of course, which will take time, money, and a work order from the Corps' planning division."

"About blasting rocks, I know nothing," Old Pierre said with an indifferent shrug. "In my day, we took the rivers, the mountains, the country, and the people as we found them. Why try to change what *le bon Dieu* made?"

"There's another possibility," Colonel Symons said, proving himself to be as hard of hearing in his own way as Old Pierre was in his. "We could build a boat-railroad around the rapids on the west bank, which is flat and fairly low. That would cost a lot of money, but the Corps can get an appropriation from Congress if we can show it's feasible. Be sure and note that possibility on your map. . . "

Next morning after the party embarked in the *bateau* and

Franklin County Historical Society
Wenatchee steamboat landing on the Columbia River.

continued its journey down the river, the current for ten miles or so was much quieter, the channel wider and the hazards to navigation so few that Colonel Symons, standing in the bow of the boat, called back to his assistant only now and then, "There's one we'll have to blast. Mark it on your chart."

Even as he recorded the hazards to navigation visible at this stage of water, Colonel Symons knew that pilots such as Captain William Polk Gray would never put their complete trust in a chart of the river, when their boat's safety was concerned. Though frequently employed by the Corps of Engineers to survey, inspect, and blast a clear channel to a specified depth, Willie Gray had declared time and again that any pilot who trusted a Corps chart of a river was bound to rip open the bottom of his boat sooner or later. Sure, a chart showing where safe water was supposed to be could be helpful. But in full spring flood a powerful river current could pick up rocks of any size, carry them downstream like bottle corks, then drop them capriciously right in the middle of what a week before had been designated as a safe channel. All a chart did was give a pilot a notion of how a certain stretch of river *ought* to be. Any change noted by the captain's sharp eye meant trouble.

Seen now from the level of the river, the immensity of this bleak desert country was awesome. Rising precipitously above the eastern shore, sheer brown lava bluffs which Colonel Symons estimated to be at least 2,000 feet high defined the course of the river. Back from the west shore, the rise was more gradual, though of equal height, with the hazy range of the ten-thousand-foot-high Cascades dimly seen in the far distance.

As they approached the landmark called "Victoria Rock," the assistant made a hasty sketch of it, which he later improved on by adding the *bateau* itself, its passengers and crew, an eagle in flight, and a couple of Indian tepees in the distance ahead on the left-hand shore. When first seen, the rock did resemble Queen Victoria, members of the survey party agreed, though close up it looked like a Greek goddess, the Egyptian sphinx, or maybe even Cleopatra. When it was suggested it ought to have an American name, a party member said,

"How abut Eagle Nest Rock?"

"Yes, that'd do fine," Colonel Symons agreed. "Looks to me like it does have an eagle's nest on top."

Rising 100 feet above the river to the left of the main channel, the flat top of the columnar, basaltic formation was crowned with a large, brushy nest, constructed by a pair of eagles. It had been there for a number of years, Old Pierre said. Since male and female eagles mated for life, the same pair probably had lived there and raised a brood of eaglets each year for a long while. Adding the *bateau*, the Indian tepees, the rock, and a bend of the river, the map draftsman sketched the area for the report.

For half a dozen miles downstream from Victoria Rock the Columbia flowed quietly through a starkly dramatic country bordered on either side by high basaltic bluffs. During past aeons in the mountain-building period, lava flows had poured down from the peaks to the west, leaving deposits in every conceivable shape lying stacked horizontally like cordwood, standing vertically like barkless trees, or curling in twisted piles helter-skelter across the ground, forming niches, grottos, and fantastic formations of all shapes.

The party passed the mouth of a low, sandy wash coming in

from the northeast, which Old Pierre called Moses Coulee. Four miles farther on, the tranquility of the river was broken by a moderately rough expanse of water called Gualquil Rapids, which offered no great obstacle to navigation. For the next seven or eight miles the river was perfectly smooth, with the Indian paddlers lifting their oars and letting the *bateau* float along unaided, while Old Pierre used his steering oar only now and then to keep the boat in the center of the current.

Passing a small stream called Crab Creek and elevations of land named Saddle Mountain and Sentinel Bluffs, the party followed a wide bend of the river first to the east, then back again to the south through a country composed of sandy, gravelly, worthless soil, fit only for scattered tufts of bunchgrass and low clumps of sagebrush.

For the next five or six miles the river was wide, deep, and sluggish in the early afternoon heat of the summer day, looking more like a lake than a river. The dead water was caused, Old Pierre said, by the damming effect of the eleven miles of obstructions in the Priest Rapids sector. He suggested that camp be made just upstream from the rapids so that the party could inspect and chart them. No, he would not walk the length of the rapids with them; his poor old legs were not up to that. But he knew the hazards of the rapids so well, he could describe them in detail, if the map-maker would just write down what he said.

Checking the information given him by Old Pierre that afternoon against the actuality of running the eleven miles of rapids the next day, Colonel Symons was amazed by its accuracy. This was what was recorded and later experienced:

The first ripple of Priest Rapids is a slight one as far as the swiftness of the water is concerned; the water, however, is shallow, flowing over immense boulders and jagged rocks, which were plainly visible from the boat and at a variety of depths below the surface. Near the left bank many of these rocks come above the water, and the whirls plainly told that many others were just below the surface. Our course lay about the middle of the stream, and the sounding pole would indicate one instant perhaps a depth of three or four feet, the next ten or twelve, and the next five or six. Through this portion of the river a steamer could go now in safety after finding and knowing a thoroughly good channel.

The second rapid is about as bad as there is on the whole river. All about, the bedrock points and islands rise up in ugly, black, jagged masses, threatening destruction to anything that touches them. The bottom, as in the first ripple, is composed of huge boulders and rocks, and the water flows swiftly over this dangerous bottom and these outcropping rocks with a depth of only three or four feet. The fall here is considerable; we passed over one fall of at least three feet.

A steamer could not ascend this rapid without the use of a line, and even then the greatest care would be necessary. A smooth stretch of water then followed, and we came to the third rapid, which was swift and shallow, with considerable bedrock jutting up near both shores. The bed of the river at this rapid is the same as it has been all along, composed of large boulders.

For about five and a half miles now the river is quiet

and slow, with rocks scattered about here and there, generally in clusters. The water is so shallow that we were able to see the bottom for a great part of the way, and is from twelve to twenty feet in depth. The fourth rapid is in this stretch of water, but is very mild in character and presents no obstruction.

We now come to a very bad portion of the river, consisting of the three lower rapids of Priest Rapids. We are able to tell from the preparations by Old Pierre and his crew that considerable danger lies along the fifth rapid, in which the water is very turbulent, boiling and roaring a great deal. This boiling and foaming is not, however, necessarily attended with great swiftness of current, for in this ripple we did not move as fast as in some others which appeared much more quiet. In fact, the tumbling over the uneven bottom which caused the agitation tended to check the velocity considerably.

The long, irregular mass near the right bank which lies along the fifth rapid continues on down the river for about two and a half miles, with only an occasional break.

A little below the fifth rapid we come to where the main channel is divided into two by another long, irregular, jagged mass of the same black basaltic rock, thrown along almost in the center of the river. We choose the right-hand channel of the two, and, after swiftly passing a few ugly-looking projecting points, we found ourselves in the sixth rapid, shooting with the speed of a race-horse down through the canal-like channel between these two long rock islands. For about a mile we tore along with the united speed of the raging torrent and our yelling Indian oarsmen. The channel seemed to have plenty of water, but is quite narrow, being about sixty to eighty feet wide. We went through it at the rate of about twenty miles an hour.

The left-hand channel is the one better suited to purposes of navigation, I believe. It is crooked and the water not so swift as in the straight-away one through which we came.

Emerging from the canal-like seventh rapid, Old Pierre threw the boat to the left to avoid some bad-looking water *dead ahead, and, after a little further tumbling and rolling about the seventh rapid, we emerged with a shout of joy from the eleven miles of Priest Rapids. We all know now that our dangers are passed, and thank God for allowing us to safely come through all the rapids.*

We soon make for shore, and camp on the right bank, having made during the morning about eighteen miles.[4]

Well satisfied with the work Old Pierre and his half-blood oarsmen had done for the river exploration party, Colonel Symons paid them in gold for their three days' labor, gave them what remained of the food and rum supplies, and sent them on their way rejoicing. Going aboard the Corps of Engineers work boat, which was moored nearby, Colonel Symons began writing a draft of what his party had learned during the past few days, which he would later summarize as the state of the river from the mouth of the Snake to above Rock Island Rapids.

Running through 130 miles of desert country as bleak and empty as God ever made, it would probably be a waste of government money and time to do the rock-blasting and channel work that would have to be done before steamboats could go upriver on a regular schedule. But that was not for him to decide. Where water flowed, bold captains would attempt to pilot their steamboats. And at that time, the boldest of them all, Captain William Polk Gray, was working in the area . . . .

Chapter 15 footnotes

1. *Report on the Upper Columbia River and the Great Plain of the Columbia*, 1881, by Thomas William Symons, Col., U.S. Army, reprint by Ye Galleon Press, Fairfield, Washington, 1967.
2. *Fur Hunters of the Far West*, by Alexander Ross, op. cit. The Symons Report retells the story and gives a vivid description of Old Pierre. I have paraphrased this description and put in dialogue the essence of what was probably said.
3. Symons Report, op. cit.
4. Ibid.

CHAPTER SIXTEEN
Captain Gray in Alaska

During most of his long career, Captain William Polk Gray was too busy piloting steamboats to do much writing, but on those rare occasions when he did put words on paper he expressed himself in a colorful style. One of his most interesting articles, which he apparently dictated and then had typed, was titled: *Narrative of a Marriage*. It began:

"During a severe storm off the Falkland Islands near Cape Horn, on a ship of which her father was captain, a girl was born at midnight June 2, 1849. When the word was passed that a little girl had come aboard, the sailors called her the 'cape pigeon' though she was named Oceana Falkland Hawthorne. The mother faded and passed away before the ship reached San Francisco."[1]

In those days, a sailing ship leaving Boston and going around the Horn to the west coast of the United States required six months to make the trip, touching land only three times during the long journey. Setting a course that took advantage of following Trade Winds both north and south of the Equator, the ship sailed for two months in a southeasterly direction to Cape Verde Island, a British possession off the coast of Africa, where it renewed its stock of provisions and fresh water at ten degrees north, then changed course and sailed southwest for two months more until it reached the Falkland Islands, another British holding at fifty-three degrees south, across as empty a stretch of ocean as existed anywhere in the world.

Because the seasons were reversed, June 2 was the beginning of winter here. Situated in a cold, gray sea 200 miles off the east coast of South America just north of the Strait of Magellan, the Falklands were a forbidding place. Steep mountains of gray and rust-red rock rose sheer from shorelines with few safe anchorages. No trees or people lived on the Falklands, though from time to time passing ships seeking fresh water or game spent a few days in tents or shacks made of whalebone as they foraged on the islands, whose only decent harbor was named Port Egmont Bay.

In those days when the master of a ship owned an interest in it and knew that the venture on which he was embarked might last two or three years, he often took his wife along to make him a home aboard. If a baby were born during the voyage, the mother probably would receive just as good a care from the ship's medicine-dispenser as she would have gotten anywhere else, for in those days doctors did not specialize on obstetrical care. In Mrs. Hawthorne's case, the mother did not survive.

"The child was taken into the hands and heart of a noble, generous woman in Sacramento," Captain Gray wrote. "Her grandparents asked that she be sent to them in Connecticut when she was nine years old. The girl was taken across the Isthmus of Panama and returned in five years to her foster mother who had married a prominent physician in Portland, where the girl finished her education at the Sisters Academy."[2]

So by the time Oceana Falkland Hawthorne met the man who would be her husband for fifty-two years, she had already gone from one coast to the other three times. Captain Gray described their meeting in 1869, when she was twenty years old.

"When the ceremony of driving the first spike in Ben Holladay's railroad on the east side of the Willamette River at Portland took place, the girl met her future husband, who was a rollicking, happy-go-lucky steamboat man.

"A party of three couples strolled down to a dock where a ship was moored. It was about eight feet down from the dock to the ship's deck. A dare was made to see who would reach the deck first. The girl instantly jumped from the dock to the deck and won the man's heart with her daring. After a few calls, they

Vancouver Public Library Collection
Canadian Development Company's stern-wheelers, *Canadian* and *Lotta Talbot* in winter quarters at Whitehorse.

became engaged, and, during the summer correspondence, it was agreed to be married in the winter holidays."

From the beginning, Captain Gray's wife-to-be seemed to know she must accept her lifetime rival—the river—for wherever water flowed in the Pacific Northwest and a pilot was needed to steer a boat, William Polk Gray would make himself available on a moment's notice.

Although the holidays were several months away, when Gray returned to Portland one evening from a lower river job in early October, he received an offer of a year's employment with two conditions: first, that he move 250 miles upriver; second, that he start the next morning. Going to Oceana Falkland's home, Gray said cheerfully,

"Nothing to stop the wedding now except fancy clothes."

"Your wish is my law," she replied (Gray wrote later), and they were married that evening.

During fifty-two years of married life, Gray claimed they "had only one row. We had been to an entertainment the night before and were awakened by the train whistling for my boat a half mile away. The cook of the boat had been fired for being drunk, so I knew I would get no breakfast aboard.

"The whistle woke us up and we jumped out of bed. My wife ran into the kitchen to lay a fire, while I put on my pants. When I reached the kitchen, my wife had taken the lids off the stove, and, in her excitement, had put a large piece of wood in first, with the kindling on top. Without a word, I took the big piece of wood out and began to re-arrange it with the kindling. She grabbed the coffee pot and hit me on the head with it."

Her reaction was so unexpected and comical, Gray said, that he laughed. Throwing her arms around him, she cried and apologized, hugging him despite the fact they both were covered with soot and ashes.

"Never mind, darling," he said, "it's worth a crack on the head to see you excited."

By this time, he added, "four kiddies were hanging about her and saying what a bad man papa was to make mama cry."

Neither of them had any financial sense, he wrote ruefully.

"The wife, a picnic for peddlers, always had an upstairs full of unused goods. The man, a picnic for promoters, was sometimes broke and at other times rich, but the home was always full of happiness when papa was home. Neither had aspirations for success in business or politics."[3]

Another article dictated after his retirement was titled:
Waters of the Northwest That I Have Navigated
(written Nov. 14, 1923 - Pasco)
The Columbia River as captain and pilot from the ocean up and into the Okanogan River.

Yukon River as captain and pilot from St. Michaels to White Horse; Willamette as capt. and pilot from mouth to Harrisburg; Fraser River as cook from Fort Langley to Fort Yale and was wrecked on Hill's bar in 1859; Stickine River as Captain and pilot from Fort Wrangell to Telegraph Creek; Puget Sound and Inland Passage as captain and pilot from Olympia to Icy Straits in Alaska; Behring Sea as captain and pilot for Isamota Pass to Nome and put my steamboat into Snake River at Nome on one tide.

Yamhill River as capt. and pilot from mouth to

McMinnville.

As master and pilot of a tug I have towed and piloted ships in and out over the Columbia River bar when there was a bar.

As captain and pilot I have run steamboats on the Snake River in Washington from its mouth to the Imnaha River and brought the steamer "Norma" down the Snake river from Huntington bridge in Oregon to Riparia, Wn. in one season.

The O.S.N. Co. wanted the hull of the steamer "Bonanza," wrecked on Rock Island rapids in the Willamette, brought into the Willamette locks for repairs and then taken across the river into the dry dock on the Oregon side. The hull drew seven feet of water. Every other captain on the river said it could not be done. I dropped the hull through Tualitin Rocks, put her into the Willamette locks where it was repaired enough to float one hour. I pulled her out of the locks, dropped her across the river close above Willamette Falls, dropped her into the Oregon City canal and into the dry dock where she sank into the "ways" before the gates could be closed. It was touch and go from start to finish and I received the thanks of the president of the company, Capt. J.C. Ainsworth, for doing something that everybody said could not be done.

In 1877 I ran the sternwheel boat "Beaver" from Seattle to Fort Wrangell and made fourteen round trips between Wrangell and Telegraph Creek on the Stickine River without knocking a hole in the boat. I refused $250 a month because the managing owner who ran on the boat as a purser would get drunk and interfere. The captain who took my place knocked her completely on his first trip down the Stickine River.

I have mushed or walked to all the creeks of the Klondike district, Eldorado, Last Chance, Hunker, Bonanza, and the Dome, looking for my pot of gold at the end of the rainbow. But a steamboat man is a poor walker and the other fellow always got there first. I claimed to be a fairly good steamboat man but thawing frozen gravel 20 or 30 feet below the surface wasn't in my line.[4]

Another piece of Captain Gray's writing after he retired was entitled:

God Bless Our Home

When the Northern Pacific railroad was being built from Ainsworth on the Snake River to Spokane Falls, the first construction engineer was H.M. McCartney, better known as Harry by everybody as he was a bright, cheerful entertainer as well as a competent engineer.

One night Harry was obliged to stay over for the night at old Wallula. Being unable to sleep because of the prior occupants of the bed, he got up about 12 o'clock and asked the landlady for a paper of pins. After Harry left the hotel the next morning the landlady found the headboard of the bedstead ornamented with the motto "Good Bless Our Home" formed by bed bugs punctured with the pins. Harry was not particularly religious either.

He named the first station north of Ainsworth "Hell To Pay," now known as Eltopia as that was the first remark made by the contractor when he arrived with his outfit, found no water, and that the water wagon had been left behind and a hot sun shining. The name "Hell To Pay" was on the first time card of the road.

Multitude

Before the completion of Dr. Baker's railroad between Wallula and Walla Walla, ox teams composed of from six to ten yoke hitched to a wagon loaded with 10,000 pounds of merchandise and a trailer loaded with nearly as heavy a load would go up from the river. The same outfit would haul wheat and flour back. Bull drivers (as they were called) took pride in every branch of their job.

Among the ox drivers was a man called "Multitude" because he could yell louder and crack his whip louder than any other driver and was several times arrested in Walla Walla for cracking his whip so loud they thought it was a pistol or gun. Other drivers could hear his voice a mile away and would prepare to fight or give him the right-of-way. He claimed he could hit a fly on the ear of an

Alaska and Polar Reions Archuves
Stern-wheeler *Ora* was one of the boats Captain Gray piloted on the Yukon River.

ox six teams away from the driver's seat. I never heard his real name but some of the old timers should remember "Multitude."[5]

Even as railroads, canals, and locks were being built along the Columbia and Snake Rivers, and Captain Gray was settling down with his family in Pasco, Washington, 350 miles inland from the sea, events were occurring far to the north that would lead him to adventures on those distant rivers. During the summer of 1897, Seattle was a badly depressed area when a piece of news reached it that made everybody sit up and take notice. Returning from Alaska, the steamer *Portland* sent a wireless shortly after she cleared Cape Flattery inbound through the Strait of Juan De Fuca. As word of the cargo spread, crowds of wild-eyed men swarmed down to the docks to meet the ship. Soon newspaper all over the Puget Sound area were screaming the sensational headline:

A TON OF GOLD ARRIVES!

The first strikes had been made on the Yukon River in Canadian territory. But soon Alaska, just across the border, would prove equally rich in gold as far north as Nome. A stampede the likes of which had never been known before ensued— with Seattle the jumping-off place where every prospector headed north would buy the ton of food, supplies, and equipment required before he disembarked at Skagway and started the terrible climb up and over Chilkoot Pass, across Bennett Lake, and then down the rapids of the Yukon River to Dawson City and the fabled riches of the Klondike.

With its mouth at St. Michaels, just south of the Arctic Circle in the Bering Sea, the Yukon River had a very short steamboat season, for the ice did not go out until mid-May and the river began to freeze over again in October. But during the few months of open water, rugged stern-wheelers and daring captains carried full loads of freight and passengers to and from the rich gold fields. As might be expected, Captain William Polk Gray was there. He later wrote:

> *Pasco - Jan. 17, 1926*
>
> *In the fall of 1900 I was Capt. of the stern wheel steamer "Robert Kerr" fitted up as a carrier of cold storage products for Dawson. We had 200 tons of storage aboard and were within 350 miles of Dawson when without warning the main shaft of the propelling wheel broke off in the middle.*
>
> *I dropped anchor and worked the boat to the bank and tied up. The winter supply of meats and vegetables for the Klondike were aboard. Ice forming on the banks would soon make $100,000 in property useless. A steamboat under command of my brother, Capt. Jas T. Gray, came down with the officers of the A.E. Co. and the crews of three other steamboats aboard that had been laid up at Dawson for the winter.*
>
> *We offered the president of the Alaska Exploration Co. $50,000 if they would tow the "Robert Kerr" to Dawson. He refused as the ice was too close and the wages of the crews of steamboats that were aboard his boat would exceed that amount if they were frozen in for the winter. But I never give up. Seeing some Alaska pine trees growing a half mile from the river bank where we lay, I had my crew cut and hew them to shape. My engineer was a splendid mechanic. We took down our hog chains and cut them for rods, bolts, and staples, jacked the old shaft together with a squared timber on each quarter, and started for Dawson under our own steam.*

Alaska and Polar Regions Archives
The *Lottie Talbot* at the Dawson City waterfront, August 12, 1899. Captain Gray brought the boat from Puget Sound, up the Inside Passage to the Bering Sea, then up the Yukon River to Whitehorse, a voyage of 2,850 miles.

Arriving at Circle City, our work showed signs of weakness and we offered the Alaska Commercial Co. steamboat $10,000 to help us to Dawson but were refused as they were afraid of the ice. But under our own power we arrived at Dawson O.K. and I caught the last boat out from there for God's Country. The Alaska Meat Co. presented me with a Swiss striking watch of which I am very proud. The following spring I went in over the ice on the Yukon, driving a one horse sled from White Horse to Dawson and took the "Kerr" under her own steam to St. Michaels where we found a new shaft from Seattle.[6]

January 23, 1926
I have thought you might not understand the size of the job we had to perform to fix that shaft to take the boat up the river, loaded with 200 tons of refrigerated stores. The shaft was of wrought iron, 26 feet long and 11 inches in diameter, made strong enough to carry the working strain

*of two 20-inch cylinders, 10-foot stroke and drive a steam-
boat 200 feet long, 35 feet wide, fully loaded up against the
current of the Yukon River.*

*No foundry or machine shop to go to and only common
tools to work with. But it was done and no one aboard had
ever heard of its being done before. The reason we offered
such large amounts to be towed to Dawson was our load
would have had to be taken by dog sled over the ice at exorbitant prices. The ice going out in the spring would destroy
the steamboat.[7]*

Several letters Captain wrote and later had typed relate past
adventures best told in his own unique style:

Pasco, Wn. July 8, 1925.
Howard Winter, Esq.
Eagle Cliff, Wn.
Dear Friend from Wrangell:

*The Wrangell Sentinel is received O.K. and I thank you
very much. I have read it through, even the want ads and
society news, and it is a surprise to learn of the development that has taken place in Alaska.*

*I was in Wrangell in '77 when the soldiers left for the
Nez Perce war. In '98 when the stampeders to the Yukon
tried to go to the Klondike by way of the Stickine River and
Lake Teslin, I took the sternwheel steamboat "Lottie
Talbot" from Seattle by way of the Inland Passage to Icy
Straits around the north end of the Pacific ocean, by Cook's
Inlet and Kodiak Island. Through the Isanooksa Pass
instead of Unamak Pass, up Behring Sea to St. Michaels
where we loaded her "guards under" with refrigerated
meats for Dawson. I changed boats with Capt. Wand of the
steamer "Ora." Took her up the Yukon to White Horse. Was
a passenger on another boat from White Horse to Lake
Bennett, railroad from Bennett to Skagway, and to Seattle
by steamship.*

*The next two years I drove a horse and sled from
Bennett to Dawson over the ice. On Easter Sunday 1900, I*

drove a horse and sled on the Yukon ice from Indian River to the "Twelve Mile House" with the thermometer showing 40 below zero. You may know from this that I know something about Alaska.

You will have to excuse my scratchy writing as I will be eighty years old next month and have a slight palsy in my hands, but my think tank is still a-working. Sometimes it works overtime and needs a couple of "stenogs" to keep up with my thoughts. If you can't read this, show it to a cross word expert.

Yours truly,
W.P. Gray [8]

Now and then he would jot down an idea he could never develop fully. Here is one of them:

Indian Canoe idea

"I have been thinking for some time of suggesting that an effort should be made to secure models of the canoes used before the advent of the white man by the Indians of the Northwest. It is well known that the famous Yankee clippers, which outsailed the ships of all other nations, were built on the model of the Chinook canoe.

"The Puget Sound, Fraser River, Queen Charlotte Island, Stickine, and Chilkoot Indians had different sizes and shaped canoes. The Eskimos have their kyaks and bidarkas. The Flatheads and Kootenais use different shapes. Think it over."

In my own research, I have discovered that the lines of the sea-going canoes built by the Chinook Indians changed after the native designers saw the first trading and whaling ships, which were built in New England in the mid-1700s. Great borrowers that the Chinooks were, the *canim tyee* (Chief Canoe-Maker) of the tribe was always ready to try a new design idea to see if it would work as well for his people as it had worked for the "Boston" captains who had sailed half way around the world so successfully. Conversely, after observing how well the Indian-built canoes survived the monstrous seas rolling in over the treacherous Columbia River Bar, which was feared by even the most experienced sailing ship captains, it is reasonable to assume that the white men tried Indian design concepts when they returned home.

Though the methods and tools used by the native craftsmen bore little resemblance to those employed in a New England shipyard, it is likely that the results would not have displeased the most meticulous master builder of a New Bedford whaler back home, who later might use some Indian techniques in a Yankee Clipper.

To begin with, the *canim tyee* chose a huge cedar tree as flawless as possible for seventy or eighty feet of its length. He then had it felled with what the Indians called a *pe-yah-cud*—a primitive axe whose blade was made of a black volcanic material called obsidian, which was incredibly sharp.

After his helpers felled the tree, the *canim tyee* scored the bark, then the workmen trimmed the branches and peeled the trunk. The hull of the big seagoing canoe was shaped slowly and carefully. After hot rocks had been used to burn out the interior and the hull had been roughly formed, the *tyee* went over it inch by inch, supervising his helpers as they used hand-chisels to remove a chip here and another there in a process taking whatever amount of time was required until the vessel took the shape he wanted.

In its design, no blueprints of any kind existed, the complete plan for the craft existing only in the *tyee's* mind. Normally sixty feet long when finished, with a raised stern and a high-peaked prow ornamented with the symbolic figure of a raven, a whale, or a mythical thunderbird, each seagoing canoe would be manned by fifty paddlers kneeling abreast twenty-five on each side, could carry five tons of cargo, and could move through the roughest kind of water with incredible ease and speed.

The balance of the canoes was perfect, achieved expertly by the skilled eye and judgment of the *canim tyee* who insisted that a wood chip be taken out here, another there, and still others at key points throughout the hull until the trim was exactly what he wanted it to be. Crucial in the construction process was the spreading of the craft's interior in order to make it exactly the right width, which was a delicate balance between load capacity and seaworthiness.

After the hull was hollowed out, it was filled with water which then was heated with red-hot stones. As the still unseasoned wood softened, carefully measured thwarts were placed so that they would act as spreaders, producing a flare. Too little spread reduced stability in heavy seas; too much might split the wood. Working without blueprints or printed directions, the only guide was the judgment of the *tyee*, whose skills had been handed down to him through a long line of canoe-builders.

"The way the Chinooks handle those big cedar canoes is something to see," Alexander Ross, a member of the original Astor party, had written many years ago. "I've watched them in rough water time and again. No matter how big the

Franklin County Historical Society
Captain William Polk Gray, age 55, in Seattle about 1900.

waves get, they never panic. When a roller strikes the windward side of a canoe, all the men on that side dig their paddles into the water clear up to their armpits, while those on the lee side lift their paddles clear. As soon as the swell passes under the canoe, the men on the lee side dig in at exactly the right instant, keeping the canoe on an even keel. All this, mind you, without anybody giving an order or a signal. They just know instinctively what to do and when to do it. They're the best canoe paddlers I've ever seen."

When Ross asked how long the big seagoing canoes could be expected to last, he was told that the one a native was showing him had been built by the grandfather-grandfather of today's *canim tyee*, which meant that must be at least 100 years old.

"How do you preserve the wood that long?" he asked incredulously. "How do you keep it from cracking above water or getting so waterlogged below that it will not float?"

"Glease. Just lub it with glease."

By then, Ross had learned that one of several letters that the Chinooks could not articulate was "r," so he had no difficulty figuring out that what the native was saying was that the cedar canoes were rubbed with grease or a similar substance such as oil. But finding out what kind of grease or oil the Indian meant required a bit more linguistic probing.

The first word the native used was *kamooks*, which he knew meant "dog." Even before Ross could ask if that meant dog grease or dog oil, the Indian added the word *pish*, which he knew meant "fish," then concluded with the word *hyas,* which he knew meant "big." Putting the three words together, he came up with the word "big-dog-fish," a name which whites and Indians alike applied to a three-foot-long shark called a dogfish, which was frequently found in these waters. Regarded as a nuisance by both whites and natives, its flesh was so distasteful that it was eaten only by starving people. But the oil of its liver—which smelled to high heaven—excelled in its preservative quality.

Chapter 16 footnotes

1. "Narative of a Marriage," Gray, 1925, p. 1, Penrose Library copy.
2. Ibid.
3. Ibid, p. 2.
4. Letter, Gray, Nov. 14, 1923, copy Penrose Library.
5. Ibid.
6. Ibid, 1926.
7. Ibid.
8. Ibid.

Captain Gray's retirement years

A t about the time Colonel Symons was completing his report on the feasibility of navigating the upper Columbia River in the summer of 1881, Captain Gray and the *Spokane* began transporting supplies and materials with which to build homes for laborers at Ainsworth, where work was about to start on a railroad bridge across the Snake just upstream from its juncture with the Columbia. In the interim, the Northern Pacific Railroad Company planned to use a ferry to transfer railroad cars across the Snake. Launching a specially equipped boat, the *Frederick K. Billings*, in May, 1881, with Captain Gray to be in command, the O.R.& N. Company brought the boat upriver from Celilo Landing in June, putting her in service on July 4, ferrying railroad cars. By the end of the year, inclines had been completed on both sides of the river, so that the rail cars could be transferred.

"Nothing has been written about the crew, which must have been at least ten to fifteen men," says Franklin County historian, Jean Carol Davis. "Nothing has been written about how many trains there were each day or each week. Or who took over when Captain Gray was away."[1]

The Snake River bridge at Ainsworth was completed in April 1884, and the *Billings* was sent to Celilo for overhaul and remodeling. It was returned to Pasco late in September 1884 and used to transfer rail cars over the Columbia River until the

Pasco-Kennewick railroad bridge was completed in 1888.

Getting their fill of wandering around the Pacific Northwest, the Gray family moved to Ainsworth in 1881, then to Pasco in March, 1885. Though Colonel Symons' report on the navigability of the upper Columbia was not very favorable to the Wenatchee area, pressure from local merchants and shippers persuaded the government to investigate the possibility of taking a steamboat through the Rock Island Rapids. In 1887, the O.R.& N. Company sent a steamer commanded by an unnamed captain, which failed to ascend the rapids. On Gray's assurance that the rapids could be conquered, if the right pilot were at the wheel, two boats were built to his specifications at Pasco in 1888. [2]

Another unnamed captain attempted to ascend the rapids, but failed. Captain Gray then was asked to take charge of the smaller steamer, *City of Ellensburg*, and try to ascend the rapids himself. Loading the boat with cordwood, equipping it with spar poles and power winches which could be used in "grass-hoppering" (literally pole-vaulting) a boat up a rapid, and inviting his aging father, William H. Gray, to come along for the ride, Captain Willie prepared to try the rapids again, well aware that the word "can't" still had found no place in the Gray family dictionary.

Not surprisingly, he took the *Ellensburg* through first Priest Rapids and then the more formidable Rock Island Rapids, using only the equipment carried aboard the boat, with no rock-blasting or expensive channel-improvement projects by the Corps of Engineers needed. Later, the sister boat, *Thomas L. Nixon*, made the same run, with both steamers serving for many years in the Wenatchee and Okanogan areas.[3]

Deciding to settle permanently in the region where three rivers, the Yakima, Columbia, and Snake, joined, Captain Gray purchased nineteen acres in Pasco from DeWitt Owen in 1885, then obtained 50,000 board feet of lumber from the Northern Pacific Company for $100 when it closed its mill in Ainsworth. After building a house in Pasco and a two-story hotel in Kennewick, he sold the leftover lumber for seventy-five dollars. When the NP moved its operations from Ainsworth to Pasco, accommodations for travelers were in short supply, so Captain

Sternwheeler *Gerome* hosts a band excursion.

Gray rented a section house, then with kitchen equipment from the *Billings*, opened a restaurant and built and furnished four sleeping rooms.

Truly, he had "swallowed the anchor" and come ashore.

In 1885 he paid homesteader Henry Gantenbein, Jr., to relinquish a 99-acre parcel, which he had surveyed and platted as "Gray's Addition" to the town of Pasco. In 1886, he was named local land agent for the Northern Pacific. He later claimed credit for being the first to utter the slogan and devise the circle symbol KEEP YOUR EYE ON PASCO, though the founder of the first local newspaper, The *Headlight*, also took credit for it.

"A good idea doesn't care who uses it," writes historian Jean Carol Davis, refusing to take sides. "Captain Gray put the slogan on rubber stamps for agents and friends to use and printed 100,000 dodgers, 2 1/2" by 5", with the words in half-inch type and a map of the area on the reverse side, to be distributed to passengers on trains."4

Franklin County Historical Society
Ainsworth Landing on the Snake River, 1906. Front, *Mountain Gem*, Captain W. P. Gray; back, *J. M. Hannaford*, Captain E. W. Baughman.

In the fall of 1888, bitter tragedy struck the Gray family when a diphtheria epidemic raged across the Pacific Northwest. Daughters Rachael A. Gray, eight years old, Catherine H. Gray, six, and Mary Gray, three, all were stricken and died within two days time. In those days, diphtheria was the dreaded killer of children, who literally choked to death.[5] In time to come, Captain Gray seldom spoke of the loss, but his wife, Oceana, was never the same afterwards. Their first daughter, Oceana Lou Gray, had died in childhood. Willetta C. Gray, born in 1875, lived to maturity and beyond, as did a son, Hawthorne C. Gray, born in 1890. But for the rest of her life, Mrs. Gray existed in a kind of daze. A friend of the family, Georgia Mae Wilkins Gallivan, later recalled,

"Mrs. Gray wore floor length black bombazine gowns, and I doubt if she was aware that in the 1920s women wore short skirts. Her dresses were reminiscent of Queen Victoria's. Mentally she drifted into and out of this world, and this had been so since the death of her children thirty years before. Sometimes she would recognize my father, more often not. On the days her memory failed, Captain Gray courteously introduced my father, whom she had known since she was nine years old."[6]

As for William Polk Gray himself, though he retired from active service as a river pilot in 1910 at the age of sixty-one, he would remain alert and active in regional affairs until the end of his long life. His particular field of interest was in Pasco promotion, where he served a term as mayor, and in river transportation, where he championed any project aimed at improving navigation.

As related earlier, in May 1895, Gray was called upon to bring the steamboat *Norma* downriver through Hell's Canyon, an adventure he did not write about until he was asked to do so many years later. For this successful feat, his brother-in-law, Jacob Kamm, and the Oregon Steam Navigation Company gave him an elaborately engraved watch, which he proudly showed off for the rest of his life, finally bequeathing it to his grandson, William. In December 1920, at the request of the U.S. Geological Survey, he wrote a long report of the trip through Hell's Canyon which is still considered a classic in the field of steamboat literature, his memory not a whit diminished by the passage of time.[7]

"My own remembrance of things past," Mrs. Gallivan wrote, "starts when I was three years old. My mother and father, Melvina and Archie Wilkins, returned to Pasco in 1918 from Spokane where I was born. The William Grays were elderly and lived in the house on the river east of the railroad bridge. My father visited them usually every Sunday. At that time, their daughter, Willetta, and her husband, Jess Sprague, lived with her parents.

"On one of my first visits after we had come to Pasco, Captain Gray took me on his bony knee and with his palsied hands removed a large, elaborately engraved watch from his vest pocket. Next he opened the cover protecting the watch face. On the inside of the cover was engraved a citation commemorating his navigation by steamboat of the Hells Canyon of the Snake River. The watch was a presentation of the Oregon Navigation Company in recognition of this historical feat. After he read me the engraved words came   the most wonderful part of all. He opened the back cover of the watch and, moving two small levers concealed in the rim, set off a tinkling of bells, a musical alarm for a sleeper, magic for a child."[8]

She described Captain Gray as being a distinguished, handsome man, always dressed formally in striped trousers, frock coat, and a gray vest, crossed by a heavy gold chain that anchored the fabulous watch. A neatly trimmed beard hid what she imagined to be a four-in-hand tie. When he attended a Chamber of Commerce luncheon at the Pence Hotel, he wore a dark Homburg and carried a cane with a deer's foot head. He, with other Pasco enthusiasts, was absolutely certain that Pasco would become a great city. So certain that he, with others, invested heavily in land and land improvements and lost heavily in the boom-bust economy of the pre-World War I era.

"Before I was in the eighth grade," she wrote, "he presented me with a deed to two corner lots in the Gray Addition. I was overwhelmed with such a gift, and tried to thank him suitably, as did my father. On our way home, my father smilingly told me that it was indeed a generous gesture, but I should realize that Captain Gray had not paid property taxes for many years. Even so, I was proud that I was a young property owner who owed back taxes."9

Hawthorne Gray, the youngest child, became a captain in the U.S. Army during World War I. Imbued with the same adventurous spirit as his father, he flew free balloons during the war, becoming so enamored with them that he stayed in the service and made a career of flying them, winning several international balloon races in Belgium after the war.

Traveling to Pasco to visit his parents, he made the journey by motorcycle, a means of travel that was not easy even by the standards of the day.

"The time of Hawthorne's last visit is fixed in my five-year-old's memory," Mrs. Gallivan wrote nostalgically. "I am standing between my father and Hawthorne during their lengthy conversation. It was sunset and Hawthorne balanced the machine he had ridden across the continent. When they finished their talk, Hawthorne started the motorcycle and rode off into the red-gold light that soon turned to dusk."

Returning to his base at Wright Field in Dayton, Ohio, Captain Gray focused his attention on setting a world record for height of a balloon ascension.

"He attained an extraordinary altitude of eight miles, a

Franklin County Historical Society
A stern-wheeler loads sacks of grain.

record," Mrs. Gallivan wrote. "However, his altimeter did not register satisfactorily for the official record. On the second attempt the eight-mile altitude was recorded, but his oxygen tanks failed. He died during his descent. Captain Hawthorne Gray is buried at Arlington National Cemetery."

She points out that the three generations of Grays—William Henry, his son William Polk, and his grandson Hawthorne—"are arresting examples of the adventurous spirit that propelled Americans. They crossed an unexplored continent, navigated untamed wild rivers, and when land and water were conquered, the third generation made the next step into the sky."[10]

Although Mrs. Gray suffered mental lapses following the death of her three daughters in 1888, a letter dated December 26, 1896, written to her daughter, Willetta, indicates that at times she was alert enough to be concerned about the welfare of her husband.

"Willetta, can you see Mr. Lyons," she wrote from Cascade Locks, where the Grays were living at that time, "and kind of talk around and see if Papa can get back on the *Billings* soon? I think he is well enough and if any one in authority could send for him, he would be glad to go back to Pasco. Don't tell any one, but just find out if Mr. Campbell is going away and who is going to take his place and mention that Papa is well now and out of work so that maybe he could come back if he was wanted but be careful how you say it. You are smart enough to know how."[11]

Exactly where Captain Gray worked for the next two years is not clear, but what is known is that after the discovery of gold in Alaska he moved the family to Seattle in 1898 and returned to the treacherous Stikine River, making five runs on the *Casca* from Fort Wrangell to Telegraph Creek and back.

"He then took the *Lottie Talbot* from the Inland (Inside) Passage, across the Bering Sea to St. Michaels, just above the mouth of the Yukon River. From there he took a load of refrigerated stores up the Yukon, across Alaska to Dawson (Dawson City, at the mouth of the Klondike), where he exchanged boats with the captain of the *Ora* and continued up the Yukon to Whitehorse, a trip of 2,850 miles."

Mrs. Gray and their son, Hawthorne, lived in Seattle while he was working on the Yukon River, historian Jean Carol Davis writes. In August 1899 she stopped in Pasco en route to Connecticut to visit their daughter Willetta. She reported that the Captain was still running a steamer on the Yukon River, but the family expected to move back to Pasco the following year.

Between 1901 and 1904, Gray acted as captain of the *Georgia Oakes*, a luxury steamer built by the Northern Pacific Company to carry mail, freight, and passengers on the placid inland waters of Coeur d'Alene Lake. He wrote nothing about his adventures there, probably because there was nothing exciting to record. Considered to be the fanciest boat on the lake, the *Georgia Oakes* had staterooms, a restaurant, a bar, and could carry six hundred passengers. The scenery was beautiful, no doubt about that, but Lake Coeur d'Alene lacked the element that long had made Captain Gray's life exciting—white water. Compared to rapids he had run on the Yukon, the Stikine, the Columbia, and the Snake, a cruise along the unrippled lake shore was tame stuff for him.

Officially retiring in 1906 at age sixty-one, Captain Gray returned to the river now and then for special occasions, such as bringing the *Undine* upriver from Portland to Lewiston in 1915, then acting as honorary Admiral on the same boat when it became the flagship of the upriver fleet during the week-long celebration at river communities in the formal opening ceremonies on May 15, 1915. The parade of boats then continued

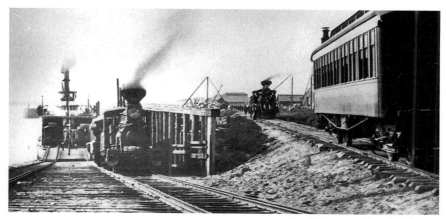

Franklin County Historical Society
A locomotive backs cars aboard the ferry *Frederick Billings* at Ainsworth, 1879.

downriver to Astoria and across the Columbia River Bar into the Pacific Ocean.[12]

After retiring from active steamboating, Captain Gray devoted most of his time to the promotion of Pasco, the development of irrigation and good roads, and, most important of all, the improvement of river transportation. He was much sought after as a speaker at Open River meetings.

"The captivating style of the Captain's speaking succeeded in holding the rapt attention of the delegates," newspaper accounts reported. As Vice President of the Open Rivers Committee for Washington state, he was a delegate to the National Rivers and Harbors Congress in Washington, D.C. in December, 1910. His address to the Open River meeting in Pasco in April 1912, was printed in many regional newspapers.

Two U.S. government vessels, *Umatilla* and *Wallowa*, worked on the upper Columbia and Snake rivers beginning in 1908 to improve shipping channels. In early October 1912, Gray accompanied Captain S.V. Winslow of the *Umatilla* in a motor launch from Pasco to Lewiston and return, no doubt running the same rapids he had been forced to swim as a thirteen-year-old boy so many years earlier. Afterwards, he wrote the *Oregonian* detailing their trip, noting the removal of boulders and the installation of wing-dams that improved channels and water depth at many points. He concluded by saying,

The end of the steamer *Hercules*.

"I would like to add a few words of commendation for the government officials and their employees who have made such a great improvement in the navigation of the Columbia and Snake rivers from Celilo to Lewiston in the past two years. . . Under the present system the steamboat pilots are consulted instead of the Corps of Engineers."

Apparently he still had not forgotten or forgiven the Corps of Engineers for leaving the broken drill bit in the river above Farewell Bend that had ripped a hole in the bottom of the *Norma* back in 1895.

While Mayor of Pasco in 1911, he tried to develop plans for a city dock, persuading Northern Pacific to deed a right-of- way so that a street could be opened to the river, and getting an architect to draw plans without charge to the city, with surveying and estimating costs done by the city engineer. The proposed port district would include Kennewick, Richland, Finley, and Burbank, with steamboat landings, docks and warehouses at several locations.

"A dam on the Snake River at Five Mile Rapids (about two miles downstream from today's Ice Harbor Dam) would provide power for port operations or for sale," historian Jean Carol Davis writes. "Nothing more was done. Captain Gray's talk about a port district at a Chamber of Commerce meeting in April, 1914, was apparently considered a joke by some members. His response was a letter to the newspaper stating that it was not a joke and he detailed his earlier plans. He stressed the development of such facilities as necessary for the economic good of the region."

But his plea fell on deaf ears, for at that place and time local businessmen seemed to feel that rail lines completed a few decades ago and the highways recently built for trucks were all the transportation facilities the region needed. Not until 1940 would the Pasco Port District be authorized.[13]

"Would Captain Gray be delighted with the rivers today?" historian Davis asks. "Would he not be proposing future development with surprising accuracy?"

Probably he would. But in his heart of hearts, he might also miss the white-water rapids he had run for so many years.

Captain William Polk Gray died just as the sun was rising on Saturday morning, October 26, 1929. He was eighty-four years old.

"The following Tuesday services for the Grand Old Man of Pasco were held at the Methodist Church," historian Davis writes. "All flags throughout the city were at half-staff and all businesses were closed during the funeral."

Several years earlier, he had written his own obituary in the form of a poem, which might well have served for all the bold river captains he had known in this lifetime. These were its first and last verses:

Yes, lay my bones in the far Northwest
Where all of my loved ones lie.
In a quiet spot let me lie in rest
When troubles have all passed by . . .

And when you have planted me deep in the ground
And all ceremonies are thru,
Just think of these words when you're strolling around,
"He kept the respect of his crew."[14]

Already, forces were at work which would alter the nature of the Columbia-Snake River system forever. The most important of these was a study authorized by Congress for the Corps of Engineers to examine and report on the development of the

Franklin County Historical Society
Open River Celebration, Pasco, Washington, May 1915.

river system for the next fifty years, telling not what should but what could be done so far as irrigation, power, and navigation of these waters was concerned. Called the "308 Report" because of the Congressional session that had approved it, the survey would be directed by Major John Butler, be completed and delivered in 1932, then would become the Bible for river development during the next fifty years.[15]

Which, as the saying goes, is another story . . .

Chapter 17 footnotes

1. *The Life and Times of Captain William Polk Gray*, by Jean Carol Davis, designed by Jaque Nielsen Sonderman, Franklin County Historical Society, Pasco, Washington, 1998, p. 10. In this excellent biography pf Captain Gray, the authors tell the story of his life illustrating it with photographs not to be found elsewhere.
2. Gray, "Letter' to Miss Coleman, May 8, 1924, copy Penrose Library.
3. Ibid.
4. *Live and Times*, op. cit., p. 13.
5. "CONGREGATIONAL CHRONICLES," (Pasco, 1889,) by Georgia Mae Gallivan, transmitted by letter to Larry Dodd, Penrose Library, August 8, 1989, p. 4.
6. Ibid p 6.
7. Gray, "Reminiscences,' op. cit.
8. Gallivan, op. cit, p. 5.
9. Ibid, p. 6.
10. Ibid, p. 7.
11. *Live and. Times*, op. cit., p. 16.
12. Ibid, p. 18.
13. Ibid, p. 20.
14. Ibid, p. 33.
15. The dam-building period began in 1938 and lasted untl 1974, while the irrigation projects contemplated began in 1946 and continued into the 1980s. By then, a serious anadromous fish loss problem not addressed in the 308 Report had arisen—and is yet to be solved.

Acknowledgments

My initial interest in steamboats on the rivers of the Pacific Northwest was stirred during the research and writing of my first novel, *Bend on the Snake*, which was published in 1949. Taking place during the gold rush to Idaho in 1860-61, its main character travels by ocean steamer from San Francisco north to the mouth of the Columbia, comes 100 miles upriver to Portland. Then must change riverboats three times as he moves up the Columbia and Snake to the Idaho gold-boom settlements 465 miles inland.

When the book sold to the movies and was filmed in the Portland area, its title was changed to *Bend on the River* and was shot in the Rooster Rock stretch of the Columbia adjacent to Mount Hood in order to display the beautiful scenery of the area. I did not object to the change in locale, nor did I mind that James Stewart was cast in the leading role. Though the filming was done in the summer of 1951, two stern-wheelers left over from their glory days on the river were still operating as tugboats, the *Henderson* and the *Portland*. The movie company leased and re-named them, gave them roles in the movie, then staged a steamboat race to publicize the movie premiere.

The *River Queen*, the working tugboat that had been gussied up to look like a stern-wheeler of the 1860s, won the race after her engineer threw some simulated pitch-filled pine knots into the boilers to give her a little extra speed, making her twin stacks throw out plumes of black smoke. Never mind that the Cinemascope camera caught an aircraft contrail in the sky 30,000 feet overhead. That was edited out, leaving the thrilling steamboat race of days gone by to excite the audience.

During the fifty years that have passed since then, I have ridden many boats on the rivers of the Northwest, but to my great regret only two of them were stern-wheelers, for their day ended in 1915. During the research for *Bend on the Snake*, I boarded one converted into a restuarant-bar tied up to the dock in Pasco. I was told it used to be a work boat named *City of Portland*, a bit of history I was never able to confirm. It was condemned and sank or burned shortly thereafter, the usual fate for laid-up steamboats, which seldom lasted long when their working days were over.

Like the popular 1920s poet, Edna St, Vincent Millay, who once wrote "There isn't a train I wouldn't take, no matter where it's going," my wife and I had a similar feeling about boats plying the rivers and sounds of the Pacific Northwest. We never bothered to ask where the boat was going; we asked only when it left.

Our favorite pursuit has been following the research trail relating the history of these steamboats, wherever it led, which has taken us to many interesting places where we've met many helpful people. Some were the authors of nonfiction books about the Pacific Northwest such as Clifford Merrill Drury, who wrote extensively about the missionary movement that took place at the same time as the riverboat era; Fred Lockley, who in the early 1920s, recorded the reminiscences of a number of early-day river captains; and writers Randall Mills, Robert Ormond Case and James A. Gibbs, who passed on fascinating tales of river adventures during the Oregon Trail days and crossing the Columbia River Bar. As I note in the book, the first steamboat came to the Northwest in 1836, but for many years thereafter potential steamboats built in the East left under sail for the long journey around the Horn, then were converted to steam operation when they entered the rivers of the West, Because some of my writings—such as the historical novel *Roll On, Columbia*—began during the age of sail, when most ships were built in New England, I was advised by Curator Anne Witty of the Columbia River Maritime Museum that to obtain information about ships built before 1850 I ought to go to the repositories on the East Coast. So in 1994 Jeanne and I spent five weeks in the Washington, D.C. area combining sight-seeing we'd long wanted to do with research at the Smithsonian and the Library of Congress. Though I had exchanged correspondence with Paula Fleming, Indian expert at the Smithsonian, over the years, I found her even more helpful in person. Later, at the

Library of Congress, ship-building expert Virginia Steele Wood, supplied me with valuable research and a piece of good advice when she said,

"To round out your research, you really should go to Boston."

So, in 1995, we spent a month there, living in a high-rise apartment building on the waterfront just a couple of blocks from the Old Oyster House. That's where Daniel Webster used to eat three dozen raw oysters for breakfast, washing each half dozen down with a glass of brandy before delivering a fiery speech at nearby Fanuiel Hall where the Massachusetts Legislature met. Still in existence, the Old Oyster House still serves great clam chowder and corn bread, our research proved, though we did not try a Daniel Webster breakfast.

During our stay, we were treated well by the historical society experts at the Boston Public Library as well as those in Salem, Gloucester and Essex. To me, seeing the launching site where a ship was built many years ago lends an authenticity to what I write about its later adventures on a distant river that can be achieved in no other way.

As I have noted in the book, Captain William Polk Gray spent sixty years piloting steamboats on the rivers of the Northwest, too busy most of the time to write about his adventures. But after retiring in Pasco, when asked to tell a reporter or historian the details of a particularly colorful exploit, he related it with remarkable clarity of detail in simple, colorful language—such as bringing the *Norma* through the rapids of Hells Canyon in 1895. In his old age, he recorded some of his other adventures in letters to friends and a young lady hoping to write the story of his life, some of which I have been given access to at Penrose Library, Whitman College, in Walla Walla. Others are at the Franklin County Historical Society in Pasco. As noted in the bibliography, the society has published a brief but excellent account of his "life and times."

My long-time friend, the late Fritz Timmen, through his work as a publicist for the Inland Empire Waterways Association, and later for the Port District in Portland and Port District of Pasco, had a unique opportunity to get details and obtain photos of steamboats on the rivers during their glory days. He took advantage of this in his book *Blow for the Landing*, which I have frequently quoted.

During the fifty years I have been writing fiction and nonfiction about the rivers of the Northwest, I have depended on repositories such as the Washington, Oregon and Idaho historical societies to supply me with facts and photos, for which I now thank them again. At regional entities such as the Franklin County Historical Society in Pasco, Washington, Administrative Assistant Sherel Webb, was most helpful, as were Lora Feucht and Mary E. White-Romero at the Nez Perce County Historical Society in Lewiston, Idaho.

Thanks to a search made for me on the Internet by archivist Larry Dodd at Penrose Library, I got in touch with the University of Alaska Rasmuson Library in Fairbanks, whose Doris Mey supplied me with photos from their files.. The same contact helped me reach the Yukon Archives in Whitehore, Yukon Territory, whose Reference Coordinator, Heather Jones sent me a number of excellent photos from their files. In both cases, I told these friendly people I would prefer to travel to their beautiful country and collect the photos in person rather than by mail, but my editor said such a trip was not in the photo budget.

Finally, I must again thank Larry Dodd, who recently retired as archivist at Penrose Library and now can add *Emiritus* to his title, for all the help he has given me over the years. But I remind him that his retirement does not mean he can quit helping me. If I keep on writing books like this one, using the new computer which he and Penrose Head Librarian Henry Yapel encouraged me to buy, I'm going to need his help more than ever.

THE AUTHOR

Bill Gulick is considered by many the dean of Northwest history writers. During a career spanning more than half a century, he has written more than thirty books, five movie scripts and more than 200 articles and stories for newspapers, national magazines and television.

A long-time Washington state resident, Gulick has won numerous regional and national awards.

Other Gulick fiction and nonfiction books available from Caxton Press include *Outlaws of the Pacific Northwest, Manhunt: the Pursuit of Harry Tracy, Snake River Country, Chief Joseph Country, A Traveler's History of Washington, They Came to a Valley* and *The Moon-eyed Appaloosa.*

BIBLIOGRAPHY

Authors

Baker, W. W., *Forty Years a Pioneer*, Lowman & Hanford Co., Seattle, 1934.

Case, Robert Ormond, *Last Mountains*, Doubleday, 1946.

Clark, R. C. *History of the Willamette Valley, Oregon*, Chicago, The S. J. Clarke Publishing Vo., 1927.

Coe, L. W., *Overland Monthly*, August 1886.

Dana, Marshal N., *Oregon Historical Quarterly*, 1915.

Davis, Jean Carol, Franklin County Historical Society, Pasco, Washington, 1998.

DeVoto, Bernard, *The Journals of Lewis and Clark*, Houghton Mifflin, 1953.

Dobie, J. Frank, *Coronado's Children*, The Southwest Press, 1930.

Drury, Clifford M., *Henry Harmon Spalding*, The Caxton Printers, 1939.

Gallivan, Georgia Mae, *Congregational Chronicles,* Pasco, Washington, 1889.

Gibbs, James A., *Pacific Graveyard*, Binfords & Mort, Portland, Oregon, 1950.
Shipwrecks of the Pacific Coast, Binfords & Mort, 1957.
Oregon's Salty Coast, Superior, Seattle, 1978.

Gray, William H., *History of Oregon, 1792-1849*, Portland, Oregon, Bancroft, San Francisco, 1870.

Gray, William Polk, *Reminiseces*, published and unpublished as noted.

Gulick, Bill, *Roadside History of Oregon*, Mountain Press, Missoula, Montana, 1991.
Roll On, Columbia, University Press of Colorado, Boulder, Colorado, 1998.

Hussey, J. A., *Champoeg: A Place of Transition*, Portland, Oregon Historical Society Press, 1967.

Irving, Washington, *Astoria*, 1837, reprint, Lipponcott, 1961

Lewis and Dryden, *Marine History of the Pacific Northwest*, 1895, reprint Antiquarian Press, 1962, New York.

Lockley Fred, *Reminiscences of Captain William Polk Gray*, Oregon Historial Society Quarterly, December, 1913.

Matthews, Mitford M., *A Dictionary of Americanisms on Historical Principles,* University of Chicago Press, 1951.

Mears, Eliot Grinnel, *Maritime Trade of the Western United States*, Stanford University Press, 1920.

Mills, Randall V., *Sternwheelers Up Columbia*, Pacific Books, Palo Alto, California, 1947.

Reynolds, Helen Baker, *Gold, Rawhide and Iron*, Pacific Books, Palo Alto, California, 1955.

Ross, Alexander, *The Fur Hunters of the Far West*, London, Smith, Elder, 1855, Reprint by University of Oklahoma Press, 1956.

Schlicke, *General George Wright, Guardian of the Pacific Coast*, University of Oklahoma Press, 1988.

Symons, Thomas William, Colonel, U.S. Army, *Report on the Upper Columbia River and the Great Plain of the Columbia, 1881*; reprint by Ye Galleon Press, Fairfield, Washington, 1967.

Thrapp, Dan L., *Encyclopedia of Frontier Biography*, The Arthur H. Clark Company, Glendale, California, 1988.

Timmen, Fritz, *Blow for the Landing*, The Caxton Printers, 1973.

Wright, E. D. *Marine History of the Pacific Northwest*, 1925

Periodicals
Idaho Yesterdays, Winter, 1961-62.
Oregon City Argus, May 19, 1855.
Oregon Historical Society Quarterly, December, 1913.

For a free Caxton catalog write to:

CAXTON PRESS
312 Main Street
Caldwell, ID 83605-3299

or

Visit our Internet Website:

www.caxtonpress.com

Caxton Press is a division of The CAXTON PRINTERS, Ltd.